THE

TIMOTHY LEARY

PROJECT

THE

TIMOTHY LEARY

PROJECT

Conceived and created by Elephant Book Company
Limited.

Library of Congress Control Number: 2017949749

ISBN: 978-1-4197-2646-0
eISBN: 978-1-68335-167-2

Printed and bound in China
10 9 8 7 6 5 4 3 2 1

Abrams books are available at special discounts when
purchased in quantity for premiums and promotions as
well as fundraising or educational use. Special editions
can also be created to specification. For details, contact
specialsales@abramsbooks.com or the address below.

ABRAMS The Art of Books
195 Broadway, New York, NY 10007
abramsbooks.com

Contents

Foreword

Getting the Timothy Leary you deserve, one piece of paper at a time

EVERYONE WANTS TO KNOW what their parents are up to growing up. As you get older and more inquisitive you naturally want to know how your birthers live in this world. What is it that they do? Who are their friends? Naturally, osmosis starts to take hold and the things our parents are into, we also get attracted to. That's the way the human condition works. Programming and metaprogramming.

During my youth, a certain mystery surrounded my upbringing. I grew up in what appeared on the outside to be a somewhat normal upper-middle-class household in Beverly Hills, California. Every morning my mom or dad would take me to school, my dad would toss the baseball with me in the backyard and on most nights they would make sure I did my homework.

Something changed at around the age of thirteen. During the 1980s, my dad supplemented his income by being an actor in a number of pretty bad B movies. On one of these assignments, I accompanied him to the set at Universal Studios. As I was standing around watching the shoot take place some guy, presumably a crewmember, stood beside me and also watched the scene being shot. Not knowing who I was, he turned and spoke to me in a very calm and deliberate manner and said, "I can't believe they have this evil disgusting man in this movie. The amount of damage he's done to this country is incredible." I'm paraphrasing of course, but that was the gist of it.

I was shocked, terrified, confused, and exhilarated. Even at that age I knew that in order to generate that kind of response from someone Timothy must have been doing something pretty exciting.

After the film-set incident, I began to take a little action to figure out what exactly Timothy Leary did for a living. I started to notice all of the books with his name on the shelf and the celebrities that hung out at our house—some of our regular visitors were fans and some people were very hung up on what he was going to say next. It was then that the realization came to me—"*he's famous!*"

Growing up in Beverly Hills in the 1980s fame was a big deal. I began to see Timothy Leary as more than a father, he was also a teacher. And I must be completely honest by saying that I was intimated by his cognitive capacity for a great many years to come.

After I read his autobiography *Flashbacks* for the first time at age fifteen, I could see that this was no ordinary man. He was a man on a mission who never wavered from what he believed to be his truth. He was fired from Harvard, lived on a commune, inspired the Beatles, and escaped from prison. At such an early age finding this stuff out was an incredible revelation and also quite bewildering.

Now when I saw him in his office, it was with new eyes. Every hour Timothy spent in front of the computer was poised and possessed, every note written in the margin of a book was deliberate and passionate, and every note, artifact and letter was tagged, filed, and stored into a box in the garage.

Watching him work, I slowly became aware that I was right in the middle of one of the great cultural movements of our times. While Timothy was not the cultural movement by himself, he was indeed one of its primary instigators and provocateurs. All of this material being thrown into these boxes was not just the work of one man, but they were documents that told the story of our times.

From the interpersonal psychology movement of the late 1950s to the cyberpunk movement of the 1990s, Timothy had a front row seat for some of the most important cultural movements of the late twentieth century. And the documentation of that viewpoint was an essential facet in the Timothy Leary legacy.

How the archives became such a well-documented repository of American culture is a tale that rivals any Hollywood adventure saga. They started off in metal bins, in shoddy boxes with not much labeling and passed their way through many hands before finally ending up in their current, and presumably final, resting place—the New York Public Library.

Technically speaking, the archives are made up of hundreds of boxes containing book drafts, research materials from Harvard, correspondence with amazing people, manifestos from the Millbrook era, random notes, personal mementos, photographs, digital archives from the 1980s and '90s, and lots of stream-of-consciousness thought starters that are quintessential Leary. I'm sure he had a good fifty book ideas that never made it past the first few pages.

Before he became the infamous 1960s counterculture rebel, Timothy was a self-respecting psychologist. He was also a self-professed "middle-class liberal robot who drove home each night and drank martinis." He had two kids, Susan and Jack, and a wife, Marianne. When Marianne committed suicide on his thirty-fifth birthday, a lightning bolt was thrust into his psyche that made his entire life's purpose about his work and almost nothing else. Sure, he would love again and find a sliver of domestic tranquility late in life, but everything would pale in comparison and priority to the triumph that was to be his life's work.

When Harvard University talked him into joining the faculty in 1959, he joined as an isolationist. He kept to himself and really didn't care about being there all that much. Timothy was looking to break out. He wanted to do something new. Naturally, in 1960, when the time came to "turn-on" and experience psychedelics for the first time at the age of forty, he was not worried about what others would think or how it might appear to the Harvard staff. Rooted in science and research, he simply did his work and wrote it all down as one big premeditated experiment in human consciousness.

When in the late 1960s, the unrest of the times reached a fever pitch due to factors ranging from the war in Vietnam to psychedelics becoming mainstream, Timothy turned from scientist to outlaw right in step with everyone else. He became the perfect man for the job of leading an antiauthoritarian crusade against the thought-police establishment.

By the time Timothy was on the run and/or imprisoned for being caught in possession of marijuana, his role as outlaw instead of a serious scientist was firmly embedded in the lexicon of popular culture. When I asked him about this, his answer to me contradicted the popular picture. He'd always tell me that his tactics, his penchant for taking on the U.S. government for control of our minds, were just as important intellectually as his groundbreaking Good Friday Experiment at Harvard in 1962. He felt that both approaches were about urging society to "think for themselves and question authority"—an ethos that was most paramount to all his work.

The transhumanist era of his post-lockup period saw many great (and heady) Leary works such as "Exo-Psychology" and "The Intelligence Agents." This time also gave birth to one of Timothy's most cutting-edge theories on the human nervous system and its associated consciousness—"The Eight-Circuit Model of Consciousness." Briefly, the model suggests that there are eight circuits of information that operate within the human nervous system, each concerned with a different sphere of activity from our primary functions through to our mystical and psychedelic experiences.

The archives of this period offer direct proof that Timothy continued to evolve his thinking. He combined his early work as a cognitive therapist with a psychedelic researcher with a transhumanist pagan and morphed it into something all his own.

Timothy was always a seeker and was always adding ingredients into the mix. In the 1970s he dabbled in space colonization, had correspondence with the cosmologist Carl Sagan, and published SMI2LE (Space Migration Intelligence Squared Life Extension). But what came next was perhaps the most interesting ingredient since LSD—the personal computer.

In 1979, I was six years old and we were one of the first homes on the block to get a personal computer. It was an Apple II+. After that event, things were never quite the same. I was never the same, our household was never the same, and Timothy was never the same.

Timothy saw computers as a way to add another dimension to his already vast output. Joi Ito, a longtime friend and the current director of the MIT Media Lab says, "I think he'd want the work remixed and integrated into every possible crazy form that we couldn't even imagine and to live forever in the DNA of technology . . ."

Because of the limitations of the early days of computing Timothy could only theorize about what he wanted to do with computers. Had he lived to see the explosion of the Web, Facebook, and Twitter, he, without question, would have created a new way to disseminate his ideas.

The groundwork of that new path, however, was laid down with the 1985 Electronic Art's release of his game "Mind Mirror." "Mind

Mirror" was a personality profiler based on Timothy's techniques for gauging interpersonal and psychological attributes. By profiling yourself and others, you could get in touch with your core qualities and look at ways of improving them. The program remained largely under the radar after 1985–86, but now it has taken on a new life as a Facebook app and can be used by searching for the "Mind Mirror Profiler" on Facebook.

After the release of *Flashbacks* in 1983, Timothy flirted with the idea that books were dead, that they were relics of the old paradigm of civilization. The archives reflect this period in exactly the same way. Whereas, the material from the 1950s–'70s was largely research- and longform-based content encapsulated in books and drafts, his works from the 1980s were more shortform and little fits and starts of great ideas. One might even say that mirrors how we see today's Internet content bubble—short and succinct bits of information for today's short-attention-span theater.

Unlike in the 1960s, Timothy was not a hands-on pioneer during these times. He was a theorist and an instigator—he actually never learned how to operate a PC all that well. In fact, I'd constantly have to show him how to do the most basic tasks even after years of use. He always chalked it up to being "a generational thing."

It didn't really matter though. From 1989 through to his death in 1996, Timothy surrounded himself with some of the youngest and brightest minds that the era had to offer. It was a full-on open-door policy salon. If you had a great idea, a good vibe, and some good grass, you could come and hang out.

When it became clear that Timothy wasn't going to be with us for too much longer, the pressure was on to get the archives in order. Right away he saw the power of the Internet and in 1995 he summoned me and some guys to make Leary.com as a place to display some of the great pieces from counterculture luminaries. However, websites were just too limited in 1995 to make a serious dent in the vast trove that the archives had to offer.

Around 1994, the 1950s–'70s material finally made its way back to our garage after being unavailable for some time, and the already growing number of hyperorganized boxes doubled in quantity. Suddenly it became tangible, real, and impossible to debate—Timothy Leary had amassed one of the great intellectual, psychological, and cultural bodies of work of the twentieth century—and there it all was in the garage.

Despite their compelling content, it took several years to find someone who was prepared to house Leary's legacy. As with all things Leary—the public simply wasn't ready yet. Then a dialogue was started with the New York Public Library (NYPL) about purchasing the archives and the results proved to be successful. Michael Horowitz, Timothy's longtime friend and archivist, commented on the acquisition that, "The New York Public Library is like the history of America and will help place Timothy in the context of the history of America that he deserves. The library is also extremely progressive and can help us explore the future of the archives."

Jennifer Ulrich, who was appointed by the New York Public Library as the chief archivist on the Leary project, came into this project with only a terse understanding of who Timothy was. But as a professional archivist she brought new meaning to the project by being objective. She is neither pro-Leary nor anti-Leary and with this slant, she has spent countless hours over the last few years pouring over every piece of paper that makes up the six hundred-plus boxes that are the archive. Ulrich acknowledges that, "What his papers will reveal remains to be seen," and she goes on to show us in this book that the possibilities of his archive are virtually as limitless as Timothy Leary's own imagination.

Timothy said upon his dying "Everyone will get the Timothy Leary they deserve." If you're looking for the acid guru you'll find him here, if you're looking for the pop culture iconoclast you'll find him here, if you're looking for the serious researcher who dedicated his life to exploring the realms of human potential you'll find him here, and if you're looking for a glimpse into the personal life of the man as a husband and father you'll find that here too. When all is said and done, I know I'll be spending a lot of time in New York getting to know him all over again, and I hope you will, too.

Zach Leary, July 2017

Preface

I FIRST HEARD ABOUT LSD and Huxley and Leary all at once from a popular magazine article in 1962. Two years later I took LSD for the first time, in a close-knit group, using Leary's *Psychedelic Experience* manual as a guide. I saw him on stage and on television, read his books, and followed news of his arrests and court cases during the later 1960s. In 1970, shortly after he was imprisoned, a conjunction of events resulted in a chance encounter with his wife, Rosemary, who was speaking at an OM Orgy/benefit on San Francisco's Great Highway. About a week later, two of us, myself and Robert Barker, became his archivists.

Our immersion in his archives was especially intense in the first half of the 1970s, when Leary was a political prisoner, jailed for a tiny amount of cannabis but really for promoting the unprecedented benefits of psychedelic drugs when properly used. After shocking the world by escaping from prison, he became a hunted fugitive and asylum seeker, was recaptured and placed under the highest bail in US history, and sent to a maximum security prison where he spent the next four years writing some of his most important books. In the most difficult of circumstances his spirit remained unbroken; he stayed productive as a thinker and writer and amazed visitors with his optimistic outlook.

His extensive, meticulously organized archives were invaluable, as we were constantly called upon to research and supply data to his lawyers, manuscript drafts to his publishers, and documentary evidence of his contributions to society to his parole board. With Leary an international fugitive, we worried that his archives might be seized, and eventually they were, in a raid at my home by the FBI. Leary's archives landed me in a Grand Jury room in 1975 in precarious circumstances, in danger of being jailed myself.

Thus the U.S. government (or more precisely, the FBI) succeeded us as his archivists for more than a year, combing through manuscript drafts of his prison book in an unsuccessful attempt to nail the people who engineered his escape. After he was released from prison and his archives were returned to him, they went into storage for the next twenty years, while new archives accumulated in his home in Los Angeles. I swapped the position of Leary archivist for bibliographer, and then editor, as our friendship evolved in the years after the intense and often stressful period of the 1970s.

The first artifact that came into my hands when we became custodians of the Timothy Leary archives was a carbon copy of Laura Huxley's personal eight-page letter sent to a handful of her closest friends describing her husband Aldous's final hours, when she gave him LSD to assist and sacramentalize his passing. The letter, dated shortly after his death (but not published until 1968), also recorded her shock at learning of President Kennedy's assassination from glancing at the television screen as she was bringing her husband—the first person Leary invited to Harvard to participate in the psilocybin experiments—the first of two 100-microgram doses of LSD. (We didn't know at the time that Kennedy himself had taken LSD, given to him by an intimate friend who received guidance on conducting trips from Leary himself.)

The archives contain voluminous records of the Harvard research projects with psilocybin, LSD, and DMT in the early 1960s. Correspondence with LSD discoverer Albert Hofmann and requisitions for supplies of the then legal mind drugs from Sandoz Pharmaceuticals. Buried within are hundreds of handwritten and mimeographed reports of participants in the first large-scale guided sessions, including divinity students and prisoners, alongside reports of the government's backlash and media propaganda that drove Leary and his associates (most importantly Richard Alpert/ Ram Dass and Ralph Metzner) from the academic world to continue their private research in Millbrook, NY. The central role of Leary during the years when psychedelics began to spread through society, resulting in the 1966 U.S. Senate hearings where he made a plea for establishing psychedelic research centers, is also documented. Likewise is the banning of these consciousness-expanding substances which were threatening the government's narrative promoting the Vietnam War and the suppression of the youth and minority protest movements rising up in the latter half of the decade.

His archives reveal the extent to which Leary was on the front lines, in communication with other dissident voices, such as Allen Ginsberg, Gary Snyder, Alan Watts, Stanley Owsley, Abbie Hoffman (the activist), Paul Krassner, Art Kleps, editors of the underground newspapers, and the more outspoken voices in underground art and film and rock music, as well as cutting-edge scientists and intellectuals, including Aldous Huxley, Albert Hofmann (who first synthesized LSD), Humphry Osmond, Marshall McLuhan, and Carl Sagan.

The Leary archives never stopped growing. We brought back what he gathered during his exile in Algeria and Switzerland. We added the ubiquitous flow of Leary-related news published in newspapers and magazines, and the manuscripts he sent us for editing. Through the periods of his interest in space migration, intelligence increase, and life-extension; the advent of new drugs like MDMA and the new underground during the "just say no" Reagan decade; and especially during the birth of the personal computer revolution ("the PC is the LSD of the '90s")—empowering individuals to think for themselves was the essence of Timothy Leary's teachings.

In 1963, as Leary and Alpert were being banished from Harvard in the controversy over LSD, they published a manifesto, "The Politics of Conscousness Expansion," in which they announced that the introduction of psilocybin and LSD in pill form was a global game-changer. In the archives we found copies of the original draft, mimeo, and offprint versions of this central text: "Make no mistake, the effect of consciousness -expanding drugs will be to transform our concepts of human nature, of human potentialities, of existence."

In an unpublished draft in the archives, Leary likened himself and his colleagues to a medical team sent to a plague area, where the plague was people "hung up" in categories: the conditioned mind thinking inside the box. Believing that LSD changed the narrative and offered an end to this psychological plague, Leary set out to advocate passionately for responsible use and further study, just as the government was criminalizing the drug. The repression sent psychedelic drugs and their users underground, delaying by some fifty years the reemergence of scientific studies of psychedelic plants and chemicals to reimprint a new paradigm that might be summed up in the popular slogan of the peace movement: "Make Love, Not War."

Working with them, I realized the monumental importance of the Leary archives to the history of the psychedelic movement that was to have a profound effect on the consciousness of the nation and beyond, upon which the fate of our planet may be inextricably linked.

Other archivists came along to continue the work: Vicki Marshall, Ron Lawrence, and Retinalogic—the team of tech-savvy young people who created timothyleary.com, one of the earliest personal websites, and uploaded many of the key documents of Leary's entire life and career preserved in his archives. The far-sighted director and curator of the New York Public Library Manuscript and Archives Division, William Stingone and Thomas Lannon, shepherded the acquisition of the Leary archives and hired Jennifer Ulrich to organize and write blogs about it.

Jennifer's immersion in the Leary archives and the expertise she gained resulted in the creation of this book, a smartly chosen and superbly annotated selection of representative archival documents that throw light on a controversial man who played a unique role in the consciousness-raising movement of the second half of the twentieth century.

One of Leary's last public acts was posting on a fledgling Internet in 1995 a simple recipe for preparing an edible marijuana bud on a Ritz cracker, which went viral and got the attention of network news—a major accomplishment for a seventy-five-year-old man decimated by cancer. On the cusp of his death, Leary was still suggesting ways to make people feel better by getting high from a plant.

Michael Horowitz, June 2017

Introduction
The Counterculture Phenomenon

TIMOTHY LEARY FIGURED LARGE in what is now understood as the counterculture phenomenon that swept through the world, particularly in the United States and Europe during the late 1960s and early 1970s. What was the counterculture? A literal definition would be: the opposite of conventional culture—a rejection of the "establishment." It represented a progression of lifestyles, discoveries, influences, experimentations, and inspirations involving mind-altering drugs, challenges to the legal system, the testing of accepted norms, and the embracing of non-Western philosophies and traditions, esoteric ideas, art, and media. Certainly, 20,000-plus hippies tripping on LSD in Golden Gate Park at the 1967 San Francisco "Gathering of the Tribes"—where Leary stated "Turn on, tune in, drop out," the phrase that was to become synonymous with him, despite being originally coined by Marshall McLuhan—did not materialize out of the ether. It is easy to think of "dropping out" or the mantra "don't trust anyone over 30,"[1] as defining this rebellion against conventional "square" society, but dig deeper, and a series of events came together to sweep away convention and replace it with experimentation. For many it was to be a psychology professor in his forties who would become the Pied Piper of this experimentation—the counterculture legend, Timothy Leary.

In America, the counterculture rose out of the Beatnik scene that was centered in Greenwich Village, New York City and the San Francisco Bay area during the 1950s. Eastern philosophies and Zen Buddhism proved popular among the Beats and bohemians, typified in Jack Kerouac's novel *Dharma Bums* (1958), a Buddhist-themed follow-up to *On the Road* (1957)—the book that marked Kerouac as the pioneer of the Beat Generation writers.

The Beatnik scene evolved into the California hippie culture of the 1960s and spread throughout the country, taken up by the baby boomers and their coming-of-age "youth movement," stereotypically characterized by copious marijuana and psychedelic drug use, hedonistic lifestyles, the dropping of social mores, free love, nakedness, and hair grown long and in its "natural" state. This "natural" way of life rejected the conventional style seen during the 1950s. From an outside perspective, it seemed as though hundreds of thousands of men and women across the United States embraced non-Western religion and fashion, gurus, yoga, sex tantras, rock 'n' roll, political protests, flower power, and an overwhelming array of mind-altering substances. While some sought to dismiss the counter-culture and its proponents in this simplistic way, this was far from the whole story. In reality, the counterculture was a movement born out of a growing discontent at a post–World War II political elite, who no longer reflected the beliefs and desires of a new generation of men and women. Collectively, it was an agitator for serious change, encompassing those urging for civil rights and equality and activists campaigning against the escalating Vietnam War and the rise in nuclear proliferation, alongside those seeking a more meaningful and enlightened path—a way of living in greater harmony with their fellow man and the planet or cosmos.

If the 1960s were characterized by optimism and idealism, the 1970s offered the continued realities of war, drug abuse, and economic woes. The new decade ushered in the comedown, when acts of personal free-dom were met with prison sentences; political demonstrations turned into armed conflict; consciousness expansion turned into looking for a fix; and sexual liberation morphed into the burgeoning pornography industry. As the Vietnam War dragged on, and the country was left reeling in the aftermath of the assassinations of John F. Kennedy (November 1963), Malcolm X (February 1965), and Martin Luther King, Jr. (April 1968). Protest movements gained more momentum:[2] women, gays and lesbians, minorities, the poor, the prison populations, the earth—everything was at stake and the fight was real. At the center of it all was a radical youth culture who left their classrooms behind and took to the streets.

The close of the Vietnam War in 1975 signaled the end of an era. The free-loving, peace-loving, radical youth culture matured and sobered up (slightly). During the late-1970s and '80s, counterculture figures settled into the new scene: yuppies replaced yippies, personal computers and video games emerged out of Silicon Valley and gained popularity, and the New Age movement grew into an industry. The counterculture became mainstream.

It is difficult to imagine just how dramatically society changed during this time. There are many generalizations that can be made about the advent of the hippie culture, but ultimately those at the heart of the counterculture wanted to change not only what people were doing, but also how they were thinking. Timothy Leary was undoubtedly among those who changed the way in which an entire generation considered the world. His quest to expand the limits of human experience and thought through consciousness-expanding drugs and philosophies resulted in psychedelic drug experiments involving some of the most influential thinkers and artists of the day. Whether they took part in "Project Leary" or not, whether they agreed with him or vehemently opposed him, Leary's role in the counterculture took on an almost mythical status, whether as the ultimate "guru" or "the most dangerous man in America."[3]

From the drug studies he led at Harvard University (1960–63), the commune he established (1963–68), his arrests for marijuana possession and subsequent imprisonment (1965–66, 1970, 1973–76), his life as a fugitive from the law (1970–73), or his born-again career as a computer enthusiast and futurist (1976–96), Leary was always a controversial figure; one whose influence was wide, touching on the lives of those he encountered and befriended, including many crucial counterculture figures: Beat authors Allen Ginsberg, William S. Burroughs, Jack Kerouac, Gregory Corso, Michael McClure, LeRoi Jones (later known as Amiri Baraka), and Gerd Stern; their drug-experimenting predecessors: Aldous Huxley, Gerald Heard, and Albert Hofmann; experimental colleagues: Richard Alpert (later known as Ram Dass), Ralph Metzner, and Paul Lee; Merry Pranksters: Ken Kesey, Ken Babbs, and Neal Cassady; yippies: Paul Krassner and Abbie Hoffman; Black Panther Eldridge Cleaver; musicians: Thelonious Monk, Dizzy Gillespie, Maynard Ferguson, John Lennon, and Yoko Ono; drugmakers: Owsley Stanley and "hippie mafia" the Brotherhood of Eternal Love; and other characters such as Robert Anton Wilson, Larry Flynt, Terry Southern, Tom Robbins, William Gibson, Keith Haring, David Byrne, and many more.

Above: Timothy Leary photographed at his home,
c. 1966.

Leary and his friend Richard Alpert toured and lectured widely, using the media to spread their message of consciousness expansion. It was Leary's dedication to this key tenet of the counterculture—that of opening one's mind—which makes him such a fascinating prism through which to view the entire countercultural movement.

Yet, how did Timothy Leary come to be such a critical and controversial figure? His early years were decidedly conventional. He was born on October 22, 1920 in Springfield, Massachusetts to Irish Catholic parents: schoolteacher Abigail (née Ferris) and dentist, Timothy F. Leary, Sr. His father left when Leary was fourteen years old. In 1938, he graduated from high school, then attended Holy Cross College, a Jesuit liberal arts college in Worcester, MA. He transferred to the United States Military Academy at West Point in 1940, but left the following year. After leaving West Point, he enlisted in the army (1942), serving as sergeant and promoted to corporal and staff psychometrician at Deshon Hospital in Butler, Pennsylvania. He received an honorary discharge in 1946. He gained degrees from the University of Alabama, and Washington State University and eventually received his PhD from the University of California, Berkeley in 1950. He had two children from his first marriage to Marianne Busch: Susan (1947–90) and Jack (b. 1949). Tragically, Marianne committed suicide on his thirty-fifth birthday (October 22, 1955).

After leaving the army, Leary returned to academia as a lecturer at the Center for Research in Personality and the Laboratory of Social Relations at Harvard University in Cambridge, MA (1959–63). In the late 1950s, he was leading a relatively conventional existence as a single father raising two children. He often traveled to Mexico, as he had done with Marianne and during his brief marriage to Mary Della Cioppa (1956–57). However, in 1960, his vacation there would change the course of his life.

In August 1960, Leary had a life-changing experience when Frank Barron, Professor of Psychology at the University of California, Berkeley, and Lothar Knauth, Professor of Anthropology from the University of Mexico, obtained and offered him psilocybin mushrooms (known colloquially as "magic mushrooms") while staying in the town of Cuernavaca. From that moment on, he dedicated his life to the study and use of psychedelics. He later wrote to colleague and Hungarian-British author Arthur Koestler, "I learned more in [those] six hours than [in] 16 years [as a psychologist]."[4] The experience was new to him, although psychedelic substances were not novel in America.

Psychedelic: prior to 1956, there was no "psychedelic"[5] there was only "inebriation," "psychic effect," and ultimately, "hallucinogen" in the western medical lexicon. Granted, the use and experimentation of medicinal plants and herbs had been practiced for millennia, but modern, Western society had not yet classified these substances in these terms until Swiss chemist, Albert Hofmann, accidentally discovered the effects of LSD-25 on April 16, 1943. Five years prior, he had synthesized LSD-25 as the 25th derivative when experimenting with lysergic acids and ergot alkaloids at Sandoz Laboratories in Switzerland. He went on to conduct self-experiments, including the infamous "Bicycle Day" (April 19, 1943) when he rode home on his bicycle under the influence of LSD. He reported his reactions to colleagues, heralding the first real research into LSD as an entity in itself.[6] Substances such as alcohol, stimulants, cannabis, opium, and other narcotics had been known and used (and abused) for quite some time—most notably by the Beats—but LSD and the group of mind-altering substances with similar chemical compounds were recognized as a different class of drugs.

Before LSD and magic mushrooms, the first psychedelic substance regularly used in the United States was the peyote cactus. Native to northern Mexico and southwestern Texas, peyote is a small, round, button-shaped cactus traditionally consumed by indigenous populations for its healing and psychoactive properties. Northern Native American groups spread its use throughout the United States during the nineteenth century[7] with the displacement and conglomeration of tribes, beginning with the Indian Removal Act in 1830 and following the establishment of the reservation system[8] in 1851. This eventually resulted in the "peyotism" practiced and protected by the Native American Church (NAC), established in 1918,[9] and later studied by infamous Harvard Botanist Richard Evans Schultes.[10] Mescaline, peyote's active ingredient, was identified and isolated by German chemist Arthur Heffter in 1897 and synthesized by Ernst Späth in 1919,[11] many years before Hofmann's discovery.

Several American writers were introduced to peyote in the 1950s through exposure to ritual use by the NAC and visits to Mexico. Beat poets Michael McClure, Gerd Stern, Philip Lamantia, William Burroughs, and Allen Ginsberg all used the cactus and publicized it to a larger audience. Many of their works were directly inspired by their peyote experiences, from Ginsberg's "Howl" (1956) and Burroughs's *Naked Lunch* (1959) to McClure's "Peyote Poem" (1958). The author (and later Merry Prankster) Ken Kesey claimed to have written the first pages of *One Flew Over the Cuckoo's Nest* (1962) after ingesting peyote buttons.[12]

Beat poet Gerd Stern recalled his initial peyote experiences in an interview for this book:

> I had started psychedelics much before acid ever appeared, with peyote in the 1940s in California. . . . Actually, once with Californian Indians and the other with a guy who was into publishing poetry, George Laite, but nobody remembers him anymore, and you know, peyote is a very different drug and also very inspiring although it's stomach-based rather than head-based and that can be a little [pause] vomitus. [laughs] But it was easy to get. You could just order it from Texas. They would send you a huge box for not very much money, but you had to process it because it was the whole plant with the root and everything. . . . They shipped it up in boxes by—what was that called—"Railroad Express" I think. It was fantastic. There was enough in the box for quite a few people to trip.[13]

After the discovery of LSD, research into these mind-altering drugs quickly gathered pace. In 1952, British psychiatrist Humphry Osmond became interested in the effects of LSD and mescaline in relation to schizophrenia and conducted patient studies at Weyburn Mental Hospital in Saskatchewan, Canada.[14] Aldous Huxley, the British author of *Brave New World* (1932) first learned about peyote and its active ingredient after visiting the United States and subsequently volunteered as a research subject for Osmond.[15] He was given mescaline in 1953 and wrote about his experience in *The Doors of Perception* (1954), influencing countless others (famously, Los Angeles rock band The Doors in 1965). Osmond himself is credited with coining the term "psychedelic" a few years later.[16]

Prior to his mescaline experience, Huxley had already explored the relationship between the mind and drugs. His quest for understanding the potential such substances held in unlocking and harnessing the power of the mind would later bring him and Leary together. In *Brave New World*, the pleasure-drug Soma is used by the World State to pacify the citizenship through "mood control;" in some ways Leary attempted to enact this with the aim of promoting positive and lasting behavioral change during his Harvard and Concord experiments in which Huxley took an active and guiding role.

British author Gerald Heard was another philosopher and intellectual in Huxley's circle with an interest in altered states of consciousness who quickly became a proponent of LSD. A radio broadcaster, journalist, and lecturer, Heard traveled with Huxley to America in 1937[17] and both men became involved with the Vedanta Society of Southern California, a spiritual movement headed by Swami Prabhavananda.[18] Heard was also friends with Bill Wilson, who had founded Alcoholics Anonymous in 1938 and who shared Heard's belief in the positive and transformative power of LSD.[19] Heard's short-lived spiritual educational center, Trabuco College (1942–47), as well as his work with Huxley at the Vedanta Society of Southern California, inspired psychologists Michael Murphy and Richard Price who established the Esalen Institute in Big Sur, California in 1962.[20] The center hosted seminars, workshops, and retreats on gestalt therapy,[21] yoga, meditation, and Eastern philosophies—giving birth to the New Age movement. Leary's coterie would become active participants at Esalen, particularly Richard Alpert, Allen Ginsberg, and Alan Watts.

A program of lectures offered by British philosopher and author of *The Way of Zen* (1957) Alan Watts was typical of the ideas explored at Esalen.

Watts emigrated from England in 1950 and became influential in the San Francisco Bay area as a radio broadcaster at the Pacifica Radio Berkeley station, KPFA. His show focused on religion, particularly Eastern traditions, psychology, and psychotherapy. Like many of his West Coast friends, Watts soon became acquainted with Timothy Leary.

These eclectic and artistic personalities paved the way and introduced others to the secrets of psychedelics, but another major player in the story was the United States government. From 1953 into the 1960s, the government secretly sponsored drug experiments using LSD and other psychoactive substances as part of a greater CIA-led covert project in mind control, known as MKUltra.[22] With the ultimate goal of

Above: The Esalen Institute, Big Sur, California. Today, Esalen remains a center for theory, research, and retreat, as it was during the 1960s when it championed the Human Potential Movement—the idea that the human race has untapped potential and that individuals realizing this potential can bring about positive change on a global scale.

countering Soviet brainwashing and interrogation techniques, MKUltra funded experiments conducted by various academic and research institutions without the participants' knowledge of what was happening or of the CIA involvement.[23]

American writer Ken Kesey participated in psychoactive drug studies from 1958 to 1960 at Menlo Park Veterans' Administration Hospital in Palo Alto, California, near the Stanford University campus where he was a graduate student in Creative Writing.

The research at Menlo was allegedly part of the MKUltra program, although Kesey was aware of the substances and was encouraged to volunteer by his neighbor Vik Lovell, to whom *Cuckoo's Nest* is dedicated.[24] However, an unknown number of people were unwittingly exposed to psychedelics during this period, courtesy of the United States government. There remains much controversy over Leary's own involvement in these CIA-sponsored drug trials and it may never be known whether Leary was an active participant or an unknowing recipient of state funds. Undoubtedly, much speculation exists over the links between his experiments and those of his colleagues, and the CIA's ongoing interest in the mind-altering power of such drugs. Robert Forte, an independent scholar and researcher of psychedelic drugs and their history and editor of Festschrift, *Timothy Leary: Outside Looking In* (1999),[25] discusses the complex web of connections surrounding these early experiments and the difficulty in separating Leary from the CIA's agenda at the time in an interview for this book:

> Was Timothy Leary a CIA agent?—is a simple question with a complex answer. The simple answer is yes, but that will not tell us very much. First, we need a bit of context, and to understand some special challenges of this inquiry. For instance, CIA "agent" is a rather broad designation. A person can be a witting or unwitting agent or asset of the CIA. The CIA employs a variety of front organizations to disguise their role in America, perhaps because it was often in violation of their charter which precluded operations in domestic affairs. The Geshickter Fund, for example, which paid for Wasson's expedition which revealed the sacred mushroom via *Life* magazine, was a front organization for the CIA. So was the Human Ecology Fund, which

supported Leary's Psilocybin Project at Harvard. Moreover, while there are well-known overt operatives and employees of the CIA, the CIA mainly works in secret. Operatives, assets or agents, will often sign an oath not to reveal their identity as employees of the CIA. And the CIA will often deny an agent is in fact an agent. Further complicating our question, many eccentric types (perhaps like Timothy Leary) for various reasons, will claim to be agents of the CIA, when they are not. If a person does not know they are being paid by the agency can we really say they are "working for the CIA"?

After the war, the Office of Strategic Service (OSS), predecessor of the CIA, split into three factions: The Harvard Psychology Clinic, The Institute of Personality Research at Berkeley (IPAR), and the Central Intelligence Agency (CIA). According to Frank Barron, Timothy's best friend and collaborator in his early career, during graduate school, "in their darker moments, they felt that they were all working for the CIA." (Frank Barron, *No Rootless Flower*, 1995)[26]

After his experience with the psychoactive drug study, Kesey and his friends threw LSD-fueled parties—the drug was still legal at the time—with acid manufactured by Owsley "Bear" Stanley and entertainment provided by the musical group the Warlocks, later renamed the Grateful Dead. Kesey is famous for his role leading the Merry Pranksters, an informal group of intellectual, mischievous, rebellious hippies, on the West Coast who became the subject of Tom Wolfe's book, *The Electric Kool-Aid Acid Test* (1968). In the summer of 1964, the Merry Pranksters, with Beat inspiration Neal Cassady behind the wheel, drove across the country in a psychedelically painted bus named *Furthur* (later corrected to *Further*) for three purposes: to champion the use of LSD; to reach New York City for the promotion of Kesey's novel, *Sometimes a Great Notion*; and to visit Timothy Leary and Richard Alpert and their commune in Millbrook, New York.[27] It was pegged as the meeting of the East and West Coast LSD scenes.

LSD and other such mind-altering substances clearly fascinated both the public and the establishment, yet their true power was unknown. Information spread through word of mouth and the relationships interwoven between different social circles—chemists, psychologists, and

Above: Owsley Stanley, aka "Bear," attends the SNACK Sunday concert (Students Need Activities, Culture, and Kicks) at Kezar Stadium on March 23, 1975 in San Francisco, California.

psychiatrists; anthropologists, philosophers, and theologians; artists, poets, and novelists. All created momentum for the "underground" knowledge of psychedelics to spread and seep into every element of the countercul- ture. The Beats, the peyote pioneers, and the early experimenters set the stage, so to speak, for Timothy Leary and Richard Alpert to determine the potential of psychedelics, through their Harvard University drug studies during the early 1960s. The resulting events saw Leary and his compa- triots spark an unprecedented escalation of drug use in the American counterculture that would virtually define a generation, and lead Leary on a personal crusade to understand the potential of the human mind.

Leary clearly realized the importance of his legacy. He appreciated the significance of his work and the key figures from this momentous period of revolutionary cultural change. He took care to save his own records from his personal life and research, and those of the organizations he founded and operated. Toward the end of his career, he also collected material regarding the counterculture to preserve for future generations. In 2011, his vision was realized when the New York Public Library acquired his personal papers.

This book came about after I was appointed Project Archivist for Leary's personal papers in 2011 and began to delve into the world of Leary and Alpert, Huxley and Ginsberg, communes and psychedelic light shows, and started to appreciate all the endless interconnections and influences associated with Leary. Before working on this project, I was already familiar with Timothy Leary the LSD guru who preached, "Turn on, tune in, drop out." He became a relic of the '60s, well liked by the underground until his death in 1996. I admit I was unaware of his academic training and predrug life, and the details of his legal struggles, and personal connections to so many artists, journalists, philosophers, and scholars leading the global vanguard. It turns out that Leary's life *is* the history of the counterculture.

Like so many stories within Leary's life, my research for this book required me to circle back through the collection to pull out items from the thousands of papers and computer files in the collection that docu- ment the development of this important cultural shift in our society. His collection not only reveals his own ideas, but those of the many artists, writers, scholars, students, journalists, authorities, institutions, publish- ers, performers, personalities, fans, and celebrities that were part of the counterculture and the mainstream's reaction to it. Selecting which items to include proved difficult as the archival material seems to contain an almost infinite number of connections.

The letters and papers offered in this book, most of which have never been published before, are intended to tell the story of the counterculture and its quest for enlightenment through first person accounts in the words of the letter writers. They serve as a unique insight into a period in history that has become obscured by its own myth-making. Importantly, my commentary throughout the following chapters acts as scene setting for the archival materials—this book is not intended to be a history of the entire counterculture, nor is it a complete biography of Timothy Leary—it is the story of the "Leary project" and the great counterculture experiment he initiated. Leary's telling of it through these documents will likely leave you with as many questions as answers, but perhaps that is the point.

AUTHOR'S NOTE

The documents in this book have been transcribed as per the originals, with the spellings, grammar, and content faithfully retained as far as it has been possible to interpret from the handwritten documents. Where necessary [sic] has been added to show that this was the author's original spelling, but we have avoided using it liberally so as not to hinder your reading or appreciation of the documents.

1

From Psychological Tests to Psychedelic Tests, 1957–61

"Everyone carries a piece of the puzzle. Nobody comes into your life by mere coincidence. Trust your instincts. Do the unexpected. Find the others . . ."

Timothy Leary (original source unknown)

FIRST AND FOREMOST, Timothy Leary was a psychologist, dedicated to exploring the workings of the mind. As scholars of psychology, Leary and his colleague Richard Alpert approached the study of the human mind and behavior by applying standard scientific methods from the field of social sciences. As professors in the Department of Social Relations at Harvard University, they were tasked with the usual duties of advising graduate students, applying for grants, and conducting research studies under the support of Harvard's Center for Research in Personality. At the time, Harvard psychologist B. F. Skinner's theories in behaviorism dominated the department. His models entailed the ideas of stimulus-response, conditioning, and reinforcement in shaping human behavior.[1]

Prior to his appointment in 1960, Leary authored a well-received monograph, *Interpersonal Diagnosis of Personality: A Functional Theory and Methodology for Personality Evaluation* (1957). This work was built on psychometric studies that he had conducted as a clinical psychologist at the Kaiser Hospital and Foundation in Oakland, California.

Some may not realize that before Leary ever dabbled in psychedelics, he received accolades for designing psychological tests. His "interpersonal circumplex" or "interpersonal behavior circle" was the first circular model for mapping interpersonal behavior.[2] Developed in collaboration with psychologist Hubert Coffey and fellow Berkeley alumni in the Kaiser Foundation Research Group (Mervin Freedman, Rolfe LaForge, and Abel Ossorio), this model used group psychotherapy sessions and psychological test data to create a vector model for personality in the context of interpersonal relationships.[3]

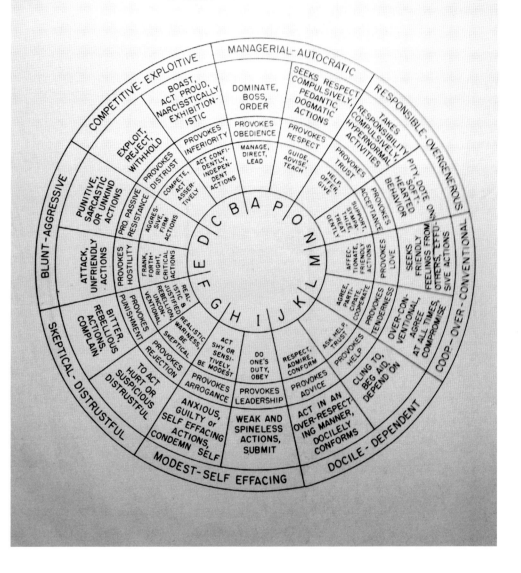

CLASSIFICATION OF INTERPERSONAL BEHAVIOR INTO
16 MECHANISMS OR REFLEXES

Page 30: Timothy Leary with sketch of behavior graph, a possible iteration developed during his work at the Kaiser Foundation in Oakland, California and his own private practice and Psychological Consultation Service during the 1950s.

Above: The "Leary Circle" graph developed by Leary to visualize his interpersonal system. Relationships and resulting behavior are classified into sixteen categories ranging in magnitude.

Visually charting the results of personality tests was a revolutionary idea. Established personality tests at the time included the MMPI (Minnesota Multiphasic Personality Inventory), which followed a linear approach for summarizing data,[4] whereas Leary's graph incorporated measurements in magnitude and direction, offering a richer, multifaceted picture of an individual's interpersonal traits, as interrelated. As he would discover post-psychedelics, a "web" would serve as an analogy to describe our interrelated relationships, including a person's reactions and, thus, personality characteristics.

Leary marketed his own product, calling it the Interpersonal System of Personality, which also incorporated the TAT (Thematic Apperception Test), a technique that uses picture interpretation to evaluate patterns of thought. Leary described his own product as a "complex combination of methods and measures for assessment of personality. . . . The raw data for the diagnoses are obtained from the MMPI, the TAT, and a test which was especially developed for interpersonal diagnosis. . . . The booklet provides space for summarizing interpersonal scores from the MMPI (at two levels) and at five or more scores from the Interpersonal Check List. The scores are standardized and plotted on the diagnostic grid. The diagnostic ratings are then used to calculate over 30 indices of conflict."[5]

Data from experiments using the model could be recorded in three booklets that Leary had specially designed: the Record Booklet of Interpersonal Diagnosis of Personality, the Record Booklet for Analysis of Group Dynamics, and the Record Booklet for Analysis of Family Dynamics, in addition to checklists, a template, and a manual.

His tests were used by other psychologists who ordered copies of his diagnostic worksheets throughout the 1960s and into the 1970s, as found in the records of his Psychological Consultation Service.[6] It is striking that experts continued to use Leary's tests even after he had been declared the "guru" of LSD. For Leary, his adventures into LSD research and his work as a psychologist went hand in hand.

Considering that Leary's training and professional career focused on the measurement of personality and behavior traits, it is not surprising that he applied these same methods to analyze and describe psychedelic substances, as seen in session report forms and later plotting circles. His social science training informed his approach to understanding the

Record Booklet For
Interpersonal Diagnosis of Personality

Subject _____ Age ____ Sex ____ Date _____ Testing # _____
LAST NAME   FIRST NAME.

Address _____ City _____ Phone _____ Education _____

Occupation _____ Marital Status _____ Occupation of Spouse _____

Referred by _____ Therapist _____ Group _____

Other _____

Identifying Codes for Clinical and Sociological Data

Sex . . . . ____ 1	Therapist. . . . . ____17	_____ ____33	Tests covered by this record:	
Age . . . . ____ 2	Type of Therapy . . . . . ____18	_____ ____34	Name	Form	Testing #
Religion . . . . ____ 3	Times Seen . . . . ____19	_____ ____35	MMPI ____ ____
Number of Siblings . . . ____ 4	Disposition . . . . ____20	_____ ____36	ICL ____ ____
Marital Status . . . . . . ____ 5	Condition . . . . ____21	_____ ____37	IFT TAT ____ ____
Number of Children . . . ____ 6		_____ ____38	____ ____ ____
	_____ ____22	_____ ____39	____ ____ ____
Subject's Occupation . . ____ 7	_____ ____23	_____ ____40	____ ____ ____
Occupation of Mother . . ____ 8	_____ ____24	_____ ____41	
Occupation of Father . . ____ 9	_____ ____25		Remarks: _____
Occupation of Spouse . . ____10		_____ ____42	_____
	_____ ____26	_____ ____43	_____
Subject's Education . . . ____11	_____ ____27	_____ ____44	_____
Mother's Education . . . ____12	_____ ____28	_____ ____45	_____
Father's Education . . . ____13		_____ ____46	_____
Spouse's Education . . . ____14	_____ ____29	_____ ____47	_____
	_____ ____30	_____ ____48	_____
Referred by . . . . ____15	_____ ____31	_____ ____49	_____
Previous Consultations ____16	_____ ____32	_____ ____50	_____

© This booklet was prepared by Timothy Leary, Ph. D., and published by the Psychological Consultation Service.

Above: This booklet accompanied the brochure and price list for "Test Booklets Manual employed in Interpersonal Diagnosis of Personality." The purpose of the "Record Booklet for Interpersonal Diagnosis of Personality" was to aid psychologists in summarizing the patient's behavior at all measurable levels of personality in order to assess relationships to the therapist, motivation for treatment, and possible types of conflict, along with the best possible treatment.

Interpersonal Diagnosis
Multi-Level Personality Pattern

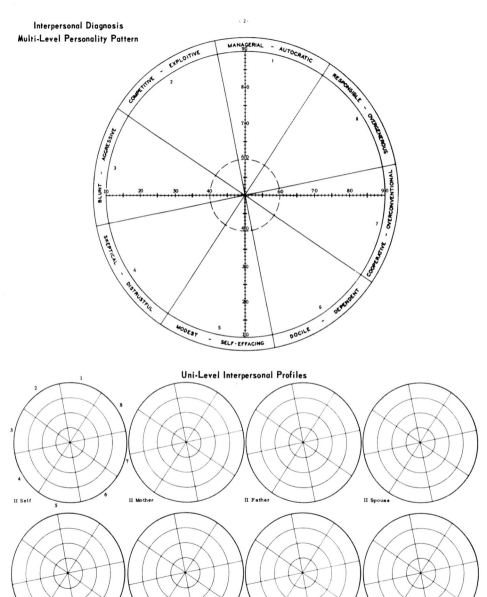

Uni-Level Interpersonal Profiles

II Self

II Mother

II Father

II Spouse

V Ideal

Above: The "Interpersonal Checklist" measures interpersonal behavior. The patient checks him or herself, his parents, his spouse, his therapist, and his ego ideal. The checklist could also be employed in the analysis of group and family dynamics.

psychedelic experience. As expected, his graphs and plotting circles become more and more unusual after the introduction of drugs.

Leary had his first experience with a hallucinogenic or psychedelic drug as a mature man—a Harvard professor in psychology, a widower, and a father of two. His wife's suicide was only five years prior. As previously mentioned, he was vacationing in Mexico that August 1960, as he had done several times before, this time in Cuernavaca—a popular haunt with his social science peers. His Berkeley colleague Frank Barron had recounted his own mushroom experience in Mexico to Leary the previous summer. Barron and linguist Lothar Knauth encouraged and prepped Leary to try it for himself.[7] Leary was by all accounts a "square": a middle-aged, single father with a solid alcohol and tobacco habit who had not as yet dabbled in psychoactive substances.[8] This was not a teenage, thrill-seeking, recreational happening. The hippie was not yet realized, the peace sign was still largely unknown outside of Britain[9] and Leary was nearly forty years old. In his autobiography *High Priest* (1968), Leary stated that "ever since that last weekend and the mushrooms, I didn't know as much anymore. I had started the slow process of throwing things out of my mind, junking mental furniture that had been clogging up my brain."[10]

Clearly, the experience for Leary was life-changing. Afterwards, he was determined to explore the potential that such drugs could offer and he began exploratory studies at Harvard that fall semester. By November 15, 1960, he wrote a report to Dave McClelland, Head of the Department of Social Relations, outlining the status of his research thus far. He stated that his aims were "to determine the conditions under which psilocybin can be used to broaden and deepen human experience; to determine which persons are benefited by the drug and in which direction; and to determine methods of making the beneficial effects durable and recoverable without subsequent exposure to the chemical."[11]

Leary's initial approach to this research was fairly typical for the time. He started as a scientist to quantify and characterize the psilocybin experience. The subjects were to "alternate between roles of observers and participants"[12] and initially consisted of two faculty members and five graduate students. The group included Timothy Leary, Frank Barron, and colleague George Litwin. Aldous Huxley also participated in the

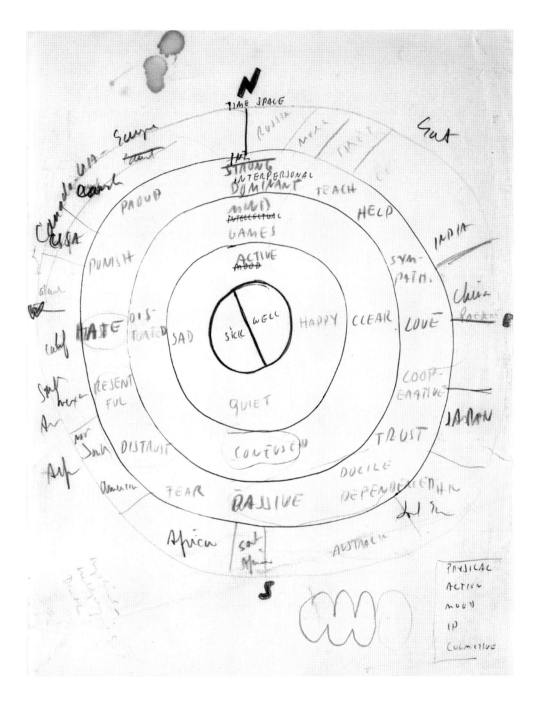

Above: Post-psychedelic "Leary Circle." Timothy Leary
continued to use the vector plotting circle throughout
his life. This appears to be reworked for characterizing
behaviors and attributes physically on the planet. The x
and y axes have been replaced by the four directions on
a space-time continuum. Not surprisingly, the East
holds positive attributes, and the West is full of hate
and distrust, c. 1962–64.

planning of meetings and drug sessions. After the first experience, it was determined to bring spouses or close friends to participate in order to reduce anxiety. Synthesized psilocybin was obtained from the Sandoz Laboratories in Switzerland, where the scientist who first discovered and ingested LSD, Albert Hofmann, worked. This was also where the CIA obtained the drugs for their experiments.[13] "The first step was to expose every member of the group to the psilocybin experience in a naturalistic setting. This was done in small groups with at least three observers present. Tape recordings of the sessions are obtained. Observers' reports, phenomenological write-ups by the subjects and tape recordings of the session, comprise the data."[14]

FROM TIMOTHY LEARY TO DR. DAVID MCCLELLAND, HARVARD | NOVEMBER 15, 1960

Dear Dave, I have received your note of November 14 in which you suggested that we put on record the design of our mushroom research. I thoroughly agree and herewith enclose a description of our current work and future plans:

Purpose of Research:
The aims of this research are:
1) To determine the conditions under which psilocybin★ can be used to broaden and deepen human experience
2) To determine which persons are benefited by the drug and in which direction
3) To determine methods of making the beneficial effects durable and recoverable without subsequent exposure to the chemical.

Among the most noticeable effects of the drug are increased sensitivity to visual experience and a voluntary and involuntary elimination of the subject–object relationship. Mystical and visionary experiences are produced.

Subjects:
There are no subjects in the classic sense. The members of the research group alternate between roles of observers and participants. All collaborate in planning and in analyzing data. The original research

team included two faculty members, and five graduate students-research assistants:

Timothy Leary   Ellen Count
Frank Barron   Eleanor Mayher
George Litwin   Sandra Raynsford
James Ciarle

Mr. Aldous Huxley has also participated in all planning sessions and in the drug experience.

After the first experience, it was agreed that allowing spouses or close friends of the members to join the group might diminish anxiety and increase the positive aspects.

*Psilocybin, a product of the Sandoz Laboratories, is the synthesized Mexican Mushroom.

Leary was fascinated by his experiments from the outset and shared his initial thoughts with Laura Huxley, Aldous's wife, who was also a psychological counselor:

TIMOTHY LEARY TO LAURA HUXLEY | NOVEMBER 18, 1960

Dear Laura, Mushroom magic continues to permeate the atmosphere here. Fascinating to see it work. Some are entranced. Many are frightened. Fear is our worst enemy. As usual.

I've talked to many people here about your "therapy" workbook and we are awaiting the promised publication.

As soon as our write-ups on the mushrooms are ready, I'll send you copies.

Sandoz Laboratories want you to have an M.D. make an application for psilocybin. They are apparently eager to have it aired for research at this time. Again the ridiculous compartmentalizations—research vs. treatment? With you as observer this platonic distinction makes no sense to me.

Enclosed are some materials for your perusal. The afternoon when Aldous participated was too active for visions but produced one of the richest, moving, raw human experiences one would ever want to be in. Food for years of thought.

Enjoyed meeting and knowing you so briefly. Hope to be able to continue our talks soon.

And please write up your work!

Best wishes, Timothy Leary

Soon after Leary's first psychedelic experience, he decided to further investigate and developed studies in set and suggestion[15] and crime reduction.[16] His colleague Richard Alpert did not have a chance to try the mushrooms in Mexico with Leary, but finally consumed synthesized psilocybin months later. By this time, Leary had contacted poets and artists to participate in his studies. Allen Ginsberg and Leary joined Alpert for his first psilocybin experience in Newton, Massachusetts in February 1961.[17] Reportedly, Alpert blissfully shoveled the snow and experienced personal revelations.[18]

Leary and Alpert—after he was on board—continued to contact individuals previously experienced in psychoactive substances, such as Albert Hofmann, Aldous Huxley, Humphry Osmond, and R. Gordon Wasson, the amateur mycologist who first wrote about Mazatec psilocybin mushroom traditions in *Life* magazine (June 10, 1957).

Other graduate students and colleagues, artists, poets, and like-minded individuals volunteered as test subjects and were administered psychotropic drugs (including synthesized psilocybin), often obtained via Hofmann and the Sandoz Laboratories. Leary and Alpert's Harvard studies included the "Psilocybin Study" (1960–62), the "Good Friday Experiment" (sometimes known as the "Marsh Chapel Experiment," a one-off experiment aimed at exploring whether psychoactive substances could catalyze the transcendent religious experience, 1962), and the "Concord Prison Experiment" (a larger study in the use of psychedelics and group psychotherapy in reducing prisoner recidivism rates, 1961–63).

By 1961, Leary was already concerned about drug prohibition and mentioned that his studies at Harvard involved graduate students regularly taking psilocybin for a semester "working through, organizing, and systematizing the results."[19] The journalist Arthur Koestler became an early advisor to Leary and Alpert and participated in their hallucinogenic drug experiments. Just before Leary tried psilocybin he gave Koestler a personality test developed by Frank Barron.

Leary was determined to apply his scientific methods of personality research and testing to the psychedelic experience, but he knew that in order to gain a clear set of results he would need a wide and varied pool of willing participants to join in his "Leary project."

ARTHUR KOESTLER   Form II B

NAME _____ DATE _____
(print)   Last   first   middle

MAJOR FIELD _____ AGE_____   SEX _____

Directions: In this test you will be given a list of briefly stated images
and asked to create for each image three symbolically equivalent or similar
images which are suggested by the stimulus image.

Example

Given image: Leaves in the wind

Possible symbolic equivalents:

    Papers on an empty street
    Driftwood in a river
    Falling stars
    Clothing in a Bendix
    Derelicts roaming over the earth

    Ten stimulus images will be presented, and for each of them
you are asked to make up other images which are similar or symbolically
equivalent. The ten stimulus images will be presented in two groups of
five each, and for each of the two groups you will have five minutes in
which to work

STOP HERE, WAIT FOR FURTHER INSTRUCTIONS

PLEASE   FINISH

This test was developed by Frank Barron, Ph.D., University of California

2
Academia, Meet Bohemia, 1960–62

"The goal of an intelligent life, according to Socrates,
is to pursue the philosophic quest—to increase
one's knowledge of self and world."

Timothy Leary, *Your Brain Is God*

ONCE LEARY AND ALPERT began to incorporate psilocybin research into their curricula at Harvard, they sought to widen their pool of test subjects and reached out to those who were already experienced with psychedelics. Leary's letters from this period are a record of how these relationships were formed and how many developed into lifelong friendships. A growing circle of friends, colleagues, graduate students, and others, began spending more time at his home in Newton, Massachusetts.

Aldous Huxley, already a good friend and experienced in drug experimentation, was fascinated by Leary's research and he too provided further connections with like-minded people. Some friendships predated Harvard: Frank Barron and Leary were college friends and it was under Barron's urging that Leary met with David McClelland, Director of the Center for Personality Research at Harvard University, leading to Leary's appointment as a Professor at Harvard.[1]

FROM TIMOTHY LEARY TO ALDOUS HUXLEY | NOVEMBER 18, 1960

Dear Aldous Huxley, Allen [sic] Watts was having lunch with your would-be host, Professor M____, but I missed seeing him. Hope to see him in New York this weekend. Enclosed are some materials for your files. Thanks for the peyote article. Frank Barron and I are beginning conversations with the research divisions of some large companies to investigate the possibility of increasing creativity of top-drawer scientists. I'll keep you posted. Hope to see you before you go back.

Sincerely yours, Timothy Leary

At the time of this letter, Huxley was a visiting Professor of Humanities at MIT[2] while battling laryngeal cancer. In early September, Huxley attended the conference, "Great Issues of Conscience in Modern Medicine" at Dartmouth College, but felt disappointed that no one discussed mind-changing drugs.[3] By December, he was completing his book *On Art and Artists*.[4]

Among the many people Leary invited to participate in his studies was Allen Ginsberg.[5] Viewing Ginsberg as his *entrée* into the New York Beats and the larger world of bohemia, Leary was able to secure introductions to those outside his usual cadre of academics. As Leary was making introductions with notable countercultural figures of the day, the Beat Generation was still in full swing. William S. Burroughs had recently published his avant-garde novel *Naked Lunch* (1959).

Ginsberg was interested in psychoactive drugs and remained eager for new experiences. He had used LSD in 1959 as a research subject at Stanford University.[6] A frequent traveler, he had also ventured to Pucallpa, Peru in the summer of 1960 to sample a medicinal brew—*ayahuasca*—under the guidance of a local healer or *curandero*.[7] Leary wrote to Ginsberg in November 1960 and the poet replied enthusiastically:

FROM ALLEN GINSBERG TO TIMOTHY LEARY | NOVEMBER 10, 1960

Dear Mr. Leary, Yes by all means! I don't know if Spiegel told you—he wrote to me you would write—I spent half a year in S. America this year and took Panisteriopsis [sic] Caapi (*Ayahuaaca* [sic], *Yange* [sic]) a number of times & kept lots of notes, mostly sort of abstract alas, but also some drawings & poems. Also I spent 2 days at Standford [sic] & had LSD a couple of times. Enclosed a piece of writing I did—about the 8th hour of the LSD. Part II Howl if you have read it, is Peyote writing.

Is Huxley there? Spiegel said he was at KIT working with mushrooms—I have never been in touch with him—show him the poem if you see & know him.

Also I have had a lot of Nitrous Oxide, Ether, Mescaline, Peyote, Marijuana, Ditran (a Datura?), (awful)—& the opiates. I'll bring up the notes I took while high.

My original interest & "stability" thru all this—or "control"—was a series of—I mean what I was looking for—was that when younger I had a series of mystical experiences—connected with reading Blake.

I have friend coming this week from S.F. and want to show him around N.Y. & am in a little confusion what I'll be doing the next few weeks. Send me a note—when you are free to have us up to C.R.P.? and I'll make plans accordingly—sometime to the end of this month?

I hope it will be OK if two of us come—another poet I live with, Peter Orlovsky, who's also had a lot of Peyote LSD & Panisteriopsis [sic], etc.

Do you know *Naked Lunch*, a very great piece of prose by W.S. Burroughs (Olympia Press, Paris)—you'll have to get it thru customs as science-privileged somehow—it's one of the most illuminating books—based on fantastically deep & extensive drug use—full of eccentric brilliant, psychic theories, satire on brainwash techniques, etc.

There is also an extensive amount of published poetry reflecting peyote insights—I'll try bring some up—almost all the younger poets have been experimenting with black market hallucinogens for 10 years.

Your letter is a great gift, since it gets me off this damned black market—I somehow had not encountered any sympathetic doctors in the East who had access to Psilocybin. Tho' I have some mushrooms I got from Gordon Wasson which I will try this week—as well as some Oloquoi [sic] seeds. The latter doesn't seem to work tho'.

Let us know when you want us to come up. I think we will need fare, or fare repaid, as I am, about, broke. OK—thanks for your letter.

Yours, Allen Ginsberg

The enclosed poem except for the marked corrections is pretty much the unchanged notes taken while still high—tho coming down by then.

Through Ginsberg, Leary made the acquaintance of William S. Burroughs while traveling to Tangier, Morocco in July 1961. On that voyage he also met Gregory Corso, Alan Ansen, and Paul Bowles. Leary and Burroughs met again in London, after attending a conference in Copenhagen in September,[8] and they maintained a lifelong friendship.

Ginsberg found some other friends who were also interested in Leary's drug studies: LeRoi Jones (later known as Amiri Baraka), a poet and publisher based in Greenwich Village whose work later became more aligned with black nationalism; Robert Lowell, former United States

Poet Laureate (1947–48) and Pulitzer Prize winner; and Gregory Corso, a close friend of Ginsberg who was living at the Beat Hotel in Paris at the time—a lodging house in the Left Bank at 9 Rue Gît-le-Cœur, frequented by many Beat poets. Ginsberg, Peter Orlovsky, Burroughs, Corso, Bowles, Ansen, and others divided their time between Paris and Tangier during the period between 1957 and 1963, forming a close-knit group.

FROM ALLEN GINSBERG TO TIMOTHY LEARY | NOVEMBER 1960

Dear Tim, The following have expressed interest: Barney Rossett, Grove Press; Leroi Jones, *Yugen* Magazine; Muriel Rukeyser (Poetess & also author); Robert Lowell.

Lowell is hesitant, and I will see him tomorrow, the rest have already agreed, so send them each a note. They all want to stay in NY. I haven't made any definite arrangements. (All are in phonebook or can be reached thru information). The first three can do it at my home, tho Rossett & Rukeyser have not visited before. Lowell as you may know has been in hospital often, mental, drinking, manic depressive, and seems interested tho tentative, worried, he has a negative-type wife—"Oh that's all we need." I hear she puts him in bughouse when he is manic and takes him out when depressive. But he's a sensitive man on his own actually.

There are lots of other people, unknown, hepcats, or minor poets, who would jump—I've worked on these first.

One problem is my natural instinct would give Clyo [psilocybin] first to friends, rather than powers, so it is rather like Work to line up people, and a disturbance. I seem not to be made for organization, no matter how weird its purpose, and the errands & phone calls & explanations of agentry, being Secret agent X-9, depress me—partly the distraction from sitting home reading Milton & writing.

In addition this week I've been entertaining a gang of Russian writers—Konstantin Simonov & Co.—so I have been extra-distracted—they should take some Cylobin while here.

I'll be here on the 14th, so come down & stay over, and/or send me postcard to say where to meet you, whatever you want.

I had a good time in Boston & inspiring week, I still have to write long Messiah poem, messiah mixed with electronics. Today I went to the dentist & had another session with laughing gas to see how it felt again & it was mysterious & great—you must try it. It feels like the universe is a mental balloon that disintegrated when you glimpse the Inevitable Pin of Nada, when the mind goes out. And that it's happened before. Life seems like an inevitable movie played backwards.

Segal was here, explaining his Roles theory, I wish he would turn on. You get Reisman?

Okokokokokokokokokokokokokok many thanks again for friendly week & I'll send you some loot when I get some, sooner or later soon—hello to Frank Charlie & Rona & babes. Love, Allen

[he appends addresses for Burroughs and Corso to this note]

Although Ginsberg traveled extensively, he was often based in his native New York City where he was surrounded by multiple artists including the jazz musicians Thelonious Monk and Dizzy Gillespie. Photographer Robert Frank was another artist who collaborated with Ginsberg and the other members of the Beat scene. Most often Frank is remembered for his acclaimed photography book, *The Americans* (1959;[9] Jack Kerouac contributed to the introduction). That same year, Frank directed a film adaptation of Kerouac's play *Beat Generation*; the film, *Pull My Daisy* (1959) featured Ginsberg, Orlovsky, and Corso.[10] In many ways, Ginsberg was Leary's recruiting officer for the Beats, enthusing to many the power and potential of psychedelics to open them up to new levels of consciousness and inspiring them to take part in Leary's great experiment by contributing their very own drug session reports:

FROM ALLEN GINSBERG TO TIMOTHY LEARY | DECEMBER 1960

Dear Tim, Lovely to get yr note & you do bounce back to adventure so enthusiastically, it's a pleasure.—I spoke to Rossett several times on the phone, he's alright and friendly, I spoke to Ann his girl on the phone for half an hour or so, she's in one piece and fine, so no worry there. Tried to see them but everybody too busy Xmas, etc.

Next, I spoke 2 nites ago to Dizzy Gillespie & Thelonious Monk who are interested. Can you send them each a short notice inviting them to call you when they get to Boston in next month? [addresses follow for Gillespie and Monk] *nov.*

Dear Tim:

The following have expressed interest:

    Barney Rossett, Grove Press, 64 University Place NYC
    Leroi Jones, Yugen Magazine, 324 E 14 Street, NYC
    Muriel Rukeyser --790 Riverside Drive (Poetess & also author
                      of biog of scientist Willard Gibbs)
    Robert Lowell--194 Riverside Drive, NYC

Lowell is hesitant, and I will see him tomorrow, the rest have already
agreed, so send them each a note. They all want to stay in NY, I haven't
made any definite arrangements. (All are in phonebook or can be reached
thru information). The first three can do it at my house, tho Rossett
& Rukeyser have not visited before. Lowell as you know maybe has been in
hospitals often, mental, drinking, manicdepressive, and seems interested
tho tentative, worried, he has a negative type wife --"Oh that's all wee
need," I hear she puts him in bughouse when he is manic and takes him out
when depressive. But he's a sensitive man on his own actually.
                                          There are lots
of other people, unknown, hepcats, or minor poets, who would jump--I've
worked on these first.
                  One problem is my natural instinct would give Cylo
first to friends, rather than powers, so it is rather like Work to line
up people, and a disturbance. I seem not to be made for organization, no
matter how wierd its purpose, and the errands&phonecalls & explanations of
agentry, being Secret agent X-9, depresses me---partly the distraction
from sitting home reading milton & writing.
                              In addition this week I've
been entertaining a gang ofRussian writers--Konstantin Simonov & Co--
so I have been extra distracted. *They should take some Cyloybin while here*

    I'll be here the 14th, so come down & stay over, and/or send me
postcard say where to meet you, whatever you want.
    I had a good time in Boston & inspiring week, I still have to write
long Messiah poem,messiah mixed with electronics. Today I went to dentist
& had another session with laughing gas to see how it felt again & it was
mysterious & great--you must try it. It feels like the universe is a
mental baloon that disintegrated when you glimpse the Inevvitable Pin
of Nada, when the mind goes out.and that it s happened before. Life
seems like an inevitable movie played backwards.
    Segal was here, explaining his Roles theory, I wish he would turn on.
You get Reisman?
            okokokokokokokok many thanks again for friendly week
            & I'll send you some loot when I get some, sooner or
            later soon------hello to Frank Charlie & Rhona & babes.

                        Love,
                        Allen

William Burroughs address
c/o Ian Summerville
Corpus Christie College
Cambridge, England
Send Cyloybin sooner

Allen

Connect both with Rosly Klein, but mainly Burroughs

Gregory Corso
9 Rue Git-le-Coeur
Paris 6, France

Page 44: Allen Ginsberg, Timothy Leary, Ralph Metzner (left to right) pose in front of a plaster Buddha in preparation for a psychedelic celebration performance at the Village Theater, New York City, c. 1965–67.

Above: In a letter to Timothy Leary, Allen Ginsberg lists individuals claiming interest in his drug studies, such as publisher Barney Rossett and poets LeRoi Jones, Robert Lowell, and Muriel Rukeyser, and goes on to suggest that his Russian poet guest, Konstantin Simonov, should also take "cyloybin" [psilocybin]. Ginsberg closes by sharing contact information for William S. Burroughs and Gregory Corso, which will further establish Leary's connection with Beat writers in the 1960s.

Gillespie says he gets to Boston often and he could call you & come over for an evening and would I think. Boy I'd like to be there for that one. But I'll probably be away. He'll be Santa Claus like Olson [famed poet Charles Olson] I think.

Thelonious Monk gets away from NY rarely & may not be able to make Boston, but do send him a note anyway so he sees the set up and maybe we or you can catch him later in the Winter in NYC if there's time.

Monk is a big child who would be delighted to get a friendly letter from a Harvard Professor, asking him if he wants to turn on. He's also a rare great deep buddhic [sic] man, I'm told. I spent nite talking with [him] last Monday and he was extraordinarily sweet tho he don't say much, ever. He did say God is dog spelt backward.

If you can get them on, you have the acknowledged Princes of Jazz at yr side.

I sent Mailer a postcard w/ yr address. Kerouac wants me to bring him some in L.I. I gave the mescaline to Robert . . . and Miles Forst, a painter.

I'm leaving for Cuba with Peter & Leroi Jones on Jan 2 and be back in 2 weeks after that I think—free trip sponsored by Cuba. Also received a check for $1,000 in mail from an anonymous foundation donor, don't know who. Enclosed find check for $40 to cover phonecall to Kerouac & a little on our excessive expenses to Boston. I'd send more to further yr project but I'm trying to keep the main body of the loot together for India. If you can send me anything to bring to Cuba—Cylocybin or Mescalien [sic]—I could turn on the poet Nicholas Guillen & maybe Castro, maybe not.

Not seen Lowell—I received proofs of my book and must work on them this week so I'm occupied—plus a mess of letters to answer & I'm doing that now. Great you got approval on seminar. YES SEND Barney [Barney Rossett, publisher at Grove Press] a little follow up note, asking for comments on the experience I guess. Make him feel good & followed up on. Strangely, I think he's publishing the Kerouac Book he put down over supper table the other nite. Change of heart of some kind.

Jesus I hope all this keeps going.

Love, Allen

Abstract expressionist painters Willem de Kooning and Franz Kline were contemporaries acquainted with Ginsberg in what was known as the "New York School"—a group of artists and poets living in New York City during the 1950s who paralleled the Beats and included poets such as Kenneth Koch and Frank O'Hara and painters Mark Rothko and Robert Motherwell.[11] Like the Beats, they were associated with jazz music and the avant-garde. Kline created his large wall paintings during this time in the late 1950s and early 1960s, before he died on May 13, 1962.[12] De Kooning's gestural work often depicted chaotic expressions of New York life and the frenetic energy of the growing drug scene:[13]

FROM ALLEN GINSBERG TO TIMOTHY LEARY | DECEMBER 31, 1960

Dear Tim, Next: the painters. The 2 big abstract-expressionists are Willem de Kooning & Franz Kline. De Kooning I haven't been able to get a hold of (don't have his address) but his phone number is LF 3-5680. He said a month ago he wanted to try mescaline-type drugs. If you're in NY while I'm gone, phone him. (I never so far have found him in). I'll send you his addr. as sooner or later for you to send him a note.

I saw Franz Kline yesterday & explained the situation, he said he was ready to turn on any-time [sic]. [address and phone no. follow] So he's all ready. Please send him a note as soon as possible (just to ratify my conversation that he was invited to participate)—and can get him sooner or later whenever there's an opportunity.

OK—out to big New Years parties tonite, hope you have a nice time with Huston Smith. Dan . . . a sort of psychological journalist who wrote about sit ins & Puerto Ricans is also now starting a series on drugs, sympathetic, with the angle that pot should be legalized. I gave him all the information & sources that I had. If you are interested in turning him on his address . . . .

I don't [know] when I leave, probably be delayed beyond the 2nd of Jan—so send mushrooms here—I can always have them forwarded or Mescalien [sic] whatever.

Burroughs has moved from Cambridge to Paris [address follows]—if you can ever connect him with Heim or anyone in Paris. Happy New Year.

OK, As ever, Allen

Ginsberg in the above letter refers to Huston Smith, Chair of the Philosophy Department at MIT, who first participated in a drug session at Leary's home on New Year's Day, 1961 with Frank Barron, who was then on the faculty at the University of California in Santa Cruz.[14] Smith wrote a session, or trip, report after this experience, "Notes on Mescalin [sic]."

Ginsberg wrote again in the new year and Orlovsky enclosed his trip report with this note:

FROM PETER ORLOVSKY AND ALLEN GINSBERG TO TIMOTHY LEARY
| JANUARY 1, 1961

Hi Timothey [sic], Here is all this reports & statements for your need to fill pill pocket.

Have been working & reading about Cuba in different books about. Still don't know if we get to go yet.

Lot of New Year parties & rain more talk with some Psychiatrist at party but forgot his name—Thanks for yr report & N.O. Brown

So maybe see you in Jan 14 or so, Peter

Dear Tim, Been reading books on Cuba and wind up much more sympathetic to Castro, especially after events of last few days. Castro's speeches real great. T. Monk has no phone that I know of, I'll send him an added note to try arrange some way of contacting you when you hit town—the 14th for real? You expect to have Cylocybin replenished by then?

Brown's piece quite strange—will you be able to contact him? He has a lot of influence on Barzum-trilling-auden set. But his piece is quite magnanimous, great in itself—last gasp of classicisms. Is it published anywhere?

I sent you Franz Kline & W. de Kooning addresses & phones last letter.

Everything among papers quite admirable. I'd heard about McFate's decision from Weston La Barre; it's being appealed alas still however. Yr report seems quite up to the mark professionally.

Not received Mes. Yet.

Busy—helping friend off junk habit—typing mss—writing dreams down—letters—about ready to get out from under soon.

No news from Cuba yet but trip not off—may go any day—or not. I may be here weekend of 14th—yr welcome to stay over here whether we're here or not.

Love, Allen

FROM ALLEN GINSBERG TO TIMOTHY LEARY | JANUARY 1961

Dear Tim, Received your letter, w/usual interest.

I spoke to Willem de Kooning yesterday, so please drop him an invitation too. [address follows]. If you phone, ring twice, hang up & ring again.

I figure Kline, de Kooning, Monk & Gillespie are the most impressive quartet imaginable for the moment so will leave it at that for a while, till they can be taken care of, not send you new names & work trouble for a while. Hope you can get these letters off.

I also wrote Osmond & Huxley asking them to connect Burroughs with Heim, or anyone in Paris.

None of my business actually, but Koestler always struck me as a little hard hearted somehow—hate myself to have him as a Final Curandero. That is, being an intellectual, he tend to organize a polemic-dogmatic-mental system around experience (as in his essay on Zen, which is very intelligent but not so magnanimous). But by all means send him batches to hand out.

Rosset's address is . . . . His girl Ann quit her job & seems generally displeased by the whole experience—not sullen, not exactly disapproving—but he has his own mind.

You have Corso's *Happy Birthday of Death?*

H.S.'s "peril of mind let loose"—well I agree with you generally. But I have had that experience of absolute fear—"suppose it decides not to keep the body going"—in Peru. It never recurred, but I can't guarantee it won't recur to me. That is there was something mysterious happening beyond what I know and later experienced. "Each incarnation is different." But at the time I was sure that if I really let go I would literally die and that might be a good idea, to get to another dimension. But I wasn't so positive it was a good idea. Really fearfully confused. Maybe you could die, like a Yoga or Buddha or something worse, or better?

Above: Allen Ginsberg leads a group of demonstrators outside the Women's House of Detention in New York City's Greenwich Village advocating the use of marijuana. Ginsberg is shown carrying a sign that reads "Pot is a Reality Kick."

Although Ginsberg's main preoccupation that January was trying to secure his trip to Cuba, his commitment to the power of drugs to open the mind was unwavering and he wrote to Leary again in January 1961 to put forward his ideas for championing the legalization of pot. During this period of his life, Ginsberg frequently traveled to Cuba, attracted to the anti-capitalist, revolutionary society once Fidel Castro had taken control in 1959. Interestingly, after the CIA staged the Bay of Pigs invasion on April 17, 1961 in an unsuccessful attempt to overthrow Castro's regime, Ginsberg reacted publicly, authoring his "Prose Contribution to Cuban Revolution" manifesto in October 1961. Another key preoccupation for Ginsberg in his letters to Leary was trying to connect Burroughs with Heim. In his letter dated January 1961 he wrote: "Burroughs is on way east in a few weeks I think—not sure. He writes he had some LSD in London, as well as an injection of another drug—what I dunno. [Burroughs] writes—"Don't flip pops is all. One must be careful of altitude sickness (siroche) and depth madness and the bends. . . . Hazards of the Silent World. . . . 'Space is silent remember' etc."

Ginsberg again picks up the theme of Cuba in his next letter, but also touches on the wider reception to Leary's work, which was beginning to attract attention within the field:

FROM ALLEN GINSBERG TO TIMOTHY LEARY | UNDATED

Dear Tim, Received the Cylocybin [sic]. Cuba trip is neither off nor on. Seems there was a reception party waiting for us to land at the Havana airport a week ago. Some bureaucratic difficulty. No telling when it will be straightened out.

Meanwhile be here probably the next weeks. I'm guarding the pills. Do you want I [sic] should take on Monk or Frank Kline or de Kooning? I feel sure I could handle those situations and send you whatever data you need. That would leave yr schedule less crowded on the 14th. I could take care of at least 1 or 2 on the list. Let me know if I should go ahead & contact them.

I gave some leftover mescaline to a painter Miles Forst who had a color sensation ball on a small amount & was very pleased . . . .

Read over all material you sent—you're going to have some correspondence business—luck[y] you have a secretary. Send me a postcard answering above, unless you be here before then—I'll likely certainly be in town & welcome you to stay here.

Heard from Osmond who sent me some interesting papers & said "I'm glad you met Leary in Cambridge. I saw him and felt that he was really interested and likely to be a valuable recruit to this strange and alive field." So despite your impressions of hesitancy at lunch with him you mentioned, he seems benevolent. His papers are pretty far out like Brown's. Also heard from Schiltes [possibly the ethnobotanist Richard Evans Schultes] who told me next time I was in Cambridge to look him up to examine his narcotics library. Said he would like to meet you sooner or later.

That really is great news about the seminar. Once that gets going there'll be no way to stop it. Maybe start one at Columbia—anyone at Columbia doing this work? We could try turning on Barzun [Jacques Barzun] the dean of Faculties.

OK, Allen

The "seminar" Ginsberg refers to was the Harvard Social Relations Department's plan for a colloquium on "Drugs, Behavior, and Mysticism" that was to be led by Frank Barron, followed by a day of poets: Kerouac, Olson, and Ginsberg. While Leary was planning this, Aldous Huxley was at the end of his career and facing a diagnosis of cancer. He was writing his last novel, *Island*, which was finally published in 1962. The following year, Huxley passed away and his wife Laura published her self-help book *You Are Not the Target*. Leary wrote to them both at the start of 1961 to let them know about the colloquium:

FROM TIMOTHY LEARY TO LAURA AND ALDOUS HUXLEY
| JANUARY 23, 1961

Dear Laura & Aldous, As you will see from the enclosed, *Harper's* is interest[ed] in the mushrooms. I'll be glad to send you the records and findings of our work if you'd like us to use them to write an essay. I've just finished surveying the psilocybin literature which I find appalling—all the investigators find psychiatric symptoms! I'm sending you under separate cover, the abstracts collected by Sandoz so you can make your own diagnosis.

Spent last weekend in New York running agapes for poets, editors and novelists. Results continue to be encouraging. Also spent some time with Gordon Wasson helping him organize his collection of mushroom papers into a bibliography. I'm acting as a literary conscience and errand-boy to get the bibliography published. It will be an important contribution.

The Harvard Social Relations Department is being "turned on" [to] poetry. During March we are running a series of colloquia on "Drugs, Behavior and Mysticism." Barron then a day for the modern poets; Kerouac, Olson, Ginsberg; then Alan Watts. Arthur Koestler says he'll come during February to try the mushrooms and his presence will add to the mystic scene. Have you read his satori experienced while in a Franco prison?

Would you let me know what you decide about the Harper's request? I'll be glad to give it a try myself if you are too busy.

Hope that you'll be able to join us in New York in September.

Best to Laura and yourself, Timothy Leary

Throughout this time of initial experimentation in the early 1960s, Leary corresponded regularly with Albert Hofmann, the discoverer of LSD at Sandoz Laboratories. Hofmann naturally held an interest in other psychoactive substances, such as ololiuqui, or the morning glory plant, the seeds of which had been used traditionally in Mexico. Hofmann and Harvard ethnobotanist Richard Evans Schultes later coauthored the book *The Plants of the Gods: Their Sacred, Healing, and Hallucinogenic Power* (1979). Hofmann and Leary regularly exchanged correspondence about this work, and Hofmann had reached out directly to Aldous Huxley, too. Hofmann and Huxley corresponded from about August 1958 (although they did not meet until 1961). Huxley's *The Perennial Philosophy* (1945) covered topics in Eastern and Western mysticism that Hofmann showed an interest in and he, Leary, and Huxley often mentioned such topics in their correspondence with one another.

FROM DR. ALBERT HOFMANN TO TIMOTHY LEARY | FEBRUARY 22, 1961

Dear Dr. Leary, I was just reading in a book by Aldous Huxley (*The Perennial Philosophy*) when your kind letter and your report on investigations with psilocybin was handed over to me. It was a friendly suggestion of Mr. Huxley to let me know the preliminary results of your studies and I should like to thank you very much for having followed his suggestion.

My own experiences with psilocybin and earlier with LSDs convinced me, as I have written to Mr. Huxley two years ago, that the use of this kind of drugs should not be restricted to pharmacology and psychiatry but that they should be studied also in respect to their faculty to open new "doors of perception." It gave me therefore a great satisfaction to study your interesting approach using psilocybin as a consciousness-expanding drug.

You have realized the importance of the environmental factor for the quality of the effects of psilocybin. Many psychiatrists who use LSD or psilocybin as a drug aid in psychotherapy don't pay due attention to this point. The results of your studies with the aim to determine the conditions under which optimum positive reactions with psilocybin occur, will also be important for the therapeutical use of this drug.

The dosage you use (up to 3036mg) seems to me extremely high. Has the psilocybin content of the tablets been checked?

I take the liberty to enclose a copy of a paper which I have read last autumn at the International Symposium on the Chemistry of Natural Products at Melbourne and a reprint of a preliminary publication on the same subject in EXPERENTIA. You may be interested to hear that we have elucidated the secret of the third important magic drug of the Aztecs, of "Ololiuqui." Surprisingly enough we have found their compounds to be closely related to LSD.

With one of the components (d-isolysergic acid amide) I experienced a mental state of complete voidness. Another Ololiuqui compound (d-lysergic acid amide) has narcotic properties. I would be pleased if the active principles of Ololiuqui could be enclosed later in your studies.

Please keep me informed on the symposium at the fall meetings of the American Psychological Association centered on psilocybin.

Looking forward to meet[ing] you in summer here in Europe.

I remain sincerely yours, Dr. A. Hofmann

Please convey my best regards to Mr. A. Huxley.

On July 25, 1961, Hofmann followed up with Leary, sending him articles on ololiuqui with the request to forward them to Aldous Huxley. Hofmann did not have Huxley's address and also asked Timothy for it. Under the suggestion of Huxley, Leary reached out to Bill Wilson of Alcoholics Anonymous about his interest in hallucinogen research. Wilson was an advocate for the use of LSD and other psychoactive substances to treat alcoholism.[15] Leary's interest in drug rehabilitation and self-help communities played out in his Concord Prison Experiment in which Leary researched the effectiveness of psilocybin coupled with group psychotherapy in the rehabilitation of inmates and reduction of recidivism rates. Leary fervently believed that the use of psilocybin could help prisoners "reset" their behavior. He worked with thirty-two subjects, all of whom were volunteers,[16] from the Massachusetts Correctional Institute at Concord, not far from Harvard. The subjects were prisoners nearing their release date, chosen specifically so Leary and his team could determine whether the treatment did indeed affect their recidivism rates. Each subject was administered doses of psilocybin in concert with group therapy and the changes were monitored through Leary's interpersonal tests. The experiment included post-parole follow-up. In Rick Doblin's study of the experiment, "Dr. Leary's Concord Prison Experiment: A 34-year Follow-Up Study," he quotes Leary as saying that in retrospect one of the key elements to the success of the experiment was the post-parole care. When asked what changes in the experimental design Leary would implement if he were to try to replicate the experiment, the first and only change he noted was, "One thing would be to set up the halfway house system. . . . A support system is really needed." In his report, Doblin discusses how ultimately, the results of the experiment remain in contention, as although there was a drop in reoffending rates, it wasn't entirely clear how significant this was or in what portion it could be attributed to the study or other factors. Nevertheless, the Concord study remains one of the more well-known experiments in the deployment of psychedelics for psychotherapeutic purposes.[17] Leary's passion for the transformative power of psychedelics was also displayed in his association with the Synanon Foundation, a drug rehabilitation program, headed by reformed alcoholic Charles Dederich.

Dear Mr. Wilson, For the past ten years I have been involved in research aimed at evaluating methods of behavior change and developing more effective methods. The conclusion of my work is that self-help is the most successful approach. For the last year I have been involved in research on hallucinogens (specifically Mexican mushrooms) attempting to develop their therapeutic possibilities. We have become convinced that these drugs are of great therapeutic value—but not in the context of the doctor-patient relationship. As you know a do-it-yourself theme permeates the LSD self-discovery.

In the course of my work I have become friendly with Aldous Huxley who suggested that we had more than one mutual interest. I should very much like to have the chance to meet you this summer. I plan to be in New York sometime in August and would like to arrange an appointment.

I shall plan to telephone you in a week or two in order to see if you can spare a couple of hours.

Sincerely yours, Timothy Leary

During 1961, Leary's work with prisoners was attracting interest from all quarters, even the most far afield and obscure ones. Anthony Brooke came from a line of "white rajahs" of Sarawak (Borneo); his family ruled the region but Brooke himself grew up in England and attended Eton and Oxford. His uncle, the Raja, passed this title on to Anthony. Having spent years serving the kingdom and opposing secessionists, he renounced his claim to the throne of Sarawak in 1951.[18] Sarawak and Borneo joined Malaysia in 1963. During the 1960s, Brooke was engaged in a worldwide peace pilgrimage, joined a commune, and developed an interest in the occult and extraterrestrial life.[19] He published an account of his experiences and spiritual theories in his 1967 book, *Revelation for the New Age*. Gerald Heard wrote a letter to Leary in 1961 in which he mentions:

I have asked a remarkable man to call on you when he passes through Boston. His name is Anthony Brooke—and he should have been Rajah of Sarawak. Brooke the IIIrd or IVth but the Briish [sic] thought that these tribes should be purely democratic and not have a benevolent leader so he is now a man without place but with dedication and charm an unusual and attractive combination. He is deeply interested in your work both because of its use of psychedelics and also because of the restitutional therapy. I know he will value very much meeting you and I know he will not waste your time but will give as good as he gets. His exact date of arrival depends on his tour schedule. He lives like an apostle in perpetual orbit, goes and sees all sorts of high ups—such as the Chinese Communists—and they recoeve [sic] him because he has given up everything, represent no one and continually advocates with frank innocency [sic] and no little skill peace, good will the anthropological approach and all the other things that men of good will know but as soon as they ate [sic] given office forget.[20]

Brooke also took it upon himself to write to Leary in November 1961 to express his desire to learn more about Leary's work:

FROM ANTHONY BROOKE TO TIMOTHY LEARY | NOVEMBER 15, 1961

Dear Dr. Leary, May I write and introduce myself as a very good friend of Gerald Heard, who has been kind enough to suggest that I get in touch with you to hear about your extraordinarily interesting work with prisoners?

You are bound to be immensely and continually busy, but I shall be in Boston between the 5th and 9th of February next, and I would be tremendously grateful if we could have a meeting and if I could hear about your work—and your views about the implications of your LSD experiments, which would seem to go pretty deep, reaching far into the whole question of the transformation of human society—a subject with which I am myself very much concerned.

It is not easy to define precisely what I do myself. As a member of the Brooke family of Sarawak (you may recall this little country was ruled by "White Rajahs" for a hundred years), my whole life pattern was changed when the country became a British colony in 1946. I was the "Rajah Muda" (or heir apparent) at the time and fought a five year campaign with Sarawak nationalities. But I now spend as much time as possible travelling around the world in different countries, including communist countries, discussing with individuals and small groups what can be done in terms of response by ordinary people in the present human situation. I am particularly interested in anything which affects "consciousness", as I believe we must look to changed [sic] attitudes rather than the intensification of activity for "salvation". Man needs a new image of himself, it would seem. I don't know what you think about this, and I don't want to lead you off into philosophical byways—but I thought I would just give you this indication of my present thinking and activity. As far as our own meeting is concerned, quite simply, I want to listen to you, and I think we might leave it at that!

I seem to be writing a long way ahead, but I shall be off on my travels again on the 27th November, and although any letter you sent after that date would eventually catch up with me, I would be immensely grateful to have some indication if you would be able to see me between the dates I have mentioned. And if you could make a definite "time" suggestion I would enter it at once in my diary and make sure nothing conflicts with it.

I hope very much we may be able to meet.

Sincerely, Anthony Brooke

P.S. Perhaps I should have added that I shall be on my way to see Gerald Heard in Los Angeles.

Meanwhile, as Leary's experiments began to gather pace and profile, he reached out to Robert Gordon Wasson. Wasson was credited for popularizing psilocybin "magic" mushrooms as an amateur ethnomycologist investigating the ritual practices of the Mazatec shaman or *curandera*, María Sabina, in Oaxaca, Mexico. He published his findings in *Life* magazine (1957) leading to an influx of outsiders to the area, essentially ending Sabina's healing practices. Leary was eager to get Wasson's insight into the more "formal" experiments that he was now immersed in, as described in his letter to Wasson on November 21, 1961, lamenting, "Mushroom activities continue to expand and the expansion brings the inevitable administrative procedures."[21]

It is clear that throughout 1961, Leary had worked to establish a network of cultural figures who were keen to collaborate with him. He was eager to not only encourage others to experiment, but to open themselves up to a higher consciousness. Like many of his contemporaries in the early 1960s, he was influenced by a range of Eastern ideologies to draw out the meaning of the psychedelic experience, including yoga, tantra, and Buddhism. His correspondence with Aldous Huxley in February 1962 shows how many in the counterculture saw Eastern beliefs as a gateway into a more enlightened world:

FROM ALDOUS HUXLEY TO TIMOTHY LEARY | FEBRUARY 2, 1962

Dear Tim, I forgot in my last letter to answer your question about Tantra. There are enormous books on the subject by 'Arthur Avalon' (Sir John Woodruffe), which one can dip into with some profit. Then there is a chapter on it in Heinrich Zimner a 'Philosophies of India.' The fullest scholarly treatment, on a manageable scale, is in Miren Eliede's various books on Yoga. See also Conze a 'Buddhist Texts.' As far as one can understand it, Tantra seems to be a strange mixture of superstition and magic with sublime philosophy and acute philosoph- ical insights. There is an endless amount of ritual and word magic.

But the basic ideal seems to me the highest possible ideal— enlightenment not apart from achieved, essentially through constant awareness. This is the ultimate yoga—being aware, conscious even of the unconscious—on every level from the physiological to the spiritual. In this context see the list of 112 exercises in awareness, extracted from a Tantrik Text and printed at the end of 'Zen Flesh Zen Blood' (now in paperback). The whole of gestalt therapy is anticipated in these exercises—and the world (as with the Vedantists and the Nirvana- addicts of the Himalayan School of Buddhists), but within the world, through the world, by means of the ordinary processes of living. Tantra teaches a yoga of [?] a yoga of eating (even eating forbidden foods and drinking forbidden drinks). The sacramentalizing of common life, so that every event may become a means whereby enlightenment can be realized, is there any . . . not merely for the abnormal, it is above all a Therapy for the much sickness of insensitiveness and ignorance which we call 'normality' or 'mental health.'

LSD and the Mushrooms should be used, it seems to me, in the context of this basic Trantrik idea of the yoga of total awareness, leading to enlightenment within the world of everyday experience—which of course becomes the world of miracle and beauty and divine mystery when experience is what it always ought to be.

Yours, Aldous Huxley

At this point, Leary's network of willing experimenters had grown exponentially and his fame had spread beyond the United States and throughout Europe. The British psychiatrist and supposed coiner of the term "psychedelics," Humphry Osmond, was arguably his counterpart across the Atlantic. He more than most had a unique insight into Leary's work and was obviously anxious to collaborate with him, as shown in this letter from June 1962:

FROM HUMPHRY OSMOND TO TIMOTHY LEARY | JUNE 1962

My dear Timothy Leary, I feel that as we met with Aldous Huxley in Nov 1960 & have corresponded you will forgive informality. I shall be in New Jersey from 27th June & in Canada & USA until 21 July.

I am very keen to meet you & hope this will be possible. I would plan to be in Boston round about 10th July—if this would suit you. I am keen to hear about your work & plans, & also hope I shall meet my old friends . . . . I am also hoping to meet Anthony Brooke in the very near future. He has been in West Africa & gotten some malaria but I understand they have been putting in suitable antimalarials . . . ."

The sheer wealth of correspondence to and from Leary during 1961–62 is testament to the fact that by the middle of 1962, Leary had fully launched his psychedelic project and was gaining momentum. Leary's great counterculture experiment was certainly well underway. Drawing in scientists, artists, musicians, poets, writers, and philosophers—it was an extraordinary example of how the 1960s spawned movements that were unlimited by geography, class, caste, and culture. It was in the pre-dawn hours of the Age of Aquarius and the forecast looked favorable. Everything seemed to be going as planned.

Above: Timothy Leary sporting a mustache in a rare
photo booth strip, date unknown.

3
From Harvard to Freedom, 1962–63

"Courage is the key to creativity and to
any relinquishing of ego structure."

Timothy Leary, *Your Brain Is God*

IT WAS INEVITABLE. In 1962, Leary and Alpert's drug research hit a snag. After the campus newspaper *The Harvard Crimson* ran stories reporting disagreements between members of the Center for Research in Personality regarding accountability in the psilocybin studies,[1] Leary faced more criticism from the Harvard community over the legality and validity of his research.[2] One key issue was the fact that researchers or "guides" took drugs alongside the participants. Following guidance from the Federal Drug Administration (FDA), Harvard determined that the drugs needed to be administered by a physician.[3] The university started to clamp down.

A memo from Dave McClelland entitled "Comments on proposal for research on psilocybin etc,"[4] and issued on February 21, 1962, made several points to Alpert, criticizing his and Leary's pilot study proposal. He stresses to them that he is more interested in long-term observational data, and not:

a) time samples of people's vocabulary (use of neologisms like "groovy," "love engineer," etc.), borrowing from language of beats, psycho-paths, drug addicts (e.g., "turn on").
b) change of clothing, haircuts, etc.
c) increased references to the "East," mysticism, vaguely religious or cosmic experiences, etc.
d) grandiosity of plans (the "gaseous ego") etc. See my earlier memo.
e) slow decrease in ability to talk about anything without bringing drugs into the conversation.

These seem to me the obvious changes. Yet you are emphasizing rather old-fashioned measurement devices like MMPI, questionnaires about hallucinations, etc.

Accusations about the selling of drugs, communal living, and unscientific methods reported in the *Crimson* did not help the public image of their experiments. Damaging headlines blared forth: on March 23, 1962, the paper ran the story "University Has Ignored Work With Psilocybin" and on December 14, 1962 it revealed "FDA Investigates Drugs at University."

During this period, Leary and Alpert sought to defend their research and refute the claims. On April 10, 1962, Leary summarized his drug studies for the department to date:

Four experiments involving Harvard graduate students had been carried out for psilocybin research. Five graduate students acted as leaders of rehabilitation groups at Concord prison. Five graduate students from the Divinity School participated in a study of religion [sic] experience. Seven graduate students were subjects in a person-perception experiment. Seventeen graduate students were subjects in a study which compared personality factors with psilocybin reaction. In all sessions the participants ingested from 10 to 30 mg of psilocybin and reported their reactions via questionnaires and written essays. Group leaders at Concord had arranged four sessions this year. The Divinity students participated in one session. The person–perception experiment was run once. The personality (set-setting) study involved two sessions. All were volunteers.[5]

In July 1962, Allen Ginsberg wrote to Leary and touched on the issues that he was beginning to have with drug supplies. His letter reflects the state of the counterculture as it continued to absorb Eastern religions and philosophies, including Buddhism and tantra. His reference to the Beat poet Gary Snyder is another example of how Leary's reach extended beyond his immediate circle into a wider group of counterculture figures who were indulging in like-minded exploration:

FROM ALLEN GINSBERG TO TIMOTHY LEARY | JULY 20, 1962

Dear Tim, Got your letter from Zihuateneho [sic]: yes saw Litwins here a few weeks ago for several days. they left us a pile of new type paylo pills & some mescaline, godsend. Though I have not done anything with them yet except give to three young Bengali po[?s] who saw colored wheels. Will be going back up to Sikkim later & meet maybe work with some Tibetan monks, I made date to do that & they were interested in trying chemicals. They are reincarnate higher-ups in the Lamaist tantric (far out) tradition & so should have something interesting to say. Meanwhile we sitting here top floor moslem hotel broke as usual waiting for various checks to arrive from City Lights [his publishers at the time] etc.

I went out to Belur Math the Vedanta center here but have not connected with anyone striking. I've lost Huxley's address, can you (Pearl [Leary's Harvard secretary, Pearl Chan]) send it to me. I'll write him a short note ask who he recommends to see here, he should know. I've been reading Ramakrishna's conversations, & many books on Tibet.

If Pearl has any pills left before the supply runs out, it might be interesting to send some to Gary Snyder. I gave him my last from Tanger [sic] (7 old candys) when he left for Japan. He is interested in finding out what his Japanese Zen colleagues would say, & he is in position to get cooperation without strain. Also he had lots experience with Peyote with Indian groups in USA as Anthro student. Says Watts in Japan was swinging & very elated & full of talk about LSD & future society built on sex tantras. Also says he wrote you at Harvard & got reply from someone else that supply was limited. But if there is any left & you've not yet contacted the Zen people directly, this be worthwhile I think.

Has Huxley sounded down his Vedanta friends, and what do they say? I mean his Indian Swami friends? Litwin told me about Heard's opinion it all had to be done in esoteric groups; also told me more about Burroughs visit & Bill wanting to be rolled around campus on wheelchair.

Calcutta very muggy & not conducive to energy, and I been down with bronchitis (after returning from Sikkim) & slight kidney stone attack & sudden allergy to Penicillin & intermittent dysentery & now worms. I'm cured of all of them but it bogged me down.

Unfortunately I've not yet connected here for Guru or run into any striking holymen, yet, but I guess there must be. The Tibetans sound like experts in their own forms of meditation however, but otherwise are sort of provincial & hung on their history-ritual which is now sort of anachronistic since they're out of office in Tibet.

What are you going to do later? Are you still with Harvard CRP? Where in India you visit? We be here at least another half year or more, wandering round. I thought to settle down in household somewhere for months but still not seen Benares, Madras, Nepal, etc so not done with educational sightseeing yet or found motive [to s]ettle.

Ok—later—love—See you here?—Allen

Mainstream news outlets picked up the story of the Harvard drug studies, and soon all of America was aware of Leary and his LSD work with students. On December 14, 1962, the *New York Times* declared "Harvard Debates Mind-Drug 'Peril'."[6] However, the furor surrounding the Harvard experiments really escalated when, despite Leary and Alpert's policy to admit only graduate students into their studies, Alpert bent the rules for an undergraduate student named Ronnie Winston, much to the displeasure of Winston's friend, Harvard newspaper reporter Andrew Weil. Andrew Weil recalled the results of his reporting on Leary and Alpert in a September 2016 interview for this book:[7]

I was the editor of the *Harvard Crimson* who sort of did the investigative reporting on Alpert and Leary that resulted, well, Leary never was fired from Harvard; he just left. And his contract ran out and was not renewed, but Alpert was fired, and that was a result of the reporting, so I would say I was deeply estranged from both of them. When I moved out to San Francisco to do my internship in 1968–69, I had a real change of heart and wanted to reconnect, and it seemed Leary would be easier to do that with, so I got a number for him. He was living in Berkeley and I called him and he gave me a big 'great' and said come over. Actually it was very easy to have a, you know . . . pick up with him . . . and he said he thought it'd be much harder for me to resolve the issues with Alpert. When Alpert was fired that was front-page news in the *New York Times*, and that was the first most

Americans had heard of LSD, or other psychedelics, so I think that that work and that explosion of publicity really spread all of [that] throughout the culture.

By late 1962, with the ethics of their research in question, Leary and Alpert moved their psychedelic experiments and studies off-campus to Leary's home in Newton Centre, Massachusetts under the auspices of the International Federation for Internal Freedom (IFIF)—later changed from "Federation" to "Foundation"—with the expressed goal of promoting research in the exploration of consciousness. They named their new research home the Freedom Center. Its mission focused on the engagement of educational, therapeutic, religious, and psychological studies using psychedelic substances.[8]

Drafted in November 1962, the organization's "Statement of Purpose"[9] was laid out:

> For the past two and a half years a group [from] Harvard University [have carried out] five research projects on the effects and applications of consciousness-expanding drugs. . . . Over 400 subjects have participated without serious negative physical or psychological consequences. Over sixty percent of our subjects have reported enduring life changes for the better. As a result of these studies and our appraisal of other research, we have come to several conclusions about the evolution of man's consciousness and the human brain, and we invite others who share our assumptions to communicate with us.

Some of the conclusions they referred to involved the limited use of humankind's brain capacity. The sixth and last conclusion addressed the need to "expand our ego and cultural games and to develop an appropriate language" in order to fully realize the capacity of consciousness.[10]

The Board of Directors included Richard Alpert, Timothy Leary, and many former participants in the Harvard experiments: Walter H. Clark, Professor of the Psychology of Religion at Andover; Paul Lee, George Litwin, Ralph Metzner, and Gunther Weil, all graduate students at Harvard University; Madison Presnell, Concord Prison Psychologist, who Leary had worked with during the Concord Prison Experiment; Huston Smith,

Philosophy Professor, Massachusetts Institute of Technology (MIT); and Zen Buddhist Alan Watts. Their aims included the establishment of other research centers across the country and the publication of *The Psychedelic Review* (1963–71). The official journal of the IFIF stated its mission and the long-term goals of the organization as "to increase the individual's control over his own mind, thereby enlarging his internal freedom."[11]

A similar organization that may have served as a model for the IFIF was the quasi-medical International Foundation for Advanced Study (IFAS), an organization which was also associated with the MKUltra study involving psychedelic drugs in Menlo Park, California. By November 1962, Leary served on the advisory board. Directors included Myron J. Stolaroff, Alfred M. Hubbard, and John C. Crouse. The other advisory board members included Abram Hoffer, Aldous Huxley, Raynor C. Johnson, and Humphry Osmond. These two organizations would soon represent oppositional approaches to psychedelic research, as the IFAS adhered to the medical-psychotherapeutic position that such drugs were powerful and potentially damaging, and the IFIF held to the educational -theological approach that these drugs were "benign agents having 'door-opening' effects of the psyche."[12] This disparity would result in the resignation of George Litwin from IFIF,[13] and likewise, Leary resigning from IFAS. Sandoz Laboratories was certainly supplying both of them at various points.

In early 1963, the controversy surrounding Leary's on-and-off campus activities had become too great for Harvard, with the *Crimson* running yet another headline on February 28, 1963, claiming that, "Alpert's 'Home' Draws Neighbors' Ire." The tipping point came when Brendan A. Maher, the Chairman of Harvard's Center for Research in Personality, received correspondence from Sandoz Laboratories about supplying drugs to Leary, at which point Maher alerted Leary in a letter dated January 30, 1963, that Harvard's name could no longer be associated with his research:

FROM BRENDAN A. MAHER, CENTER FOR RESEARCH IN
PERSONALITY, HARVARD TO TIMOTHY LEARY | JANUARY 30, 1963

Dear Tim, The two letters enclosed were addressed to the Center here and were therefore passed to me for attention. The letter from Sandoz appears to be in response to some inquiry on your part and I

SEVENTY-FIVE CENTS

The Harvard Review

DRUGS
and the MIND

FEATURING . . .

RICHARD ALPERT & TIMOTHY LEARY
*THE POLITICS OF CONSCIOUSNESS
EXPANSION*

R. GORDON WASSON
MUSHROOM RITES OF MEXICO

RICHARD EVANS SCHULTES
HALLUCINOGENIC PLANTS

*PSYCHEDELICS: A CAVEAT
'UP' ON PSILOCYBIN*

ALSO . . .

DRUGS AND THE ARTIST
An Exclusive Portfolio

HARVARD REPORTS * * * BOOKS

VOL. I
NUMBER 4

imagine that the same is true of the other although there is no identi-fication on it. I have been quite disturbed by the content of the letter from Sandoz and have discussed the implications of it with Dr. Bales who, I understand, will be writing to you on the same topic shortly.

If I understand the Sandoz' letter, they are replying to what they imagine to be an inquiry on behalf of the University, as at 5 Divinity Avenue, seeking to arrange for a supply of psilocybin and LSD to be sent here. As the form of greeting is "gentlemen," and they make reference to the supply of these drugs to "your University" there seems to be little doubt that they are under the impression that they are dealing with some activity that is being sponsored or authorized by the University. I am at a loss to understand why this should be the case, especially as Dr. Alpert had already assured me that Sandoz has already been instructed to the effect that there was no further connection between the University and the psilocybin activities. As long ago as last July he showed me a carbon of a letter in which this request had been conveyed to Sandoz and we understood that the Center would not be involved further with any matters dealing with the ordering, shipping or receipt of these supplies.

In view of these recent developments, I must repeat my request that the name and facilities of the Center not be used for matters connected with the psilocybin activities. It is my understanding that facilities now exist for you through the machinery of your own non-profit corporation and I cannot understand therefore why this kind of situation should still be occurring. Could you please reaffirm your instructions to Messrs. Sandoz and other suppliers that these drugs are not to be directed or received at 5 Divinity Avenue. I appreciate your cooperation in this matter.

Sincerely yours, Brendan A. Maher,

Chairman, Center for Research in Personality

Leary was not deterred and on February 13, 1963 he simply wrote to Albert Hofmann at Sandoz Laboratories explaining that all shipments were to be sent to the Medical Director of the IFIF, Madison Presnell, and labeled in accordance with the FDA. He sent Hofmann payment of $10,000 for 100 grams of LSD-25 and 1 kilogram of psilocybin. That amount would equal 1–2 million "hits" of LSD. In this letter he also updated Hofmann on his progress:

> Our project has been expanding rapidly and there are a growing number of researchers who are joining with us to study the social and personal applications of these drugs. We are pleased with the contributions our research project has made to this new field. For example, *Life* magazine, as part of a series on "Behavior," sent a team of writers and photographers to spend three days with us. You will be glad to hear that they seemed to understand very well the broad, social implications of consciousness-expansion.[14]

The IFIF organization promoted the formation of additional Freedom Centers, or "cells" throughout the country. In March 1963, Ken Kesey, along with Vic Lovell and Jane Burton, neighbors of Kesey near Stanford University and fellow Pranksters, wrote to the IFIF to request information and supplies to start their own cell or research group. In retrospect, they may not have needed any such help, as reported by American journalist Tom Wolfe in his stylistically groundbreaking book *The Electric Kool-Aid Acid Test* (1968) Kesey and his friends were already hosting parties featuring an LSD-spiked fruit drink. In tribute to the IFIF, Kesey and the Merry Pranksters, while driving across the country in the *Furthur* bus, named their "research" group the Intrepid Search for Inner Space (ISIS).[15]

As well as responding to individual groups like Kesey's, the IFIF responded to and supported the work of other, more formal groups, such as the Synanon Foundation in Santa Monica, California. Founded by Dr. Manfred Spaulding, a former addict and inmate, the mission of this early self-help organization to treat addiction naturally aligned with the work of the IFIF and Leary's previous experiences with the rehabilitative powers of psychedelics during the Concord Prison Study. Although the Concord study proved inconclusive, other scientists theorized that psychedelics could serve as a treatment for addiction. This opinion was also shared by Bill Wilson of Alcoholics Anonymous, who Leary had previously written to. A note from the IFIF correspondence files indicates how Dr. Spaulding sought support from the organization to establish a Synanon House in Boston:

All of below are
members —

IFIF

March 12, 1963

Dr. Ralph Metzner
c/o IFIF
Zero Emerson Place
Boston 14, Mass

Dear Dr. Metzer:

    The persons listed below would like to form an IFIF research group. Please send us all necessary information, application materials, FDA forms, etc.

                                    Sincerely,

                                    Victor R. Lovell
                                    5 Perry Ave.
                                    Menlo Park, Calif.

                                    Mr and Mrs, James Wolpman
                                    4 Perry Ave.
                                    Menlo Park, Calif.

                                    Mr. and Mrs. Ken Kesey
                                    9 Perry Ave.
                                    Menlo Park, Calif.

                                    Jane Burton
                                    7 Perry Ave.
                                    Menlo Park, Calif.

                                    Chloe Scott
                                    180 Stanford Ave.
                                    Menlo Park, Calif.

Above: Letter of inquiry to Ralph Metzner in Boston, Massachusetts c/o the IFIF organization, from the neighbors on Perry Avenue, Menlo Park, California: Ken Kesey, Victor Lovell, James Wolpman, Jane Burton, Chloe Scott, and others, March 12, 1963. The group requested materials to form their own research group, which inevitably happened in their Merry Prankster–style.

FREEDOM CENTER's most recent interest is the active support of the Synanon Foundation, the well-known behavior-change program for drug addiction. To this end, Freedom Center has supported Dr. Manfred Spaulding, a former addict and inmate, who has been campaigning actively for the establishment of a Synanon House in Boston. Dr. Spaulding is currently at the Synanon Foundation in Santa Monica, California, where he is studying the Synanon philosophy and methods. Further support from Freedom Center for the establishment of such a Synanon House in Boston is forthcoming.[16]

The group participated in the "Synanon game" or a "Dissipation" that involved "violent verbalization" and physical tickling and jabbing—all aimed at increasing insight and self-awareness.[17] The Synanon Foundation and Dr. Spaulding evolved into the "Church of Synanon" but, unlike many of the other psychedelic churches that sprung up in response to LSD criminalization, Synanon took a cultish turn and eventually disbanded in 1991.[18]

Leary consistently believed in the transformative and creative utility of drugs, but may have rejected the Synanon approach as intimated in a letter to his friend Michael Horowitz[19] in which he reflected on the life of science fiction author Philip K. Dick, "I re-read the Phil Dick interview and felt very sad at this loneliness and fear and the hardness of his resolution. He went to Canada to kill himself, ended up in a synonon [sic] scene; got hard and pessimistic, cured his psychosis and is now a normal neurotic. Too bad." Although Leary thought Dick's trajectory was unfortunate, the novelist went on to write one of his most well-regarded novels, *A Scanner Darkly* (1977), featuring the world of psychedelics, addiction and rehabilitation, narcotic double agents, surveillance, and overall paranoia. It could have been ripped from the pages of Timothy Leary's life story, or that of any number of counterculture figures.

In the meantime, Richard Alpert, who had been formally removed from his post after the fallout from the Ronnie Winston debacle, tried to state his case against dismissal to Harvard President Nathan Pusey, and champion the development of the IFIF for the purposes of continuing psychedelic studies, in a letter dated May 15, 1963:

FROM RICHARD ALPERT TO PRESIDENT NATHAN PUSEY, HARVARD
| MAY 15, 1963

Dear President Pusey, At our meeting last Tuesday, you advised me that you would bring the matter of the termination of my contract before the Corporation at its next meeting. This issue is not entirely separable from the views of the University toward our research in general. Therefore, I am taking this opportunity to bring to the attention of you and the members of the Corporation some of the cogent matters associated with our work. By this means, I hope to prevent the broader issues from being totally submerged beneath the myriad lesser decisions (e.g., my contract) which have to date constituted Harvard's official "position" and expressed concern.

We have carried out our studies of psychedelic (mind-manifesting) materials at the University from the Autumn of 1960 until the end of 1962, when the association of our research with Harvard was formally terminated. Consequently we organized I.F.I.F. [International Federation for Internal Freedom], through which we have continued our research activities. During the period when the research was affiliated with Harvard, we worked safely with over four hundred subjects in a series of studies at the Concord Reformatory, within the local religious community, and at the University. These studies explored the effects of altering states of consciousness on 1) the creative process, 2) the religious experience, 3) the rate of learning, 4) behavior change, 5) aesthetic experience, 6) interpersonal relations, and 7) flexibility of thought process. Some of our efforts have been directed toward the development of adequate models for conceptualization of these profound mind-manifesting experiences (very much in the tradition of William James). Our preliminary research, as well as studies pursued by others in the field, indicates that psychedelics are among the most powerful consciousness-altering substances known to man and certainly deserve our most serious and creative attention. . . ."

In the summer of 1963, the IFIF set up a research center at Hotel Catalina in Zihuatanejo, Mexico, a town located on the Pacific coast north of Acapulco in the state of Guerrero. The IFIF chose an idyllic setting to establish a center that was focused on demonstrating the value of psychedelic drugs while training others to lead or conduct their own sessions. It was a vision conceived as early as 1962, as evidenced in a letter[20] to Leary from Gerald Heard dated July 17, 1962:

FROM GERALD HEARD TO TIMOTHY LEARY | JULY 17, 1962

Dear Tim, Delighted to get your Zihuatanejo letter. We greatly enjoyed our afternoon with you and hope Hotel Catalina looks promising for your purposes.

As you say The Trinity of the 3 Ps Police, Priest, Paymaster (Banker) is always against the journey of the soul but the current of consciousness is against the 3. For better or worse—better if you and the con: chanq: [meaning here is unclear] suggest do it—worse if the politician is bought enough and his dark way to get in on the act. In either case police first and paymaster have had their day. Did you see that Glen Seaborg head of the A.E.C., asked what would be the big breakthrough in the next 30 years, said in the consciousness changing drugs.

We are off to visit Sandoz et al. due to start in a week. Hofman [sic] wrote to say he'll be in Mexico looking up the mushrooms. I guess you'll meet him thereupon.

Michael joins in affectionate greetings and best wishes,
Love, Gerald

In March 1963, Leary wrote to Albert Hofmann to inform him about the imminent opening of the Zihuatanejo Center and to raise concerns about supplies and attitudes at Sandoz Laboratories:

FROM TIMOTHY LEARY TO ALBERT HOFMANN | MARCH 6, 1963

Dear Dr. Hofmann, So much happens each week it is difficult to keep you informed. We have phoned Dr. Henze, but feel rather discouraged by his response. It is our impression that Sandoz S.S.A. is not interested in large scale use of LSD and psilocybin. We are hopeful of obtaining Hanover's help in preparing our application to be an import-sponsor. We expect that matters will move slowly. Our strategy is two fold: 1. to apply quickly as import-sponsor, 2. to continue to organize IFIF research groups qualified to execute educational, therapeutic, religious, psychological studies. We now have fifty such groups ready and this number grows as fast as we can organize them. The first wave of IFIF groups will be led by men who have had considerable experience with consciousness-expanding drugs. We have over twenty medical doctors who have to [?]. We shall soon have a nationwide chain of serious and respectable outlets waiting for supplies, and pressure for Food and Drug Administration action will generate from these sources.

At the same time we have decided to put considerable energy into our Mexican program. We are working there with DANDA, S.A., the largest psychological consulting company in Mexico. Our associates there have been very successful in obtaining enthusiastic support of Mexican psychiatrists, scientists. Our attorney, Lic. Armando Calvo, is setting up IFIF-Mexico, a non-profit research foundation. We're setting up a research laboratory in Mexico City to conduct cell, tissue and animal work. I am moving to Mexico May 1 and am taking out resident papers. A group of ten IFIF staff will be coming with me there and the Zihuatanejo Center will be in operation after May 1. We are now purchasing trucks, hotel supplies, etc. to be transported to Mexico next month.

Now—we wish to place an order for 100 grams of LSD to be sent to our Mexican operation for research there. There are several alternatives among which you can choose . . . ."

Of the five thousand applications to take part in the research at Hotel Catalina, five hundred were accepted.[21] Joseph J. Downing, Program Chief of the San Mateo County Mental Health Services and Clinical Associate Professor of Psychiatry and Preventive Medicine at Stanford University School of Medicine, observed the behavior and social interaction of participants under the use of psychedelics, mostly LSD, and reported his observations in the book *Utopiates* (1964) edited by Richard Blum. During his stay from May 1 to June 16, 1963, Downing observed thirty-five guests, and described the nature of the studies and "experiments in transpersonative living." Transpersonative[22] related to the enhanced interpersonal sensitivity, perceptivity, insight, and reduced defensiveness observed during the group use of psychedelics.[23] Although not a member of the IFIF, Downing's observations at Hotel Catalina served as one of the first reports on group psychedelic experience by a psychiatrist.

Interestingly during this period, concerns started to surface about the effects of adulterated drugs and in May 1963 Aldous Huxley wrote twice to warn Leary at Zihuatanejo about a green liquid LSD produced by Bernard Copley. He claimed that the green liquid was tested by Hofmann and found to be only sixty percent pure LSD. He pleaded with Leary to not take the risk of using low quality product for his work. Copley and Bernard Roseman were later convicted in 1966 for mislabeling and importing LSD in a case that involved one user having to be hospitalized:[24]

FROM ALDOUS HUXLEY TO TIMOTHY LEARY | MAY 26, 1963

Dear Tim, An acquaintance of mine has just called me to say that he has recently come back from Europe, where he showed Albert Hofmann a specimen of [Bernard] Copley's green LSD. Hofmann tested it and found that the liquid [was] only 60% LSD, but he could not in the time at his disposal say what the remaining 40% consisted of. Nothing too good if me may judge [?] what happened to the two local users of the stuff that I happen to know of—Dr. Dunn, now in Norwalk, Pe[rry?] Bevin, now a suicide. I don't know if you bought any of this material from R and C. If so, for god's sake don't use it— or use it only after very careful testing (not on yourself, preferable!) Hofmann also told my informant that LSD in highest form cannot stand up to exposure to the air—and I understand that the green stuff is not in airtight ampules. This alone ma[y be?] disturbing. the 40% solution with god knows what is very [?] indeed. So please be careful. It would be disastrous if someone became physically ill or mentally [deranged?] as a result of ingesting this material while staying at Zihuatanejo. It would be far better to suspend operations than to run the risk of doing sessions harm by using doctored material obtained from a dubious source.

Ever yours, A. Huxley

The purpose of the group sessions at Zihuatanejo as presented by the IFIF was to "produce ecstatic experience, to expand consciousness, and to provide the subject with the most memorable, revelatory, life-changing experience of his life."[25] The idea was that these transformative psychedelic experiences would allow the "patient" to be liberated from their ingrained inhibitions that had been created through socialization, illusions or, in Leary's words, "games." There was a sense that these drugs allowed people to become a truer version of themselves, freed from the falsity or game-playing that society thrust upon them. As Downing wrote, patients showed that on LSD, "In neurophysiological terms, established learned, or imprinted, neural patterns are unlearned, or erased, permitting new learning based on present, accurate perceptions rather than on past, irrelevant memories."[26] Instruction in self-awareness of the individual's own game-playing in order to achieve a "no games" setting, and eventually, "real" behavior change, was theorized and practiced by Leary and his cohorts for years to come.

The end of Zihuatanejo and the Freedom Center was predicted in a letter from Professor Richard Marsh to Richard Alpert, sent with Marsh's notes on Alpert's sessions at Zihuatanejo. The police were swarming Hotel Catalina and the Mexican authorities did not support the IFIF research. Ralph Metzner had left, and the center was essentially falling apart.

On June 16, 1963, the Mexican authorities shut down[27] the center and the experiment in transpersonative-living needed to be relocated. According to the psychiatrist Downing, the center attracted negative press for a few reasons: IFIF's own misplaced attempts to publicize the endeavor; not securing the good intentions of the psychiatric advisors to the local Mexican health officials; supposed Oaxacan informers wishing to protect the native religious customs; and retaliation from an uninvited guest.[28]

Leary tried to move operations to other localities in the Caribbean, but the negative press[29] in Mexico[30] preceded them, thwarting their plans for another "Island Institute," as inspired by the Aldous Huxley utopian-themed novel, *Island* (1962)[31] which likewise featured drug-inspired enlightenment, free love, and communal living. After Leary and his organization relocated to Millbrook, New York, Huxley's book continued to serve as a model for transcendental communities to act "as psychedelic training centers."[32]

4
The Trip Reports

"Did you imagine that there could be emotions in heaven? Emotions are closely tied to ego games. Check your emotions at the door to paradise."

Timothy Leary, *The Politics of Ecstasy*

D ESCRIBING THE EFFECTS of psychedelics has proved a chal-
lenge ever since Albert Hofmann rode his bicycle after ingesting
LSD on April 19, 1943. Aldous Huxley reportedly first experienced
mescaline in 1953 and subsequently wrote about his experience in 1954
in his book *The Doors of Perception*. Hofmann described his "bicycle trip"
a bit later in his book *LSD: My Problem Child*, first published in German
in 1979. Some of Leary's fellow experimenters attempted to write while
under the influence—with varying results—but many would describe
the account later in "acid diaries" or "trip reports." A number of these
were sent to Leary as part of his research projects.

As seen in Leary's earlier clinical research, he was a social scientist who
applied standard methods to the research of personality and behavior,
shown in his interpersonal workbooks, plotting circles, questionnaires,
and MMPI and TAT tests. One important method of acquiring feedback
was through self-reporting. Although subjective, these reports provided
invaluable input and often colorful stories. After reading a number of
these reports, one can see why Leary and Alpert sought participants
from various vocations and backgrounds. While some indicated universal
experiences, each was unique. Granted, these were not the first clinical
studies of hallucinogens. As previously noted, Ken Kesey famously participated—several years prior to Leary's experiments—in the CIA-led
LSD and mind-control research at Menlo Veteran's Hospital, which was
documented as part of a larger program. So, although these may not
be the first, they do represent the early trip reports of the American
counterculture, now a classic genre within the psychedelic community.

Descriptions one might expect from trip reports include mystic visions, telepathy, astral projections, and other versions of "ego-death," in which the person's sense of self completely vanishes, and the essence or "soul" is left at one with the universe. Surprisingly, none of these reports describe mandala visions.

This selection represents a handful of the variety of scholars and artists handpicked by Leary to contribute to his great counterculture experiment. Many more survive written by participants from official Harvard studies, such as the Concord Prison Experiment (written by prisoners) or others involving former student volunteers.

Most of these reports were submitted directly to and logged by Leary from 1961 to 1964 and formed part of the Psilocybin Study.

Ralph Metzner

A graduate student at Harvard University, Metzner is known as a collaborator and principal investigator for the psilocybin studies conducted under the guidance of Leary and Alpert. He served on the Board of Directors for the independent research organization, the International Federation for Internal Freedom, and coauthored *The Psychedelic Experience* (1964). He was the third, less public partner in the psychedelic trio with Leary and Alpert.

RALPH METZNER TRIP REPORT #17 | UNDATED

The stated purpose of the session was total loss of self; I had experienced this before but briefly, sporadically and with no clear recognition of its implications. I had died "gamey" deaths e.g. through self-torture or choking in my own game-traps, but these had been terrifying and did not involve any insights except afterwards knowledge of how I could do myself in.

Tim was the guru and we started off in silence, Tim reading some passages from the manual. We had agreed that if I felt fear I would say so, rather than try to struggle against it by myself. For one hour nothing happened, I was restless and angry at myself for not being able to let myself go. I was thinking too much and too hard.

Then Tim lit the candle, opened a beer and we sat there creating an atmosphere of quiet sensory awareness with nothing else to distract. I looked at Tim's face and it became the face of God. Then it changed and half of it became ugly and distorted. I felt like a piece of protoplasm half of which is stuck to a rock and the other half is already floating in the ocean. My mind was already cradled in the void but occasionally I would slip back with fear and distress.

R: "I keep losing it."

T: "How do you lose it? With your mind? How do you get it?"

R: "It just comes."

R: "I see divinity in half of your face, but the other half changes to horrible."

T: "Remember that it comes from you just like the fear and pretty soon you will be able to see divinity in the whole face or in the candle or the cigarette or the following day if you are good."

Tim went and sat by the door and again I tried to reach it by the other way of emptying the mind. But I couldn't. I got discouraged and was thinking I could reach this state only with Tim or with someone. I lay on the floor and saw hallucinations; fearful aspects would start to emerge and I remembered the admonition that they were in my own mind only, so I told them to go away which they did. Then suddenly I realized I could do this not only with relatively trivial demons but with all my fears. My mind opened about 360 degrees and I felt exhilarated as never before. I thought about how absurd it was that my fears of someone should interfere with the relationship between that person and myself. I sat up and looked at Tim and he took one look and said: YOU made it. I told him about the fears insight and he added: "Not only the fear but the love is in the mind too and the point is you have to know your own mind otherwise it scares the shit out of you." We talked a lot about [a] way of maintaining the state where everything shines with a divine radiance and the difficulties of living at that level. All this time, for about 2–3 hours, although I was using my mind and thinking, talking, there was no ego. I could with total dispassion examine various relationships that "Ralph Metzner" had with parents, friends, parts of himself etc. People who walked into the room were accepting my own mental products; they were really walking around in my mind. This state is hard to maintain when people play fast, hard games around you and a couple of times I got lost again momentarily.

There is a strange paradox in the finding that as you put more and more of the phenomena you thought were external inside your head, your ego vanishes.

RALPH METZNER TRIP REPORT #23 | UNDATED

We started off a small group—Barbara, Susan, Bill, myself. I took dexamil and marihuana, since I would still be tolerant to consciousness-expanding drugs. Also I wanted to see how far I could get on this plus contact. Everyone else was on mescaline.

Read the invocation to the Buddhas asking for protection. Everyone very relaxed, quiet. Could feel the dex pushing me up and the pot pulling me down. Barbara singing quietly. Then she sat on the floor and started to move her hands like a Balinese temple dancer, saying someone was pulling her strings. She was sitting in enraptured trance seeing the Void ("clear soup" she called it), a log, a Mary Magdalene.

Was following her visions with my own, but they were not always the same: a lot of food imagery that I've never had before; also very realistic as opposed to fantastic imagery of the mushrooms; i.e., breakfast foods, people known to me, etc.

Bill analyzing his own hang-ups, somewhat lonely I thought but impossible to bring closer. Susan sending out magic electric nonverbal vibrations. George comes in, glowing, quiet, receptive, great. Then Dick, Buster, Foster, Mike, later Max and Dick, Fred. Gets too crowded. The straight people not quite able to swing into the mood of the session which was very delicate and nonverbal.

Allen Ginsberg

American poet Allen Ginsberg was one of the first Beatnik artists Leary recruited for his studies and, as seen in his letters, was indispensable in introducing Leary to other Beats, including Jack Kerouac and William Burroughs. The two went on to maintain a close friendship throughout their lives. Leary's papers contain a few of Ginsberg's trip reports. In this early report, he speaks glowingly of synthetic psilocybin. He was an experienced drug user, having taken LSD years earlier, and had experienced similar transcendental experiences without drugs.

ALLEN GINSBERG TRIP REPORT | JANUARY 1961

Have had experience with Mescaline, LSD 23, and Psilocybin. The mushroom synthetic seems to me the easiest on the body physically, and the most controllable in dosage. The effects are generally similar, subjectively, Psilocybin seems to me to be some sort of psychic godsend—it offers unparalleled opportunity to catalyze awareness of otherwise unconscious psychic processes—to widen the areas of human consciousness—to deepen reification of ideas and identification of real objects—to perceive the inner organization of natural objects and human art-works—to enter the significance and aesthetic organization of music, painting, poetry, architecture; it seems to make philosophy make sense; it aids consciousness to contemplate itself and serves some of the most delightful functions of the mind—as if, turning up the volume on a receiving set background and FM stations can be heard. The affects are not unnatural, I have experienced similar things without the use of chemical catalysts, and correspond to what I as a poet have called previously "aesthetic," "poetic," "transcendental" or "Cosmic consciousness." I think it will help Mankind grow.

Ginsberg offers a thorough, multitrip report of a session including participants Peter Orlovsky (his partner), Timothy Leary, and Jack Kerouac. Ginsberg claimed to have typed for fourteen hours, weeks after his drug session:

ALLEN GINSBERG TRIP REPORT | UNDATED

The first time I took Psilocybin—10 pills I think—was in a fireside-social setting in Cambridge with a number of people I did not know well, as well as a few friends present. After an hour when the chemical effects began to be noticeable to me, I withdrew into visual introspection and regarded all intrapersonal activity as a plot and affront to my desire to contemplate my own mind. I lay down on a large comfortable couch next to my companion Peter Orlovsky and drifted off into a reverie about the origin of the universe which involved the visualization of a sort of octipus of darkeness [sic] breaking through out of the primal void. The presence of this creature became increasingly real and I felt a sort of hissing at the back of my mind—I allowed myself to be inundated by the Presence and it was a scary feeling—I became nauseus [sic]—my usual reaction to anxiety-provoking situations—I went to the bathroom but did not vomit, then returned to [the] fireside where I was approached by a young lady (Sandra Raynesford) who wanted to make my acquaintance, whom I took to be a sort of reptilian Deva (Hindu imaginary presence)—I listened to her talking and realized after a while she was haranguing me politely and insistently about my apparent coldness and remove from the fair sex. After a while I went upstairs and listened to another sort of hepcat (Gunther Weil) describing his conception of the human universe—a bunch of beings each preoccupied with their special project or "thing" as he described it. He looked like a caracture [sic] creature of a Pfeiffer or Steig cartoon—in fact so much so that I thought I'd wandered into a cartoon universe with this fellow sitting on a bedroom rug in a richly furnished house gesturing toward the window—caracture gesture of hand and cartoon mustache [sic] on his face— "Everybody, sees his own thing, some people got music, some people got houses, some poetry, some jobs, everyone his own thing, some got bombs—and everybody's entitled to respect for his thing." How awful I thought, and drew a picture of this monstrous product of social psychology with [h]is mustache explaining his "Thing." I began to see myself through [h]is eyes with my own thing in mind and wrote down on a piece of paper "I am a horse's ass." Suddenly felt this understanding was absolutely right, one of the keys to my existence, and began thinking of my father; as if I were one of a line of horses' asses. The effects slowly wore off and I spent several hours talking.

II

Several nights later I took a larger dose of 18 and went upstairs with Orlovsky to a separate room, took off all my clothes and lay in bed listening to music. As my awareness expanded I saw myself laying in bed, with the alternative of withdrawing into mystic introspection and vomit, or swallowing back my vomit, opening my eyes and living in the present universe. I felt intimidated by the knowledge that I had not reached yet a perfect understanding with my creator, whoever he be, God, Christ or Bhudda [sic]—the figure of the Octipus as before—suddenly however realized they were all imaginary beings I was inventing to substitute for the fear of being myself that One which I dreamed of—Prof. Leary came into my room, looked in my eyes and said I was a great man—That determined me to make an effort to live in the here and now—I got nauseous soon after—sat up in bed naked and swallowed down the vomit that besieged me from my stomach as if an independent being down there were rebelling at being dragged into existence—Orlovsky was naked in bed with me and his erotic gestures looked reptilian as if out of hindu-deva statuary—his lidded eyes and hooked nose almost like a blue Krishna Statue from the wrong plane of existence not consonant with 1960 USA . . . .

I took some Benzedrine type—methedrine—and ten mushrooms and sat down to write, several weeks later—stayed at my desk for 14 hours typing anything that came into my head—it all came out organized—a development of thoughts outlined above from earlier mushroom experiences and other natural experiences, political and cosmic thoughts—a mixture of subconscious and rational surrealist flow—"Here am I old Betty Boop whopsing [sic] it up again behind the old skull-microphone wondering what nightmare movie we put on this time again etc." This discharge of a unconsciously organized material seems to form a perfect endpiece for a long political-prophetic poem I have been taking notes on for the last 3 years.

Peter Orlovsky

Poet and partner to Allen Ginsberg, Orlovsky was one of the artist-types recruited by Leary to participate in his early psilocybin studies. He described his session to Leary in a poetical letter:

Dear Dr. Timothy Leary, Experiences with Psilocybin in me have been very tastey & eatable & when the affects come on, wham, I am in the middle of this ever grower larger and larger cosmos of vibrating hums of wishes & desires & mistroy plays as in Shaskerpiere, about to enter the stage & speack in the play. Somehow these pills make the soul more real: painful soul realness coming or frighten soul realness coming or joy or sw[e]lling love & sence of consciousness of the universe as one vast conscious & it also helps the fantassys to roal with out hinderounce because awareness pushes the soul love to ballon hights of outer space galixies [sic] & this psilocybin is helps to reach unknown areares of the mind & soul & love of this vast consciousness.

All the fearing fantassys I get I don't mind because I realise they are only dream fantassys in my mind & I wanted to summon the angeles of heaven to come to aid of earth worrey people & the tents of angeles were preparing to depart & enter earth thru the horn of some vast horn.

Are we Gods ball in his back pocket or are we God with this sun in our heart brain that beams high when on psilocybin.

Something beautiful happens & I want more of it.

The experiments on the mind of those who want to experiment must continue & this wing of pills helps to send feelers out feeling around in the universe like when yr really high & sence something going on seems I was an insect squeezeing out of a dusty ancient book, all kind of book t[o]uched by universe thumbs.

Psilocybin is also good of mixing with people & friends & helps do so on a more important and deeper level of talking and feeling with others around you so I recommend its social importance as extremely helpful & vastly interesting.

Also it makes for fuller sense of being decendant from animal creatures of long ago past—like I felt when high, I was a reptile of some kind & this sense relation harmony is very interesting, feels good at [text undecipherable—2 words] when yr feeling good so I am glad I [text finishes abruptly]

Okay timothy here

You are, you want more????

Your flower, Peter

Jack Kerouac

Like Ginsberg, Kerouac was already well experienced with drugs. He participated in this psilocybin session with fellow Beat Bob Donlin, as well as Peter Orlovsky. He compared the side effects as better than that of mescaline for his multiple-day trip. Like many writers and artists,

Kerouac had traveled to Mexico, and recalled a time imbibing the popular fermented agave drink pulque in Mexico City. He felt he reached satori—the Buddhist term for awakening. Interestingly, he found psilocybin to be a worthwhile memory aid:

JACK KEROUAC TRIP REPORT | 1961

Mainly I felt like a floating Khan on a magic carpet with my interesting lieutenants and god . . . some ancient feeling about old geheuls in the grass, and temples, exactly also like the sensation I got drunk on pulque floating in the Xochimilco gardens on barges laden with flowers and singers . . . some old Golden Age dream of man, very nice. But that is the lament of hallucination in this acid called mushrooms (Amanita?) The bad physical side-effects involved (for me) stiffening of elbow and knee joints, a swelling of the eyelid, shortness of breath or rather anxiety about breathing itself. No heart palpitations like in Mescaline, however. I felt that Donlin was asking for too many more "fives" all the time (in the [?] they'd say he has an oil-burning habit, or is "hog")—But under the sympathetic influence of the drug or whatever it is called I kept agreeing with all his demands. In that sense there's a lot of brainwash implicit in SMs. So I do think we took too much. Yet there were no side evil effects.

In fact I came home and had the first serious long talk with my mother, for 3 days and 3 nights (not consecutive) but we sat talking about everything yet went about the routine of washing, sleeping, eating, cleaning up the yard and house, and returning to long talk chairs at proper time. That was great. I learned I loved her more than I thought. The mushroom high carried on for exactly till Wednesday Jan. 18th (and remember I first chewed the first pills Friday night the 13th). I kept i[t] alive by drinking Christian Brothers port on the rocks. Suddenly on Friday the 20th (day of Inauguration) it started all up again, on port, but very mushroomy, and that was a swinging day, yakking in bars, bookstores, home around Northport (which I never do).

My report is endless, exactly. But here, remember what we were saying? "What? what did you say?" (to have a mumble repeated, the mumble being of excruciating importance.) And "Who are you?"

Page 86: Leary taking part in an illuminated show as part of the psychedelic performances, designed to visualize the experience of a trip.

Above: Neal Cassady and Jack Kerouac, San Francisco, California, 1952. Photograph by Carolyn Cassady.

"Are you sure?""I'm not here."—"What are we doing here?"—"Where are we?"—"What's going on?"—"Am I going to die?"—"No""I can't see you, you're a ghost"—"You're the Holy Ghost"—"Walking on water wasn't built in a day"—"We're just laying around here doing nothing wasn't built in a day"—"We're just laying around here doing nothing"—"Even if I knew how to break your leg" (utilizing Zean koan (Zen) about Baso (T'ang master d.788)) "even if I knew how to break your leg I wouldn't do it—besides you haven't got a leg. Who said you had a leg? You? Who are you? I cant see you! You're not there! I don't see [?]tin! I hate you! Why? Because I love you!" "I love you anyway."

We were at the extremest [sic] poin[t] goofing on a cloud watching the movie of existence.

Owing to the residue of Sacred Mushroom hallucination I woke up briefly the other quiet morning (Thursday 19th) feeling that everybody in my neighborhood was sleeping trustfully around me because they knew I was the Master of Trust in Heaven (for instance).

Everybody seemed innocent. Lafcadio became St. Innocent the Patriarch of Holy Russia. Donlin became the Paraclete, whom [you] waved over my head by an astonishing show of physical strenth [sic] (remember!) It was a definite Satori. Full of Psychi clairvoyance (but you must remember that it is not half as good as the peaceful ecstasy of simple Samadhi trance as I described that in the Dharma Bums). When I yelled out the window at the three Porto Rican teenage boys walking in the snow "Avante Con Dios!" I had no idea where the word "avante" came from, Allen said it meant "Forward with." Clairvoyance there. I saw you, Leary, as a Jesuit Father. Donlin called you Doctor Leary. I saw Allen as Sariputra (the Indian saint). My old idea of St. Peter (about Peter Orlovsky) was strengthened. I saw Peter's sister Marie as Ste. Catherine. Bob Kaufman as Michoscan Indian chief. I saw communists all around us (especially that . . . and others). Pearl became a Lotus of indescribable beauty sitting there in the form of a Buddha woman Bhikkushini. When someone mentioned people being electricity I said "Consolidated Coils." Divine run-outs in my head, like when I went to pee I said to the toilet "It's all your fault!" and could never leave the group without feeling that they were still with me (in the toilet.) Finally told my mother "C'est la Sainte Esprit" and she agreed. My old convocation that nothing ever happened was strenthened [sic] (ow). I felt like a silly [angel] but now I know I'm only a mutterer in old paths, as before. I kept saying, however, to all kinds of people "What an interesting person you are!" and it was true. Finally I said "I think I'll take a shit out the window" in desperation, it was impossible to go on in such ecstasy and excitement. Jokes were the Sacred Jokes of Heaven. the low dog of Dublin, Bob Donlin, was there by design, I'd say, to keep the good old Irish joking going, otherwise we would all have been too serious, I say.

In sum, there is temporary addiction but no withdrawal symptoms whatever. The faculty of remembering names and what one has learned, is heightened so fantastically that we could develop the greatest scholars and scientists in the world with this stuff. There's no harm in Sacred Mushrooms and much good will come of it. (For instance, I remembered historical details I'd completely forgotten before the mushrooms, and names names millions of names and categroies [sic] and data).

Brion Gysin

British artist Brion Gysin engaged in a mushroom session and wrote a report for Leary. He touched on a "flicker apparatus" and being "turned on" by Harry Smith's movies sans drugs. Harry Smith was a San Francisco–based experimental filmmaker known for abstract animation works. This letter precedes Leary's introduction to his psilocybin research, presented to his psychologist peers at the 14th International Congress of Applied Psychology in Copenhagen, Denmark (August 13–19, 1961). Huxley also lectured on "Visionary Experience"—the only time both presented at the same event.[1] Leary had imagined that the congress would be "turned on to visionary matters" in which Aldous Huxley was a speaker. Unfortunately, this was wishful thinking and Leary received a negative reception to his talk, "How to Change Behavior."[2]

At the time of this letter, Gysin and Beat author William S. Burroughs were collaborating on their "cut-up" technique, in which text on paper is cut and physically rearranged to create a new composition. Their work appeared in literary journals and was published in the book, *The Third Mind* (English edition, 1978).

FROM TIMOTHY LEARY TO BRION GYSIN | MARCH 13, 1961

Dear Brion Gysin, Thanks for the reports on your mushroom experiences. The intensity of reaction is as expected with the moderate doses you took. I find that 10 pills (20 mg.) equals about 200 mg. of mescaline. Individual differences and social context can play havoc with such estimates, however.

I'm grateful to you for your description of the flicker apparatus [a reference to Gysin's "dream machine"]. I wrote Burroughs about Harry Smith's movies which turned me on without drugs. I'll set up a trial over the weekend to see what happens.

We have become interested in the issue of which modality gets expanded under mushrooms. Some people are warmly concerned with visual reactions—others respond most to religious and philosophic issues—others to interpersonal dramas. My concern is to tape out more specifically who, when and how these variations take place. The more modalities it is possible to intensify the better and I'm pleased to hear of your interest in the auditory.

I'll send you some more mushrooms in a couple of days. Sandos [sic] Laboratories have been delayed in making up new batches but have promised some by week's end. We are beginning our studies in State prisons. The inmates are volunteering enthusiastically and the staff as well! We have to spend considerable time training our staff members before we get to the inmates. Maybe the staff needs it more!

I'm chairman of a symposium at the International Congress of Psychology, Copenhagen—August. Drugs will be discussed in my symposium and in at least one other. Aldous Huxley and Harry Murray (both friends of mine) are giving two keynote speeches—so the Congress will be well turned on to visionary matters. Perhaps you'd like to take in the Congress. In any case I hope to have the chance to discuss these matters with you in Paris—June.

We are pursuing the idea of a mushroom anthology and hope you and Burroughs will be contributors.

Best wishes, Timothy Leary

Paul Lee

Harvard Divinity School student Paul Lee was one of the participants in the Good Friday Experiment, conducted at Marsh Chapel in Boston, Massachusetts. For the one-day double-blind experiment, graduate student Walter Pahnke led a study to ascertain if participants would undergo a religious experience in a chapel setting after ingesting psilocybin. Lee was given the placebo, but he did engage in other drug sessions later on. Some at the session experienced sadness. He regretted not having a tape recorder as he realized that he would not be able to remember everything.

PAUL LEE TRIP REPORT ENTITLED "THE MUSHROOM" | FEBRUARY 26, 1962

We gathered at Ralph's at about 6:00 and took the mushroom (4 pills) about 6:30. Ernie and Michael and Ralph and I. The first impact was an overwhelming sense of having been through exactly the same situation before. Michael told a joke that made no sense and touched off an explosion of laughter. I had the impression of being dropped into my chair like a bomb and when the invisible debris cleared I saw Michael bathed in blood. He had said that he had seen the following written on a toilet wall that day: "Jane has mental health." We all laughed like idiots even though no one knew what he was laughing about. I managed to regain perspective and got up and found some paper and wrote down some notes in order to remember. I'm exceedingly sorry that I did not continue to do so. I have very little recollection of the following experiences. There was a tremendous amount of laughter throughout and I wonder if this doesn't function as a protective or defensive measure. Ernie often set us off. I had a number of tremendous responses to the music and remember one particular time dancing and laughing uproariously in the middle of the room. I remember Ernie asking Michael and myself to go into the bedroom where we saw a display of wheat under a bright light-pit looked like a gold sculpting. I found it hard to maintain my attention because of the intensity of color and the vibrating character of the wheat. A number of times I wondered what Ernie was doing. I thought at one point he was exposing himself to Ralph and his wife in the kitchen. I remember him making some reference to "it's all sexual" or something like that. Ralph's wife entered into the group in a magnificent way and I enjoyed her immensely. She was very vivid and dramatic and I remember her asking me at one point if I wanted to worship her foot and I tried to say but couldn't get it out that I certainly could worship her foot and for the sake of the foot not just because it was part of her body. I was ready to worship the foot itself. I considered this a particularly romantic thing to think and was a little sorry I couldn't say it. I have a recollection of responding to her beyond proprietary, although my doing so was completely spontaneous and natural. I had the feeling finally that Ralph was exceedingly aware of what was going on and didn't know what to do about it, except be somewhat embarrassed. Under the influence of the drug such interpersonal dynamics are transparently obvious and cannot help but be noticed and acknowledged. I again had the impression of the room being a vast sensorium, where all nuances and subtleties are vividly and emphatically experienced!

One's intuitive powers are increased dramatically, which leads to qualities of understanding and communion and affection. I responded profoundly to this character of the experience. During the last hour it seemed as if we reached a kind of easy plateau where we all sat around and chatted. The group dynamics were beautiful. I felt as if we were tapping a huge reservoir and that I had greater access to its power than the others, although when they exercised power I felt supportive. I thought that we all shared this power and could utilize or give expression to as much as we wanted. It was during this time that Michael tried to take a directing hand in things and I contested him and oer' leapt him. It was like an exercise in power gymnastics and I enjoyed the dynamics of it immensely, repeating such words as wonderful beautiful in order to express my enjoyment and appreciation. Ernie kept repeating phrases that we outlawed which was funny. I again had a tremendous amount of sinus drainage, almost more than the previous time—although there was nothing revelatory about it . . . .

In another report, Lee bemoans his session due to the other participants, excepting Huston Smith. His report is several pages long:

PAUL LEE TRIP REPORT ENTITLED "LSD . . . OR, GETTING AND BEING BOMBED CHEMICALLY"

Although I happily and enthusiastically looked forward to taking the drug and felt very animated about this adventure, the experience began to very quickly take on a nightmarish quality due to the violent reaction of Beverly. I had the feeling that we would more or less "be on our own" and that the experiences of the others would not encroach upon or obtrude upon mine. We would be mutually engaged in a private or at least solitudinous [sic] exploration. I was sadly mistaken. Nevertheless, I found myself "beyond" their psychological problems and self-revelations and unwilling to be drawn into their respective dramas, even though I felt that demands were being made upon me that called for some kind of response (sympathy, concern, commiseration, etc.) but a response that distracted me from enjoying my own realms. Therefore, I gave no such response. I suppose I anticipated more for an aesthetic experience (this is said in retrospect—I have a firm recollection of not knowing then what to anticipate and being rather elated about it) rather like going to a symphony and maybe smiling and nodding appreciatively every once in a while at my fellow participants. Gene and Walter were immediately responsive to Beverly and Charlene started to feel very badly about Beverly's crying exemplified by her saying: "Why are they subjecting this girl to such suffering." All of this was compounded by Beverly's vomiting, which seemed particularly violent and disturbing. (Beverly almost immediately hallucinated [2 words unreadable] and cried and cried.)

My overall initial viewpoint was that the others (Beverly, Gene, Walter esp.) were seeing themselves for the first time as others saw them (as I saw them) and I had a profound sense of participating in their insight even though this was due to no activity on my part. I was an observer, but an overwhelmingly interested and appreciative one. I thought at any moment they might come over and gasp at me how they stood revealed and what a tremendous experience it was for them and how they would understand that this was somehow confirmatory of what I had known all along. Related to this then was the lack of any impulse whatsoever in myself to understand myself revealed in a unique and original way. I did not preclude this, but

I considered the dimension of psychological problems or personal self-awareness of this sort to be an indulgence (or a decision) that militated against the experience and exploration of other dimensions. Why drink ginger ale when you can have champagne? I considered their histrionics as somewhat phoney (an indulgence) and depressing. The latter because they needed such an occasion to come to such insight about themselves, which I felt I already had and could go on from. This raised [f]or me the theme of judgment (or profound critical self-appraisal) which I consider to be an enormously important dimension, the experiential impact of which may receive for the first time under the drug.

Another way of saying the above leads to my first really profound experience. I had the impression that the others were sharing my perceptions, that, indeed, there was suddenly no difference between subject and object (the room had become one large sensorium where all emotions and feelings were made available and were shared). But this is possibly tantamount to saying that I was related to the others as in a dream, wherein one associated with others, but where it can be said about those of whom one dreams that they experience nothing of this. They were undergoing what I was perceiving in a dream-like way, but they were experiencing it differently from me. We were separated. This latter occurred to me finally when I suddenly realized that they weren't really learning from their being exposed and opened, and then I was overcome with a pained regret and awareness that events were repeating themselves. I bemoaned the fact that something serious had happened and that it would not really be appropriated properly.

It is obvious the extent to which I was aware of the experiences of the others and how I envied Huston who was like some ancient Indian monkey off on his own cloud.

Timothy Leary
Not surprisingly, Leary wrote long descriptions of his experiences under the influence of psychotropic substances. This one is presumably his first, reflecting on that initial life-changing experience in Mexico.

TIMOTHY LEARY TRIP REPORT ENTITLED "REMEMBRANCES"
SUMMARY | UNDATED

In August 1960, on a sunny afternoon in the colorful garden of a Mexican villa, I ate seven mushrooms, the so-called "sacred mushrooms" of Mexico. For the next five hours, I was spun through a visionary journey which could be described in many extravagant metaphors but which was, above all, the deepest educational and religious experience of my life. No language exists to describe the speed-of-light transformations of energy which are experienced after taking consciousness-expanding protein, such as the mushrooms, peyote, LSD, etc. One crude attempt might be made to describe the experience in terms of three classes of images.

The internal flow of archetypical forms. I found myself caught up in an endless flow of colored forms, microbiological shapes, cellular acrobatics, capillary whirling. My cortex was tuned in to molecular processes which were completely new and strange—a Niagara of abstract designs. My mind swooped in and out of this evolutionary stream, creating cosmological visions. Dozens of mythical and Darwinian insights dashed into awareness. I was permitted to glance back down the flow of time and to perceive how the life energy continually manifests itself in forms, always changing and reforming. Microscopic images merged with primal created myths. There was incredible emotional ecstasy. New physical sensations pulsed throughout my body—the glow of life was felt flooding along my veins. I merged into a timeless ocean of fluid electricity, the endless flow of life. There was a feeling of intense self-less love. I was an ecstatic part of all life. The memory of former delusions of selfhood brought about exultant laughter. Floating down the evolutionary river, there came a sense of limitless, self-less power, the delight of flowing plasticity—the astounding discovery that consciousness can tune in to an infinite number of organic levels. There are billions of cellular processes in our bodies, each with its universe of experience. The simple joys and pains of my familiar personality represented one set of experiences—a repetitious, dusty set. As I slipped into the fire-flow of biological energy, hundreds of new experiential sets flashed by. At times there was panic and desperate desire to return to the familiar, to shut off the flow. I would wrench myself away from the visionary flow, the ecstasy would cease . . . .

George and Ann Litwin

George Litwin met Timothy Leary when he was was a PhD student and the Research Assistant to the Chairman of the Department of Psychology. Litwin was conducting research on the psychological effects of mescaline in a hospital setting. Leary was assigned to be his Faculty Advisor, and they spent many hours discussing the research that Litwin was doing. According to Litwin, initially Leary was strongly opposed to the use of drugs—his experience is that they were used to control behavior. For this book, George Litwin recorded his experiences of the first psychedelic session he participated in with Leary.

THE FIRST PSYCHEDELIC SESSION IN CAMBRIDGE
INTRODUCTION

Contrary to popular belief, the first psychedelic session in Cambridge during the Leary era was not with LSD but with psilocybin, an extract of the active ingredient in the psilocybe mushroom that grows in Mexico and Mesoamerica.

During the summer, Tim had stayed in Mexico with a colleague, Frank Barron, and they decided to hire a curandera who was experienced in taking psilocybe mushrooms and guiding sessions. She was older, and from the region north of Oaxaca in the mountains. Timothy had a very positive experience with the psilocybe mushrooms.

When he returned in the fall, he rushed up to me, and said we must immediately begin research on these mind-expanding chemicals, such as the psilocybe mushroom from Mexico. He selected me because I had done prior research with mescaline, and had spent a number of hours with him discussing the details of the mescaline sessions, and the possibilities for using this class of chemicals to expand consciousness and awareness of both self and environment.

We sat down that very afternoon and wrote a letter to Sandoz Pharmaceuticals, the company that first extracted the psilocybin from the mushroom, and then synthesized it in the laboratory. We expected a package of forms to fill out. Instead Sandoz sent us a large bottle of psilocybin pills and a brief note saying we should report back to them on any results we found. Timothy took the pills for safe-keeping. Several weeks later, he called me on a Sunday afternoon and said, "Aldous Huxley is visiting and he wants to try psilocybin. I think we will do the session this afternoon. Do you want to join us?"

I immediately jumped in my Volvo and raced over to the house on Grant Avenue that Tim was renting from a Harvard faculty member on leave. It was a lovely home, with a large library that had both books and windows. There were comfortable couches all around. Timothy seemed quite excited, and Aldous Huxley sat calmly, introduced himself to me and said how interested he was in the possibilities of the mushroom.

THE SESSION

After a brief discussion of the ground rules, we passed around the bottle of psilocybin. The ground rules we set were, we had to stay together, in sight of each other. We had to be peaceful and non-violent; otherwise we should expect some sort of intervention. We also agreed that we would not interfere with each others' experience, but share what we thought was possible afterward.

The psilocybin experience seemed to last three or four hours. It wore off slowly, so it is hard to put an exact time on it. As I re-experience it and imagine what happened, I can think of the experience in several phases. I have some notes in an old notebook, but they are just words I wrote down, and it is hard to interpret them.

After about 45 minutes I began to experience the effect of the psilocybin. The first effect was that my perception began to change; the walls became brighter, the room became bigger. Then I noticed the walls were waving as I walked around. I sat down to steady myself and the waving was reduced. I realized that I had disconnected some of my most basic perceptual processes. For example, I experienced a wavy motion that seemed to turn liquid eyeballs into stable objects. This is a brain orientation that happens early on in life and I felt I was reexperiencing this time when we learn to see things by interpreting our sensory input.

I closed my eyes for a few minutes and I had a great flash of images flashing by. I could barely see them they went by so fast, but they looked a lot like old photographs I had seen as a child—of my family, of my family's family, picnicking, playing baseball, etc. I sat in a more upright position and began some very regular breathing. After a while the flow of images slowed down, and I could begin to recognize particular pictures. As I saw the pictures, I felt drawn into them and often became part of them. They were pictures that represented experiences to me, and I was reexperiencing these times of fear, or happiness. The kinds of images that came up included being locked in the trunk of a car with a ten-year-old dog, being thrown into the bathtub with five fish, and playing baseball with my father. There were a number of experiences in which I had felt great fear, but also experiences when I had felt great joy. Mostly they were experiences that had been very emotional to me at the time.

This went on for perhaps an hour; I reexperienced whole segments of my life. Since that time, I see it as a review that has helped me integrate who I am, where I came from, and what I am here to do. Then I seemed to fall into unconsciousness for a while. I don't remember anything but darkness.

When I awoke, I opened my eyes and the room was filled with a great light. It was brighter than anything I had ever imagined, yet it didn't have a single bright source, like the sun. Each object emanated light of different color and intensity. It was a very positive experience. My brain said I was living in the future—this is what the future would be like. Perhaps this is true; I have no evidence of it.

The experience of great light continued for a substantial time and people began to come and go. They moved very slowly and very gracefully. When someone touched me, it was the gentlest touch and I felt better all over immediately just from the touch.

All of this made it seem like I was experiencing, if not the future, the evolution of our species; while these were people, they were extraordinary people, beautiful, gentle, graceful and full of light.

As the light experience gradually passed, I recognized the space I was in originally—the library, and I saw that each thing in it was a living form, full of light if you chose to see it that way. It has changed my view of many things. I tend to treat the world as composed of living things, both animate and inanimate.

THE AFTERMATH

The session ended with no particular ceremony. We got together one-by-one in the kitchen for a drink of water, or milk. Timothy talked about his experience, which had been quite strong. He compared it with his experience with the mushroom, which he thought was even more powerful—probably containing a greater dosage of psilocybin. Like each of us, he re-experienced parts of his life, particularly parts that were particularly painful. As I understand it, his first wife committed suicide. I doubt that this is something that Timothy, or anyone, could easily recover from.

This past, which contained both guilt and brilliant insight, came up in many of the sessions I had with Timothy. It was his theme. Did he have a reason to keep on living? Could he justify taking up space, and air and water, and food? Or was he already dead, and just failed to complete the passing?

Aldous compared the psilocybin experience with other psychedelic experiences he had had. He was quite knowledgeable about psychedelics, having experienced peyote with the Navajo, and LSD on several occasions. He said he thought the psilocybin was much gentler and less disturbing than drugs such as LSD. In that light he thought it might have a positive social value.

His discussion of his experience with LSD led me to realize that one could take a higher dosage and have a truly ego-shattering experience from which it might be difficult to put together the pieces. With the lower dosages of psilocybin that we took (four to eight milligrams) there was perhaps a slow dissolution of the ego and the regulatory mechanisms that make it up, but it was not destructive and it was quite comfortable to return to who we had been before—albeit with some changes in perception and attitude.

George's then wife Ann wrote a very long description (nine pages) of her experience after consuming ten pills of synthetic psilocybin. She claimed that she was "probably the most depressed the day after" that she had ever been, and "eventually had to work these thoughts through with George who said that I had been reaching for what the Buddist

[sic] calls nirvana and when you attain that state you cannot love others, and this is largely what I felt."

Stage 1

I felt quite apprehensive about taking a drug previous to this session and only took four pills at first, followed twenty minutes later by four more. I had no noticeable reaction, in spite of the fact that others were commenting on colors of things in the room, which had not changed for me. I did not feel suggestable then or later. I did feel more relaxed. One of the first effects was a warm tingling heavy feeling of my body. By this time I was lying down on the couch. I had covered my head with an orange blanket which Tim Leary gave me to screen out the laughter of those who had found something to laugh at. A kitten was sitting on my hand and it took tremendous effort to remove him. Just previous to these first effects I had taken two more pills making a total of ten pills. I had my eyes closed under the blanket and could see furry animals, spiders with many legs, birds with rainbow-like feathers. I much preferred the colors of the inside world to what I saw when I uncovered my head and removed the kitten. The trees outside the window did change into different shapes but retained their usual color, one flower in the bouquet of flowers on the table was singularly beautiful and, what I think was Lynn's shoe, took the shape of a nicely colored snake. I covered my head again.

Huston Smith

Smith was a scholar of comparative religion and known for his work, *The World's Religions* (1958). He was a professor in the Philosophy Department at MIT in Boston (1958–73) at the time when Leary and Alpert were at Harvard (1960–63). Earlier in his career, he was influenced by Gerald Heard and Aldous Huxley,[3] relationships that brought him to the acquaintance of Leary and, naturally, his drug studies.

HUSTON SMITH TRIP REPORT ENTITLED "NOTES ON MESCALIN" |
JANUARY 1, 1961

New Year's Day, 1961. Eleanor and I reached the home of Dr. Timothy Leary in Newton about 12:30. Present in addition to Timothy were Dr. George Alexander, a psychiatrist, and Frank Barron, research psychologist.

After pleasantries, Tim produced a capsule container, saying one was a very mild dose, two an average dose, three above average. We were to take from one to three as we wished. Eleanor took two [Note: Eleanor states that she took three pills at this session, while Huston took two] at once; I took one and a second about a half hour later when nothing seemed to be happening.

I would judge about an hour after my first pill I noticed mounting tension in my legs which turned into tremors. Went into the living room and lay down on the couch. The tremors turned into twitches, though they were seldom actually visible.

It would be impossible for me to fix a time when I passed into the visionary stage—the transition was absolutely imperceptible. From here on time becomes largely irrelevant. With great effort I might be able to reconstruct the order in which the following thought-feelings occurred, but there seems to be no point in trying to do so.

The whole world into which I was ushered was strange, weird, uncanny, significant, and terrifying beyond belief. Two things struck me especially. (1) The mescalin [Note: although Huston refers to mescaline here, his wife Kendra states it was psilocybin that he took] acted as a psychological prism. It was as though the infinitely complex and layered psychological ingredients which normally are smelted down into a single band was weak, nondescript sensation-impressions were now being refracted, spread out as if by spectroscope, into about five layers. And the odd thing was that one was aware of them all to some degree simultaneously and could move back and forth among [them] at will, choosing to attend to, concentrate upon, whichever one [you] wished. Thus I could hear the soft conversation of Tim and George Alexander in the study adjoining . . . .

Huston and his wife Eleanor (also known as Kendra), took two pills (average dose according to Leary) in the company of psychiatrist George Alexander and psychologist Frank Barron at Leary's home in Newton. Smith wrote of this first experience:

> I realized how utterly impossible it would be for me to describe them on the morrow when I lost this world of perception as I knew I would. I knew this because I know how impossible it would be right then to describe what I saw to Tim or Eleanor. With all this came the clearest realization I have had as to what literary genius would consist of. I[t] would consist of the ingenious use of words to bridge as far as possible the gulf between the normal state of existence and the world I was now in.

He also wrote, "It should not be assumed from what I have written that the experience was for me pleasurable. The two accurate words are significance and terror." Although Smith thought such tests were dangerous, he continued to participate. In a session several days later, Smith was still at a loss for words.

HUSTON SMITH TRIP REPORT ENTITLED "RECOLLECTIONS OF LSD"
| JANUARY 6, 1962

To begin with, the usual: the experience is so fantastic in both its novelty and its power as to beggar all possibility of adequate depiction through words. The most that can be hoped for by way of description is an approximation, and only those who have had the drug can know how far removed from actuality the approximation must be.

The things that can be said easily and unequivocally are: (1) My physical symptoms were a pronounced quaking which centered in my lower limbs, climaxing (I would judge) about 1½ hours after taking the drug but continuing off and on for about five hours; a slight stomach cramp for about ten hours; the feeling of physical depletion—having been wrung through a ringer—on coming out of the spell; and inability to sleep (bright flashes of light) until 3am. (2) No disorientation; a[t] no point did I lose awareness of who I was, where I was, or the group experience that was underway. (3) Considerable apprehension, but no real terror or paranoia [this time].

Now to the difficult part. The best way I can describe the experience as a whole is to liken it to an emotional-reflective-visual kaleidoscope, with the words listed in order of decreasing importance—mood and emotion most important, thought next, visual (internal, of the sort you can get with your eyes closed) least. Experience involving these three components kept dissolving continuously from one pattern to another.

Emotionally the patterns ranged from serene contentment and mild euphoria to apprehension which boardered [sic] on, but never quite slipped into, alarm. But overwhelmingly they involved (a) astonishment at the absolutely incredible immensity, complexity, intensity and extravagance of being, existence, the cosmos, call it what you will. Ontological shock, I suppose. (b) The most acute sense of the poignancy, fragility, preciousness, and significance of all life and history. The latter was accompanied by a powerful sense of the responsibility of all for all—all this, it must be pointed out, while lying comfortably and privately on one's own flat back.

Intellectually, the dominant impression was that of entering into the vary [sic] marrow of existence. Instead of looking at a painting, I was climbing into it, almost through it, as if to view it from behind. So too with being in general. It was as if each of the billion atoms of experience which under normal circumstances are summarized and averaged into crude, indiscriminate wholesale impression was now being seen and savored for itself. The other clear sense was that of cosmic relativity. Perhaps all experience never gets summarized in any inclusive overview. Perhaps all there is, is this everlasting congerie of an infinite number of discrete points-of-view, each summarizing the whole from [h]is perspective with the sum of all perspective running the entire gamut from terror to absolute assurance and ecstasy.

During the supper, after the two groups had gathered together, I found myself disinclined to speak much, And the reason seemed clear—and still does. Several times a thought began to take shape. But immediately one saw three or four feasible (and very different) ways any overt expression of it could be taken: straightforward, platitudinous, farcical, too personally revelatory to be publically broadcast, etc. As language seemed too gross and clumsy to screen out the senses I did not intend, it seemed, not so much more prudent as more truthful in the sense of not multiplying misunderstanding, to remain for the most part quiet.

Felt clean—cleansed, actually—clear and happy the next day; the reverse to about equal degree the day following: normal, thereafter.

In another session, later that year on November 25, his experience was not so joyous:

HUSTON SMITH TRIP REPORT ENTITLED "NOTES ON PSILOCYBIN"
| NOVEMBER 25, 1962

Friday, Nov. 25. Took 8 capsules, together with Neal Grossman, an MIT junior, who is doing independent study course with me on atypical stages of awareness.

Very powerful sense throughout of the widely alternative ways in which reality can be viewed. In terms of organization[,] or experience, emphasis, and mood. As to mood, mine ran a wide gamut.

Major moods:
- Considerable dislike of the experience. Impatience to be through with it. Asking myself if I really want ever to take it again.
- Everything, even Beethoven playing at the moment, seeming funny. Explosive laughter. Though not as intense in this mood as Neal, or as I was the time with Raynor and Mary Johnson.
- Feeling that everything in the universe is exactly [right and] as it should be.
- Intense affection for my family.
- Sense of the tremendous significance of life and history. Importance and rightness of behaving decently and responsibly.

Other thoughts, very vivid at the time:
- In this condition you discover who you are at base. In my case, family man, teacher, etc.
- How easily attention can swing from one frame of reference to another. Merely through speaking or hearing a word.
- At one point I felt certain I [had] come upon an important theoretical point regarding personality and its structure. Felt I could put it into words if I tried. But decided not to try at the moment. Now I can't recollect what it was.

- Strong physical sensation while going under. Limbs felt very light. Slight headache while coming out. Feeling of enormous physical depletion 6–8 hours after taking it, but this passed in a couple of hours. Slept soundly and dreamlessly, and awoke feeling very well.
- A couple of extraordinary visual sensations. One relating to trees. Back branches swayed forward until they came in front of the fore branches & vice versa. Neal's nose would at times look as large as that on a clown's mask. [handwritten arrow pointing this to move before preceding point]

He was not impressed by the visuals. They seemed like "an intrusion, a distraction from significance, which for me was all important."[4]

As evidenced by Huston, not all sessions were ecstatic experiences with inspirational revelations. Despite their best efforts at set and setting, blessings, and the reading of Leary's *Manual*, some trips went south. The administration and supervision of a psychedelic session sometimes fell apart.

Gunther Weil was a graduate student participating in the Harvard experiments and described how in one of his sessions in April 1961, the room was filled with depression:

My impatience to take the mushroom shortly after a few of the others had begun now strikes me as being a bit strange. Although I usually enjoy the experiences a great deal I don't believe that this really explains my actions on that morning. In some way the mushroom became an escape from the barrenness and isolation of the room. In another way, it freed me from worrying about the depressive atmosphere as an observer. Yet its most immediate effect was one of depression.

An insidious depression filled the room for the first hour or more. If anyone of us was not subject to the same feeling, the feeling itself—collectively—was enough to deter a strong expression of any contrary feelings. Tim was perhaps the first to put his finger on the problem. Perhaps he was then feeling what I was later to experience with great intensity. Being caged, trapped, pacing like panthers, we all seemed to be pacing at once at one point. What was simply an experimental room became the whole prison for me. It was later to become the whole universe. And it was finally to become a womb . . .

5
Millbrook, 1963–64

"We saw ourselves as anthropologists from the twenty-first century inhabiting a time module set somewhere in the dark ages of the 1960s. On this space colony we were attempting to create a new paganism and a new dedication to life as art."

Timothy Leary on the Castalia Foundation in Millbrook, New York; quoted in *Storming Heaven: LSD and the American Dream* (1998) by Jay Stevens, p. 208

LUCKILY, WHEN ONE DOOR CLOSES, another one opens. Without a home for the IFIF, Peggy, Billy and Tommy Hitchcock—heirs to the Mellon family fortune—offered to host the research on their family estate in Millbrook, New York (also known as the "Dieterich Manor"). Leary had first become acquainted with Peggy at a New York City artist's "salon" in early 1962. Peggy and her brothers became consciousness-expanding enthusiasts and helped to fund the IFIF after it was pushed out of Zihuatanejo, Mexico.[1]

At this time, the organization changed its name to the Castalia Foundation, based on the fictional society created by Nobel Prize–winning novelist Hermann Hesse in his book *The Glass Bead Game* (1943).[2] The story involves a futuristic society of mystic game players in the fictional place Castalia. In an homage to Hesse, Leary and Metzner wrote that he was a "master guide" to the psychedelic experience, whose books served as manuals toward LSD sessions.[3]

As with the Newton Centre home, many people lived at and visited Millbrook, such as jazz musician Maynard Ferguson and his wife Flo, Richard Alpert, Leary and his children, the Hitchcocks, and other people previously associated with the drug studies at Harvard, such as Ralph Metzner, British researcher Michael Hollingshead, along with a rotating flow of characters. In June 1964 Ken Kesey and his Merry Pranksters pitched up on their *Furthur* (now *Further*) bus. Prankster Ken Babbs recalled their trip to Millbrook in an interview for this book:

Psychic-Drug Testers Living in Retreat

2 Scientists in LSD Dispute Accepted in Upstate Village

Debate Over Right to Change Normal States Is Pressed

Special to The New York Times

MILLBROOK, N. Y., Dec. 14 — When they moved to this quiet Dutchess County village of 1,700 inhabitants in August, Timothy Leary and Richard Alpert made no splash in the placid waters of its disposition. They were generally regarded as agreeable men of neighborly demeanor and only vaguely remarkable background.

Most residents did not begin to be fully aware of the men's renown until one after another of the major national magazines (Look, Esquire, Time, The Saturday Evening Post and others) appeared at the village newsstand with long, mostly uncomplimentary, articles on the work the two men have done with hallucinogenic drugs.

Fascination with the effects that such drugs produce in the human consciousness cost them their positions as lecturers at Harvard earlier this year. Dr. Leary attempted to carry on his work by opening a combined resort and psychic drug research center in Mexico. This foundered in June when the Mexican Government expelled him for engaging in activities not permitted to a tourist.

The two psychologists are now living deep inside an enclosed 2,500-acre estate here. They have established another of their "transcendental" multifamily communities," with seven adults, six children, three dogs and seven cats, in a rented 53-room house with 10 baths. Dr. Alpert, 32 years old, is a bachelor, but Dr. Leary, 43, is married and has two children.

Another psychologist, Dr. Ralph Metzner, 27, and his family are working and living with them in a house at the end of a long private roadway lined with craggy old trees on an estate that once employed several dozen gardeners but has not been manicured lately.

The house is an old white wood mansion with a wraparound porch and a red brick chimney running up the front side. A big iron bell and a pumpkin flank the entrances to the porch.

Men Collate Research

The doctors say that they are doing no active research with what they call the "consciousness-expanding drugs." They are having no sessions in which doses of lysergic acid diethylamide (LSD), psilocybin or mescaline induce visions, hallucinations or mystical experiences in subjects.

They cannot now legally get the restricted drugs, which were available to them as members of the Harvard faculty and in Mexico. They have only some morning glory seeds that have similar properties. They did not

want to say when they had last been in a transport by their use.

Dr. Leary and Dr. Alpert are living in retreat from what they regard as the unwarranted hostility of the medical and psychological professions. They are living on savings, income from writing and the contributions of a few supporters. They are consolidating the results of their former very extensive research and are speaking occasionally before college and professional groups.

Dr. Leary has been president of the International Federation for Internal Freedom, but he said it was dissolved yesterday because restrictions on the use of the drugs had made it impossible for the group to set up centers where people could come for sessions.

He said that 500 persons had signed up for sessions in Mexico in beautiful surroundings. Dr. Leary said that "the setting in which a person takes the drug is what is crucial to the kind of experience he will have."

Although not very widely used, LSD is generally available to psychiatrists as an experimental therapeutic agent.

"Our debate with psychiatrists about the use and control of psychedelic (mind opening)

drugs involves the right, right now, of thoughtful Americans to change their own consciousness," they say in a paper completed this week. The paper adds:

"The LSD experience is so novel and so powerful that the more you think you know about the mind, the more astounded and even frightened you'll be when your consciousness starts to flip you out of your mind. A new profession of psychedelic guides will inevitably develop to supervise these experiences."

Proponents say that the after benefits include a new understanding of beauty and art, in more ability to be oneself, and a greater understanding of human relationships. Some speak of finding new directions for their lives.

Dr. Alpert said they had found that it was not psychiatrists and physicians who were interested in such changes of consciousness but writers, scholars, philosophers, artists, theologians and divinity school students.

At Harvard, the experiments the men were doing exerted a powerful attraction on students. Many of them sought eagerly to enlist as subjects, a fact that appalled the guardians of

that institution, especially when some of the rebuffed students began to obtain hallucinogenic drugs from bootleggers who came to hawk them near Harvard Yard.

Now the 60-acre campus of Bennett College, a stylish and expensive two-year girls' school, is in walking distance of the former Harvard lecturers' transcendental manor.

"As a precautionary measure," the president, Donald A. Eldridge, has declared the estate "out of bounds" for Bennett's 330 students, who have been made to understand that expulsion might follow any violation of this rule.

There has been a good deal of talk in the village lately but residents have not been shaken in their equanimity. Many seem to regard the men and their work as separate entities; they like the former and are reserved about the latter.

The village newspaper, The Millbrook Round Table, seems to have set the tone of public reaction in an editorial it ran last month under the title, "No Witch Hunt Here."

It commended the men for "a wise and fair decision" in promising to eschew research here and it asked that both they and their families be accepted "solely on the basis of their actions in Millbrook," not by magazine reports.

The Rev. Edwin Daniels, minister of the Federated Church, said that people had been "very curious" and "somewhat concerned" since the magazine articles appeared in late October and early November.

Both men have a good deal of personal charm. They laugh readily and can be very entertaining in conversation.

"Before any of us knew who they were, they came into our stores and they were very, very pleasant people and we got to know them and like them very much," said Edward Maggiacomo, president of the Businessmen's Association.

"When the articles came out in The Saturday Evening Post and Esquire it didn't faze me a bit, nor any of the men. The relationship was exactly the same, just as if the articles were not printed," he said.

John Kading, owner for 20 years of the Corner News Store at the center of the small shopping section, said, "You can't meet finer people." He said he had not heard his customers speak "one solitary word" against the men.

George T. Whalen, a real estate and insurance man who is regarded as the most important businessman in town, was brief. "No statement from me," he said icily.

The New York Times

Dr. Richard Alpert, left, and Dr. Timothy Leary chat with Mr. Leary's daughter Susan on street in Millbrook, N. Y.

Page 118: Leary holding his fingers in a chanting position while standing outdoors at Millbrook, 1967.

Above: Leary and Richard Alpert shown smiling with Leary's daughter Susan in Millbrook, New York in this *New York Times* article, published December 15, 1963. The LSD research and the Millbrook commune is described as positive and accepted by the local community, as evidenced by testimonials.

At Millbrook in June 1964, when we took the bus, *Further*, driven by Neal Cassady, Allen Ginsberg at his side giving directions, north from Madhattan [sic], winding through country roads, stopped at the gatehouse and were serenaded by Maynard Ferguson who then gave Kesey directions to the Peggy Hitchcock Mansion, home of IFIF; were greeted by Richard Alpert in a swirl of green from a smoke grenade we threw from the bus.

When we were leaving Millbrook, Leary shook Kesey's and my hands and told us we were cohorts, doing the same work and we would continue to do it together whenever we had the chance.

Millbrook essentially became a commune, with Leary and his gang continuing sessions and leading others through workshops, in the journey towards achieving ecstasy and heightened states of consciousness. The Millbrook brochure described the weekend workshops as providing "external support for consciousness expansion." The programs were also designed to create a "balance between verbal and nonverbal, between the didactic seminar and the experimental laboratory." The Castalia Foundation hosted an open house every Sunday and the cost per participant was a minimum of $75 per weekend. The brochure stated:

THE CASTALIA FOUNDATION, MILLBROOK, WELCOME BROCHURE

Location: The setting for the weekend workshops is a large estate in the mid-Hudson Valley, two hours by car or train from New York City. The house and grounds have been arranged to provide external support for consciousness expansion.

Schedule: Weekend workshops begin at 6:30 Friday evening, and end on Sunday afternoon following lunch. The programs vary from weekend to weekend depending upon the special skills of the staff members in attendance. However, the schedule for each weekend provides for a balance between verbal and nonverbal, between didactic seminar and the experimental laboratory.

Recommended Dress: Informal. Women bring slacks.

Facilties [sic]: In addition to the seminar rooms and living rooms, the houses and grounds contain a meditation house, forest paths, lake for swimming, vegetable gardens, art and photographic facilities, music

Beloved
guests

1. Please limit the attempt to capture audiences for your personal drama.

2. Obey laws of the land. No drugs. Please sign statement of non-posession of drugs.

3. Please keep Castalia green. A $5.00 a day "contribution" is requested.

Above and overleaf: Sign advising guests on behavior and participation at the Millbrook commune occupied by the Castalia Foundation, the organization which superseded the IFIF.

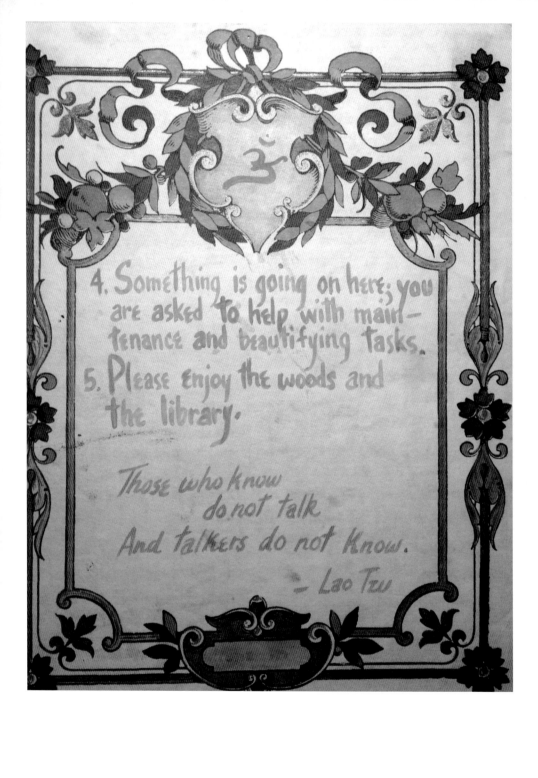

4. Something is going on here; you are asked to help with main-tenance and beautifying tasks.

5. Please enjoy the woods and the library.

Those who know
         do not talk
And talkers do not know.

                — Lao Tzu

Location: The setting for the weekend workshops is a large estate in the mid-Hudson Valley, two hours by car or train from New York City. The house and grounds have been arranged to provide external support for consciousness expansion.

Schedule: Weekend workshops begin at 6:30 Friday evening, and end on Sunday afternoon following lunch. The programs vary from weekend to weekend depending upon the special skills of the staff members in attendance. However, the schedule for each weekend provides for a balance between verbal and non-verbal, between the didactic seminar and the experimental laboratory.

Recommended Dress: Informal. Women bring slacks.

Facilities: In addition to the seminar rooms and living rooms, the houses and grounds contain a meditation house, forest paths, lake for swimming, vegetable gardens, art and photographic facilities, music and book libraries of relevant selections both Eastern and Western, and a library of tape lectures and experiential films.

Financial Arrangement: Each participant is invited to contribute a minimum of seventy-five (75) dollars per weekend to the Castalia Foundation (a non-profit foundation).

Reservations: If you are interested in attending one of these workshops, please write the Castalia Foundation, briefly describing (1) your reasons for wishing to attend, (2) your previous experience in consciousness expansion, (3) any special interest in relevant theories and methods. Also give preferred dates.

Open House: There will be open house at the Castalia Foundation every Sunday afternoon from 4 PM to 6 PM only.

CASTALIA FOUNDATION
BOX 175
MILLBROOK
NEW YORK 12545

and book libraries of relevant selections both Eastern and Western, and a library of tape lectures and experiential films.

Financial Arrangement: Each participant is invited to contribute a minimum of seventy-five (75) dollars per weekend to the Castalia Foundation (a nonprofit organization).

Reservations: If you are interested in attending one of these workshops, please write to the Castalia Foundation, briefly describing (1) your reasons for wishing to attend, (2) your previous experience in consciousness expansion, (3) any special interest in relevant theories and methods. Also give preferred dates.

Open House: There will be open house at the Castalia Foundation every Sunday afternoon from 4PM to 6PM only.

Leary's inner circle continued to advocate for his work at Millbrook and many of his acquaintances—although not necessarily part of the commune itself—still kept him abreast of their own experimentation. In January 1964, Alan Watts wrote to Leary about his experience with some "enhanced" gingerbread and touched on the memorial service for Aldous Huxley, who had died the previous year:

FROM ALAN WATTS TO TIMOTHY LEARY | JANUARY 27, 1964

Dear Tim, Many thanks for all your news. At present I'm completely absorbed in finishing my book BEYOND THEOLOGY: THE ART OF GODMANSHIP. Alas, I simply can't manage anything else until after March 1st—when we will be coming East for about 6 weeks. I wish very much I could do the tribute to Aldous, but there just isn't the time . . . . When we reach N.Y. I will call you and make arrangements for a visit to Millbrook. I must tell you about a most extraordinary voyage with the aid of some grass in gingerbread. What a waste to smoke it!

Our love to you all, Alan

At Millbrook, the ongoing experiments into consciousness expansion went hand in hand with an emphasis on spiritual exploration that was a touchstone for much of the counterculture movement. Leary and his research team developed forms to record the journey of a

Above: The porch at Millbrook, c. 1966, below the
fantastic painted façade of the house.

Billy —

If you could leave some (1)
it would make possible session tomorrow
for Susan etc.

Sorry I didn't see you

Above: Note to Billy Hitchcock from unknown author, requesting LSD for drug session. One of the Millbrook estate owners, William "Billy" Mellon Hitchcock and his siblings, Tommy and Peggy, all became interested in the psychedelic drug research begun by the IFIF and continued to support Leary's work for many years.

FIRST BARDO	**Non-game Trancendence**	Cosmic future				
		Human future				
		Personal future				
		Present				
		Personal post			X X X X X X X X	
		Human past				
		Cosmic past				
		Timeless-ness	X X X X X X X X X 7			
		Void-unity-silence				
		Biological lifeflow				
		Biological self				
		Biological differences				
		Beyond space-time				
		Beyond words				
2nd BARDO	**Halfway Stages**	Hallucination revelation				
		Immediate sensation				
		Game involvement				
THIRD BARDO REALITY CONTACT	**Social Games**	Philosophic-religious				
		Intellectual				
		Social-political				
		Aesthetic	X X X X X X			
		Recreational	X X X X X X X X			
		Occupational				
	Self Games	Mind gam games				
		Interpersonal				
		Mood affects				
		Body games				
		Repression				
		Action				

person during their experimentation from the shedding of earthly "games" to what was termed the "Bardo" levels, a Tibetan concept associated with the transition from death to rebirth, which Leary believed offered the idea of a psychic realm that could be explored via the psychedelic experience.

Leary, Alpert, and others involved in this research were preoccupied with games manifested from personality. While at Millbrook, Leary, Metzner, and Alpert wrote *The Psychedelic Experience: A Manual Based on the Tibetan Book of the Dead* (1964). In the book, games are termed as "behavioral sequences defined by roles, rules, rituals, goals, strategies, values, language, characteristic space-time locations, and characteristic patterns of movement. Any behavior not having these nine features is nongame: this includes physiological reflexes, spontaneous play, and transcendent awareness."

While residing in Sausalito, California, Alan Watts wrote an effusive letter to Leary after reading the proofs of *The Psychedelic Experience*, declaring it to be one of the few psychiatry books which attempts to classify the states of consciousness. He also described his recent trip to Oaxaca in southern Mexico and mentions how interested R. Gordon Wasson was in observing the Mexican culture. Wasson was the amateur mycologist who had previously published an article in *Life* magazine detailing his encounter with *curandera* María Sabina and her use of psilocybin mushrooms in traditional Mazatec healing services. Ironically, rumor had it that after the article two women reportedly conspired to tip off the authorities in an effort to protect the mushroom cult and that this move played a part in the ousting of Leary and the IFIF from Zihuatanejo, Mexico. Interestingly, there has in recent years been much speculation on conspiracy theory websites about whether Wasson's trip to Mexico as detailed in the *Life* article was part or wholly funded by the CIA as a precursor to or part of the MKUltra experiments. This speculation is largely due to the presence of a letter in the CIA archives from Allen Dulles, CIA Director at the time to Wasson, the receipt of which is acknowledged by his secretary on June 3, 1960.[4] However, the letter itself offers no evidence for these claims.

FROM ALAN WATTS TO TIMOTHY LEARY | JULY 4, 1964

Dear Tim, How are things with you these days? I have been busy (May–June) with lectures and what not, but have had one or two interesting trips.

You have presumably heard about the very unfortunate Rose-man-Copley case. Altogether a mess. They weren't at all cool, and the judge was hopelessly prejudiced. Sentencing is set for Monday. It will take a year to get it before the appellate court, and bail is rather unlikely.

Jano and I are planning to go to Mexico towards the end of July and to be there throughout August. Our final destination is Oaxaca, and I'm wondering if there's anyone we ought to see there. I'm not so interested in actually taking the mushrooms as in observing the culture that uses them, and also in getting a look at other "outsiders" (such as Wasson) who are devotees. Someone, I quite forget whom, told me of two ladies taking a protective attitude to the Oaxaca cult who were instrumental in getting the Mexican government to quash your project at Zihuatanejo. Do you know who they are?

I very much enjoyed reading the proofs of THE PSYCHEDELIC EXPERIENCE. In some ways this is the first really deep psychiatric book in that it describes and tries to classify states of consciousness which ordinary psychiatry ignores, despite the fact that understanding all levels of consciousness should be its main business. Please be sure to see that the publisher lets me have a review copy.

Love from us both to you all, Alan

Leary and his fellow researchers were determined to gather data that chimed with their theories in *The Psychedelic Experience*. One key way they attempted to do this was documented in the form of "mood charts." The participants tried to measure their levels of ecstasy and "collaboration attitude" ranging from "Hung up angle" to "Buddha [sic]" levels in both group and single settings.

Some of the exercises created under the auspices of the IFIF were carried over and developed at Millbrook. Like at Hotel Catalina, self-awareness and removal of game-play was a goal achieved through work-shops and role-playing.

CASTALIA FOUNDATION, MILLBROOK, NEW YORK, WORKSHOP
MATERIAL | JANUARY 1964

How to play transpersonative living: visitors' contract

Definition:

A game is a temporary social arrangement with goals, roles, rules, rituals, values, strategies, space-time characteristics, all of which are subject to revision. Ecstatogenic games are voluntary and the contract explicit.

You have been invited to participate in the game of transpersonative living during the length of your stay at Millbrook. This means you have joined a culture which may be, in many ways, quite novel and puzzling to you. This explicit contract is designed to lessen your "culture shock" and to insure an ecstatic visit.

Goals:

1) To establish and maintain, for as long as possible and for as many people as possible, the highest level of interpersonal unity possible.

2) To encourage each person to move effectively and ecstatically towards his own personal goals and to be able to climb out of his personal game at will. An interweaving of community and individual goals is carried on.

Roles:

While there are many roles involved in running such a complicated enterprise, in this contract we are solely concerned with the roles involved in the short-term visitor game.

The role that has been most comfortable to you and which was of most use to you on the planet is of little utility and, indeed, an awkward handicap to you here. This is the game of "you." No one here is eager to play the game of "you" or the game of "guest" with you. There will be little interest manifested in your thoughts, values, opinions, accomplishments, nor in the history and complexity of your personality. You will find total acceptance but little verbal reassurance.

This approach was influenced by the work of Greek-Armenian philosopher George Ivanovitch Gurdjieff, who theorized that people were generally not fully aware and thus, not tapping into the full potential of human consciousness. He proposed methods to wake up the mind and connect with the true power of consciousness. His work paralleled

Buddhist and yogic principles of the mind-body connection, being "in the moment," and general mindfulness. He visited the United States in 1924 to demonstrate his techniques. His work *Beelzebub's Tales to His Grandson*, published in English after his death in 1950, helped to introduce his teachings to the West.[5] Castalia incorporated Gurdjieff-inspired methods into their own exercises during their experiential workshops.

CASTALIA FOUNDATION, MILLBROOK, NEW YORK, WORKSHOP MATERIAL

Experiential workshops: background

In each generation a few men stumble upon the riddle of consciousness and its solution; they discover, once again, that beyond the ordinary world of macroscopic, tangible, material things, there are endless levels of energy transformations accessible to consciousness. They learn again the age-old lesson taught by mystics and philosophers of East and West: that most of mankind is sleepwalking, moving somnambulistically through a world of rote perceptions. They learn that it is possible to "come to," to awake, to be liberated from the prison of illusory perceptions and conflicting emotions. As have many internal explorers of the past, they become dedicated to the process of consciousness expansion, to the ideal of maximum awareness and internal freedom.

The first step is the realization that there is more: that man's brain, his 13-billion-celled computer, is capable of limitless new dimensions of awareness and knowledge. In short that man does not use his head.

The second step is the realization that you have to go out of your mind to use your head; that you have to pass beyond everything you have learned in order to become acquainted with the new areas of consciousness. Ignorance of this fact is the veil which shuts man within the narrow confines of his acquired, artifactual concepts of "reality," and prevents him from coming to know his own true nature.

The third step (once the first two realizations have taken place) is the practical-theoretical. How can consciousness be expanded? What is the range of possibilities outside of our current verbal-cognitive models of experience? What light do the new insights shed on our view of man and his place in the universe? And, perhaps most important, how can the new levels be maintained?

Name Dich Date 21

			Saturday		Sunday		Monday		Tuesday		Wednesday		Thursday		Friday	
			Self	Grp	Self	Grp	Self	Grp	Self	Grp	Self	Grp	Self	Grp	Self	Grp
Mood	Ecstatic	7	X													
		6		Y												
		5	X	X												
		4														
		3	X													
		2		X												
	Anguished	1														
Collaboration attitude	Budda	7														
		6	X	Y												
		5														
		4	X	XX												
		3	X													
		2														
	Hung-up angle	1														

Name Ralph   Date Sat 14

			SATURDAY		SUNDAY		MONDAY		TUESDAY		WEDNESDAY		THURSDAY		FRIDAY	
			SELF	GRP	SELF	GRP	SELF	GRP	SELF	GRP	SELF	GRP	SELF	GRP	SELF	GRP
	ECSTATIC	8	X	X					X	X	X	X						
		6				X				X			X		X	X		X
		5	X		XX			X				XX					X	
MOOD	NEUTRAL	4		X	X	X	X		X	X			X		X	X	X
		3	X							X	X						X	X
COLLAB- oration	AVERAGE	2							X				X	X		X	X
	ANGUISHED	1		X		X	X	X						X		X
	BUDDA ANGLE	7	X	X		X				X	X						
		6	X		XX	X		X	X		X		X	X	X	X
		5	X	X			XX	X	X		X				X	X
		4	X		X		X		X	X	X			X	X	X
		3		X								X		X	
		2						X				X		
		1	X	X		X			X		X	X	X	X

Name Tim   Date _____

			Saturday		Sunday		Monday		Tuesday		Wednesday		Thursday		Friday	
			Self	Grp	Self	Grp	Self	Grp	Self	Grp	Self	Grp	Self	Grp	Self	Grp
	Ecstatic	7														
		6	X	X												
		5	X	XX												
Mood		4														
		3	X													
		2														
	Anguished	1														
	Budda	7														
		6	X	XX												
Collab- oration attitude		5	X	X												
		4														
		3														
		2														
	Hung-up angle	1														

CASTALIA FOUNDATION

MILLBROOK SUMMER SCHOOL

PSYCHEDELIC TRAINING COURSES.....

will be conducted at Millbrook, New York from June 19th through August 28th, 1966.

PURPOSES

1. To produce psychedelic experiences (without drugs).

2. To teach methods of running psychedelic sessions.

3. To teach recognition of different levels of consciousness and how to direct consciousness in order to reach specified levels.

4. To teach psychedelic language--techniques of communicating psychedelic experiences.

BACKGROUND

Since 1960 a large and rapidly growing group of psychologists, philosophers and artists, working first in the Harvard area and later at Zihuatenjo, Mexico and Millbrook, N. Y. has been studying psychedelic plants and drugs, and their effects, and the applications of these experiences.

This network of investigators is larger, has conducted more psychedelic sessions, has published more reports--in the form of books, essays, paintings, movies, sound-light projections--than any similar group in the world.

The results of these studies can be stated simply:

1. Psychedelic plants and drugs are the most powerful releasers of neurological energy ever known to man.

2. Almost no one in our society, at the present time, has the specific knowledge and general wisdom to use these agents.

Above: Leary with Rosemary Woodruff standing next
to him during a communal dinner at Millbrook on
June 16, 1967.

For those concerned with the "third step" questions, a series of weekend workshops in consciousness expansion have been instituted by the Castalia Foundation, a nonprofit corporation.

The weekends themselves were tightly scheduled and came with their own rules:

CASTALIA FOUNDATION, MILLBROOK, NEW YORK, MESSAGE #1

Welcome to an experiential weekend

Your weekend in Millbrook has been planned to provide a series of novel and consciousness-expanding experiences.

The first step in the process of going beyond your routine and familiar patterns is a period of *absolute silence*.

Shortly after your arrival at Castalia you will be given further instructions. Please do not engage in conversation of any kind. The breaking of peace is particularly announced.

For now: LOOK, LISTEN (to the nonverbal energy around you), EXPERIENCE DIRECTLY.

CASTALIA FOUNDATION, MILLBROOK, NEW YORK, TENTATIVE
SCHEDULE

Friday

8–10: dinner

10–12: informal discussion and orientation

12–12.30: meditation w. I Ching in Hermitage

Saturday

7.30: rise

7.45: stretching and breathing exercises

8–9: breakfast

9–10: work in fields

10.30–12.30: seminar in ecstatics and psychedelics (T.L.)

1–2: lunch

2–3: siesta

3–5: miscellaneous presentations by visiting staff or specially prepared by regular staff (e.g. tantra, Guerdjieff [sic], sufi, karate, hatha yoga,

Above: Timothy Leary and Nena von Schlebrügge's
wedding portrait, Millbrook, New York, 1964.
Photographer unknown.

taoism, mythology, etc.) try to involve special interest of participants
5–7: creative communication (each participant tries to communicate
some aspect of his experience so far in words, music, painting, photography, dance. These will be shared with the group)
sunset: meditation on porch
8–10: dinner
10–11: white stag
11–12.30: music session; with slides, films, tranart, when available. (Japanese,
Buddhist, Mexican, Dervish, Stockhausen, Cage, Indian, Laura Huxley)

While residing at Millbrook, Timothy Leary met Nena von Schlebrügge,
an international fashion model, at a party in Cambridge, Massachusetts.
Living and working in New York City, her interest in Indian and Eastern
teachings brought her to Millbrook on July 4, 1964. The following weekend she returned, supposedly consumed LSD with Leary, and they were
swiftly engaged.[6] The wedding was held in the Grace Chapel in the town
of Millbrook on December 12, 1964. It was a large affair with many New
York personalities in attendance, such as the photographer and writer Diane
Arbus, the jazz musician Charles Mingus, and celebrity hairdresser/performer
Monti Rock III. The reception champagne was spiked with LSD.[7] Guest
Don Alan "D.A." Pennebaker captured the pre-wedding preparations in
the documentary, *You're Nobody Till Somebody Loves You*. He applied the
"direct cinema" style which he had developed in documentary filmmaking
during the early 1960s. A year later, Pennebaker filmed Bob Dylan's British
tour, resulting in his iconic documentary *Don't Look Back* (released 1967).

This was Leary's third marriage. It ended in divorce in 1966. The
following year, von Schlebrügge married Buddhist Robert Thurman.

While Leary was away on his honeymoon with Nena in India, Alpert
held down the fort at Millbrook. He wrote to Leary to keep him abreast
of LSD session planning and the Gurdjieff exercises. Millbrook residents
at the time included Maynard Ferguson and his wife Flo, painter Allen
Atwell, jazz musician Dick Katz, and poet Allen Cohen (founder of the
San Francisco Oracle). Leary later used Atwell's work to illustrate his autobiography, *High Priest* (1968). Millbrook didn't have a monopoly on the
practices of Gurdjieff; nearby in Warwick, New York, Willem A. Nyland
would give lectures in a barn.[8]

FROM RICHARD ALPERT TO TIMOTHY LEARY AND NENA VON SCHLEBRÜGGE | UNDATED (LIKELY C. DECEMBER 1964–EARLY 1965)

Dear Tim and Nena, Millbrook is one of the greatest myths being lived out, and you two are the other.

What is going on here is quite extraordinary. We are now down to seven in our climbing party (Bittan, Shelah, Susan, Allen, Bjorn, and Michael) and the group is really starting to get a new identity. I can feel the freshness developing in all the inmates. Our two hour meetings a day are too much—being a mixture of Guerdjieff [sic] exercises, Meher Baba, LSD Session planning, and the back ward of the menniger clinic. But we all feel the human ring being tempered. Next week will be our second group session (since last one we have dropped Tom from the climbing party for many reasons too obvious to mention). And since our last one everybody has had at least one session (all sessions are programmed in the house) or will have—Bittan is having a big one with me Sunday night. Bjorn and Shelah had a great one last night, and Michael (joined by Britte) had what he called "the second real LSD session I've ever had," Allen is voyaging tonight, and Susan and I are doing guiding for outsiders (a writer, a doctor, and David this week). About two or three extra sessions a week.

I am just engineering a loan from Billy [Hitchcock], using stock of Dabid's Company as collateral, to increase the effectiveness of the Castalia weekend seminars.

The legislative committee is underway (I have Tom doing library research). I was invited to be an actor in an Italian movie but I asked for 300 a day and they couldn't afford me. Too bad—I would love to become an Italian movie star. The group will be shooting up here early in April. Anyway . . . they are quite taken with us as representatives of the future.

We saw the wedding movies and they are great—especially the footage of Monty explaining this scene to two girls on the way up.

Speaking at Cornell, in Chicago on TV, at City College, at Princeton . . . on Poughkeepsie radio and Westinghouse . . . teaching Billy to fly—we are getting a twin-engined six seat plane with supercharger (goes 280 mph with supercharger). Jonathon's barn burned down with his helicopter in it (insured of course for much more than he was about to sell it for), diamonds may yet be a girl's best friend, and our new Japanese bath is too much. Peggy may marry Lou (haven't seen her since she is back—they did Grossingers last weekend.)

Maynard and Flo want to move back in, Van is most loving and fun—very tied up with Carol, Allen Atwell is painting Van's living room into the showcase of N.Y.C., and is moving up here Friday to take over the red playroom as his studio . . . Billy Onley is working in Poughkeepsie and will live nearby. Dick Katz is bringing up movies for the weekend and working on psychedelic films on his NOMH grant this year—will join with us late spring. Al Cohen runs hypnosis and suggestion great these days, Bjorn is completely into autosuggestion, I will run Felix session in next few weeks, Mario never made it into the group (at his own choice) and drops by mostly weekends, guests number twenty every nonseminar weekend. I have gone to two Nyland meetings—very hot and stuffy in there—but interesting nevertheless; Bertha is very loving. Jack now has not only Peter as [a] friend but also John—Susan's old boyfriend. John is a hip kid and Jack is learning much quickly. But still stays in the game with Peter and school scene. His report card was pretty good (a bit weak in Algebra and Spanish) but he is at his best this year. He is buying and selling and trading guns with his school friends . . . but still asks permission to kill anything. We can't get Bjorn to steal one of Billy H's cows . . . Robber-baron, i.e. . . . only Michael and Bittan and I are eating dinner tonight. Everyone else is in New York or out . . . and Bittan is making us Yorkshire pudding she just announced. We take pictures of each of us for each new group session.

At any rate don't rush home. We have a most extraordinary experiment going on here, which if I am not entirely wrong, is going to tell us something new. We are creating a stable group base camp for internal exploration for each of us. From this camp I think we can explore amazing pockets in each of us. This group is an absolutely amazing storehouse of human experience. But many of the scenes are like something out of Tennessee Williams. But what I want to say is that I'd really like a few months to try this out without starting any new games here. So don't rush back. . . . Because Bittan isn't yet strong enough that she won't fall back into the game with Nena (that doesn't take into account change on Nena's part. But I have no word from Nena indicating anything whatsoever). . . . Furthermore I just want to remind both of you that you represent an experiment in which we are all deeply involved. There is enough support both financial, chemical, and emotional to leave you both free to form an entirely new concept of the man-woman relationship. Where [sic] you to come back with less than that I would feel that you got caught in sangsara.[9] Don't miss the opportunity—you haven't spent enough time . . . take six months at least . . . before you return to being Tim and Nena. Ah but that comes from somebody tired of shifting scenes for the moment . . . just an old hang-up attachment of wanting to live something out to its approximated conclusion.

The Millbrook commune remained the center of Leary and Alpert's activities, the Castalia Foundation, and successor organizations. The mission of the IFIF and Castalia, and likewise that of Leary and Alpert, was to educate and train others to conduct their own sessions in mind-exploration. Not satisfied with simply waiting for the people to visit and participate in the weekend workshop at Millbrook, they knew that in order to spread their message, they needed to employ various avenues for reaching the public. This took the usual forms: press releases, lectures, magazine interviews, etc., but not surprisingly, they would again call on artists, mystics, and performers to solve the problem of translating, communicating, and simulating the psychedelic experience.

LSD

For a Better LIFE !!

Hear

Richard Alpert Ph.D.

Wed. Jan. 25th

Disneyland Hotel - 7:30 p.m.

Lecture on "A Journey Into An Awareness"

$2⁵⁰

Hear about the marvelous potentials of these chemicals for solving human problems!

See and feel the rapture of a psychedelic LIGHT SHOW engineered by Jim Morrisett!

Hear and be inspired by knowing the magic of the human mind - unfettered, touching the st

Know that LSD is not dangerous when properly used, and that it should be legalized
    so that the proper guidance be available!

Because - six million (6,000,000) people can't be wrong!

6
Acid Tent Revival, 1965–67

"Grow with the flow."

Timothy Leary, *Your Brain Is God*

ONCE CASTALIA WAS ESTABLISHED and Leary had returned from his honeymoon, he, Alpert, and Metzner sought to spread the message of their findings surrounding LSD and consciousness expansion. In 1965, they left Millbrook for a lecture tour that took in venues on university campuses, town halls, hotels, and other locales, earning fees for Castalia and, later, for their next venture: the League for Spiritual Discovery (L.S.D.). The letters they subsequently received from audience members who wrote letters to Castalia to request information, offer praise, or to inquire into the subject and the organization were a clear indication of the influence their ideas were gaining within the counterculture movement.

The lecture tour developed further. The artist collective USCO (standing for "the company of us"), stationed across the river from Millbrook in an old church in the town of Garnerville, Rockland County, New York, put on a performance with Castalia to raise funds for the organization. Subsequently Castalia approached USCO, asking them to collaborate with them on new shows in New York City, melding their innovative psychedelic performances, using projections, strobes, and other lighting effects to accompany Leary's lectures. USCO and Leary's team produced the Psychedelic Explorations at the New Theatre in New York City as an attempt to simulate the LSD experience, showcase psychedelic art, and raise money for Castalia.

USCO had been founded by the American poet Gerd Stern and artist Michael Callahan. In an example of the "small world" of counterculture, Stern had been acquainted with Allen Ginsberg years earlier when he

THE STUDENT COMMITTEE FOR DISTINGUISHED
SPEAKERS IN PSYCHOLOGY PRESENTS

A DISCUSSION OF L S D

AND

CONSCIOUSNESS EXPANSION

BY

DR. RICHARD ALPERT

WEDNESDAY MARCH 10, 1965, 3:45 P.M.
HORACE MANN AUDITORIUM, TEACHERS COLLEGE

Dr. Alpert received his P.hD. at Stanford and taught at Harvard. Among his
publications is The Psychodelic Experience by Timothy Leary, Ralph Metzner and
Richard Alpert.

The discussion will be followed by refreshments.

Page 144: Poster advertising Richard Alpert's lecture on "A Journey Into An Awareness" including a light show at the Disneyland Hotel, Anaheim, California, c. 1966–67.

Above: Poster advertising Richard Alpert's lecture on "A Discussion of LSD and Consciousness Expansion," at Horace Mann auditorium, Teachers College, New York City, March 10, 1965.

befriended him while hospitalized by the New York State Psychiatric Institute at Columbia Presbyterian Hospital, New York City in 1949. Stern
was admitted under false pretenses by the urgings of his father to clean
up his homeless lifestyle. Ginsberg's infamous stint resulted from his plea
bargain after his arrest with stolen goods as a Columbia College student.[1]
Additionally, Carl Solomon was hospitalized with them after throwing
potato salad at the novelist Wallace Markfield during his lecture at New
York University.[2] Ginsberg's experience at the hospital provided inspiration
for his poem "Howl," which he dedicated to Solomon.[3] Solomon became
a poet in his own right, and worked for his uncle, A. A. Wyn, a publisher
who established Ace Books, which first published William S. Burroughs's
Junkie (1953). In turn, they were all to play a part in the "Leary project."

The artists of USCO lived communally and followed the principles
of group ownership, not attributing their works individually. Gerd Stern,
the founder of USCO, explains:[4]

[Steve Durkee[5]] was a very talented painter and he bought into what
I and Michael Callahan were doing in intermedia and he wanted to
be part of it and he was. We considered all the work that was done.
Sometimes at the church building there were wives and husbands and
everyone was working together and eventually we had fifty people
living in that building, it was nuts.

The idea of communal collaboration between artists and people
came to me long before and in California from a woman, Grace
Clemens, who I was involved with at KPFA, Pacifica, where I was
one of the founders with Lou Hill . . . she was into Jung a great deal.
But the person who wrote about traditional societies and how artists
didn't sign things was Ananda Coomaraswamy who was at the end
of his life an art historian in Boston at the Museum of Art. He wrote
a lot and I read it through Grace, about how artists behave and how
they weren't anything special. And I loved it. So, when Michael and
Stephen and I got together, I said "let's call it the company of us,
abbreviated USCO, and we're not going to sign anything." That was
very much unlike Stephen and his immersion in the art world he had.
Allan Stone was his gallery and Allan Stone was the first to show my
work in New York, but Steve understood the concept and loved it.

Right now there are 20–30 from large to small USCO works, paintings sculptures, audio visual things and they're owned by Intermedia Foundation which we formed in 1968. I don't consider them the property of any of the people. . . .

There were many points of commonality with Castalia, and drug experimentation was regularly practiced by USCO artists as a way of opening and freeing the mind to achieve an artistic transcendence. Leary's desire to collaborate with the USCO collective was an example of one of the many ways in which he reached out beyond his inner circle to bring his ideas into the wider consciousness. Stern recently shared his memories about his first meeting Leary:[6]

> I met him when he and Alpert were still at Cambridge, Mass., when they were at Harvard, and I just met them through mutual friends who lived up near there and they were working for David McClelland who was the head of the sociology department, who later I worked for. Many years later I mean; I had an appointment through him at Harvard he also worked with Intermedia Systems Corp. and in fact he was on our Board. I worked for him and his two sons worked for me. He has been dead for a long time but he was an amazing person. He dealt with achievement motivation that came from his mentor Professor Murray, anyway . . . you know he hired both of them and then he had to fire both of them 'cause, you know, there were students involved taking psychedelics which was definitely a no-no. I know some of those people quite well . . . one of those students in the Chapel experiments [also known as the Good Friday Experiment] was Paul Lee who's in Santa Cruz, who became a good friend of mine who gave me a job at Santa Cruz teaching again a long time ago after I worked for McClelland.

The idea for the Psychedelic Explorations was born out of the relationship between Millbrook and USCO, as Stern recalls:[7]

> When I met them we didn't take anything together. It wasn't until they moved to Millbrook when we were across the river from USCO that

. . . we spent a lot of time at Millbrook and I think three times we did multimedia at Millbrook and then . . . when they had to raise money, we did the psychedelic theater which was, you know about, at the New Theatre that was a problem. The psychedelic theater was sponsored by one of the Hitchcocks, the Hitchcocks owned Millbrook, they were people I knew fairly well: Peggy, Tommy, and . . . and they were deeply into acid both from an education point of view and commercial point of view. Well Billy, Billy sold psychedelics later on and nearly got into a lot trouble with the authorities but they come from a wealthy family.

Anyway, the psychedelic theater, they approached us, I mean Richard and Timothy did, to do it with them, to do the multimedia, and Timothy was to lecture during the evenings. Timothy was an excruciatingly boring lecturer and he just never got it. At one point, during a [lecture] [we] were so bored that we broadcast the screams of Antonin Artaud over his voice who was kinda a madman that I had gotten from Radio Française through friends of mine, but eventually Ralph Metzner came up to the control booth and said you're breaking your contract with us and we will have to stop you but we didn't stop. We didn't care about breaking the contract, we did have multimedia, and all the money went to the Castalia Foundation because we all agreed that they needed it. And it was at that time five dollars was the admission and I can't remember we did three or four nights maybe five and it was full and Timothy and I agreed that we would not allow anyone in without paying admission and do you know Harry Smith, he's dead, he's an artist. Somebody we knew. He could be pretty maddening, very loud, and he came in and said, "I ain't payin' anything I know these guys" so I looked at Timothy and said to Timothy here's five dollars for Harry cause if he starts screaming it's going to be terrible for all of us. He was kinda terrible during that evening but it was kinda the scenes in those days.

Stern remembers how the shows received a lot of attention when they were first put on in New York:[8]

The psychedelic theater created quite a stir in New York. Anybody who had any interest was there at least once, not every time because each time was different but not much different. There is a guy named Richard Aldcroft and he put together a kaleidoscopic projector with a plastic drum that turned around and had all kind of bits of negatives and colored things and projected [them] and he was one of the artists that we let him be part of the New Theatre and Isaac Abrams and he's still a good friend of mine. He put together the first psychedelic gallery. Timothy came to the opening. Isaac decided—he had very early psychedelic experiences—he decided that none of the painters who were painting out of the psychedelic movement were painting what he saw, so he started painting. He started as self taught . . . he is still doing psychedelic painting. But he was another one of the artists who showed at the New Theatre.

These [performances] were in NYC oh not in the village . . . on the Westside Theatre, Billy Hitchcock knew the people who owned it . . . the New Theatre. It was a nice place, we had huge screens and also gave time to other psychedelic artists to perform which was the first time people could appreciate it. Most of those people are not still around, most of them are dead. The end of it was that Timothy said to me "we're gonna keep doing this but we're not going to keep doing it with you, because the next time we do this we're going to have the birth of Jesus do it from the beginning to the end, not all this mess that you think is psychedelic." We thought that was the funniest thing 'cause we thought our techniques were more [true to the] psychedelic experience than starting [and just going] to the end would be. They did do that. They went to the Filmore East and 2nd Ave and Jackie Cassen did it with them and I thought it was boring stuff. They did the life of the Buddha and the life of Jesus on separate evenings.

Timothy generally had a problem 'cause he was very much a literalist. Another thing was that he came across psychedelics late in the game, and he was really an alcoholic and he drank every day and he could, he had an enormous Irish-type capacity and it certainly disturbed us because we were not into alcohol . . . we were into smoking pot and taking psychedelics.

We were into the media stuff and they loved using media and it was Timothy's fantasy that using media was like an analog to the experience and we never believed that. We didn't think that what we

PSYCHEDELIC EXPLORATIONS

Presented by Castalia Foundation and USCO

New Theatre   154 E. 54 St.   July 19, 1965

******

Polarized Light Sculptures
by Jackie Cassen

Acrylic and Aniline Projections
by Don Snyder

Presented in collaboration with
CODA GALLERIES
89 East 10th St.

******

Random Analog Projections
by Richard Aldcroft

Automatic re-organization of
selected forms
******

The projections and sound are comprised of various
modern materials using contemporary technology.
Nonetheless, we believe them to be in the true
traditions of transcendental art media of the past,
particularly these that utilize the principles of
light waves -- reflection, refraction, magnification
and polarization.

Above: Flyer for Psychedelic Explorations performance
at the New Theatre in New York City, 1965. Castalia
and artist collective USCO developed performances as
an attempt to simulate the LSD experience, showcase
psychedelic art, and raise money for Castalia.

Above: Leary and Ginsberg participating in the
Psychedelic Explorations.

were doing was like being on a trip. But he wanted the media to simulate a trip. But that was not what we considered scientific or artistic
'cause what we were doing [was] based on kind of a motivation of
using the multiplicity of media 'cause we used up to thirty channels
of sound and light and whatever, you know: slides, film, oscilloscope,
etc., etc. and the first multi-media that I did started in San Francisco,
not New York. It had nothing to do with psychedelics, called "Who
Are You and What's Happening?"

So, there was a kind of misunderstanding with what we had, with
Timothy on the kind of fantasy and illusion side, and with Richard on
the side of . . . We weren't into getting lots of other people involved
in psychedelics, and Richard wanted to get everybody involved.
More [so] than Timothy. Richard later on, he lived in California with
Barbara and Steve, who moved out there—the Durkees, and Steve
and he was on the lecture circuit lecturing about "LSD: illusion or
reality" was the name of what they did. Steve, I know because he told
me, was not even aware that Richard was selling acid out of theater
dressing room. [laughs]

Taking the Castalia message out of Millbrook to the people, Leary and
Metzner decided to focus on their Gurdjieff-style exercises and lectures
without USCO in a touring show known as the "Psychedelic Sessions."
These programs were more intimate and humble affairs. One nine-hour
session was held in Washington, D.C. in late October 1965. At the cost
of $40, participants engaged in programmed exercises and meditation,
watched a film of a psychedelic experience, observed slide shows, tapes,
and records while sitting or lying on the floor in order to simulate the
psychedelic drug experience.[9]

By 1966, LSD use had skyrocketed along with marijuana and other
drugs, particularly among the younger population, causing some Americans to panic. Intrepid West Coast chemist Owsley Stanley reportedly
made over one million hits of acid between 1965 and 1967.[10] *Playboy*
magazine published an extensive interview with Leary in 1966. When
asked, he admitted to experiencing over three hundred LSD sessions.[11]

All too soon, Leary found himself defending LSD in press releases,
interviews, and multiple Senate Committee hearings.

PSYCHEDELIC SESSIONS

TIMOTHY LEARY & RALPH METZNER

FALL AND WINTER 1965/66

IN

NEW YORK, BOSTON, PHILADELPHIA, PITTSBURGH, CLEVELAND, CINCINNATI, DETROIT, CHICAGO

The LSD Conference

June 13-18, 1966

Above: Planned as a five-day program on the UC
Berkeley campus, the event was relocated at the
last minute to San Francisco due to the concerns of
school officials.

On June 13–18, 1966, the University of California, San Francisco hosted the "LSD Conference," purportedly to "clarify the factual background of the controversy, and to present major research findings on various aspects of the use of these drugs." Directed by Richard Baker, a Harvard dropout turned *roshi* for the San Francisco Zen Center,[12] the advisory committee consisted of Richard Alpert, Frank Barron, the psychiatrist and LSD researcher Sidney Cohen, MIT Professor Paul Lee, and religious scholar Huston Smith. It was during this conference that Leary was questioned about whether he had suffered brain damage after consuming LSD 311 times (as he had admitted to *Playboy*; Alpert had reportedly had 318 doses) to which he responded that he would undergo any and all tests to prove he was fine.[13] Leary spoke before USCO staged a sample of their psychedelic theater performance "We Are All One Media-Mix." It featured thirty audio-visual channels and thirty feet of scaffolding which Leary stood on during the Thursday night of the conference.[14]

Before the start of the event, Dr. Sidney Cohen (who was then Chief of Psychosomatic Medicine at the Veterans Administration Hospital in Los Angeles) told the press, that the trouble with drugs stemmed from teenage abuse and that the beneficial application of LSD will be lost, just as hypnosis was lost to the vaudeville scene.[15] Dr. Cohen had written about the benefits of applying LSD to psychotherapy, but warned against the black market and abuse in his book *The Beyond Within: The LSD Story*, which was published in 1964. By 1976, he wrote *The Therapeutic Potential of Marihuana* and commented on substance abuse and addiction in general. Prior to appearing at the LSD conference, Cohen had conducted LSD research sponsored by the National Institutes of Health and had testified before Senator Robert Kennedy's subcommittee to a prevalence of LSD-precipitated psychiatric admissions.[16] The conference expressly stated its desire to cut through the controversy in the conference program:

The controversy over LSD and related drugs such as mescaline (peyote) and psilocybin has been heated and widespread; but the issues and the facts are seldom made clear. The purpose of *The LSD Conference* is to clarify the factual background of the controversy, and to present major research findings on various aspects of the use of these drugs.

The aspects to be discussed include the psychological, social, anthropological, philosophical, pharmacological, legal, religious, scientific, artistic, and therapeutic.

LSD and related drugs, sometimes called psychedelic or hallucinogenic, are not generally considered habit-forming. Whether they are psychologically habit-forming is more open to question. Estimates of the number of persons who have taken them in this country range from 100,000 to over a million. Intellectuals and persons in the professions are thought to constitute a majority of those who have used psychedelic drugs. Other users include persons who are interested primarily in religious experiences. Still another group is said to be young people who use the drugs to experience an unusual state of consciousness. . . .

There is sure to be continuing and widening controversy over the significance and potential of the LSD-type drugs for the individual and society, and over the moral, religious, and health problems they raise. No single answer to these questions will be universally accepted; but there is an urgent need for the kind of knowledge that will make informed and intelligent discussion possible. The aim of *The LSD Conference*—the first comprehensive survey of this subject and the first open to the public—is to provide some of this knowledge.

The six-day international conference involved other people who had previously engaged in Leary's drug studies, such as Huston Smith. He addressed the conference on "The Religious Significance of Artificially Induced Religious Experiences." Frank Barron spoke at the opening session about the desperate need for more research. Paul Lee presented the topic, "The Myth about Psychedelic Drugs." It was his first visit to California, and a memorable one.

Lee described this event in a recent interview:[17]

I met Richard Baker who was a priest at the Zen Center but also doing programs at UC Berkeley Extension and that was 1965 and so I said you should do a conference on LSD, that's the hot new topic. So, he organized it; I helped him. I gave him a list names of who should be invited, and they all were—most of our group in the East in New England at Harvard.

Above: An advertisement for Leary's spoken-word album
entitled *L.S.D.*, released by Pixie Records in 1966.

I was moving to Santa Cruz that fall to take up duties at UCSC. I thought that the week that Baker organized around LSD was my reception committee, kinda like a party to welcome me to California. That was really fun.

The first day I was there the day before the conference started, the Grateful Dead had thrown a party at a big estate in Marin County. I didn't know anything about them. I didn't know anything about the psychedelic group in San Francisco it was all a huge . . . The first thing I thought was: who gave them permission to look like that? We were all still wearing Brooks Brothers suits in Cambridge and here were these heads who were wild and woolly. That was a big eye-opener. At the party, almost everybody was nude. And Owsley, who made the acid in California, was handing out acid tabs and I declined 'cause I had to give the opening address at the conference the next morning and I wasn't even sure what I was going to say. But I finally decided I was going to just describe the party. This is the way of the future. This is psychedelic style and I simply described what I saw. For instance, they rolled joints in newspapers. That was innovative, I thought.

Then the [Grateful] Dead came out and played and one guy from the audience went and put his head in the speaker and I thought—he's blowing his brains out—who is that? That was Neal Cassady.

[After that time] I moved to Santa Cruz and took up teaching duties. I was a little worried about my teaching career 'cause Leary and Alpert got kicked out of Harvard and there were some other friends that had career problems because they were identified with psychedelics. Santa Cruz seemed to me to be open for the expressed purpose for students to take drugs. I didn't want to be a Leary at Santa Cruz and encourage people to turn on 'cause I had misgivings about it as soon as I found the first student casualty that never recovered from taking LSD, that really cautioned me about the tyranny of being hip.

Despite Leary's attempts to defend the psychotherapeutic benefits of the drug, LSD was scrutinized over the course of several United States government hearings. On May 17–18, 1966, New York Senator Robert F. Kennedy—a progressive Democrat, who had helped draft

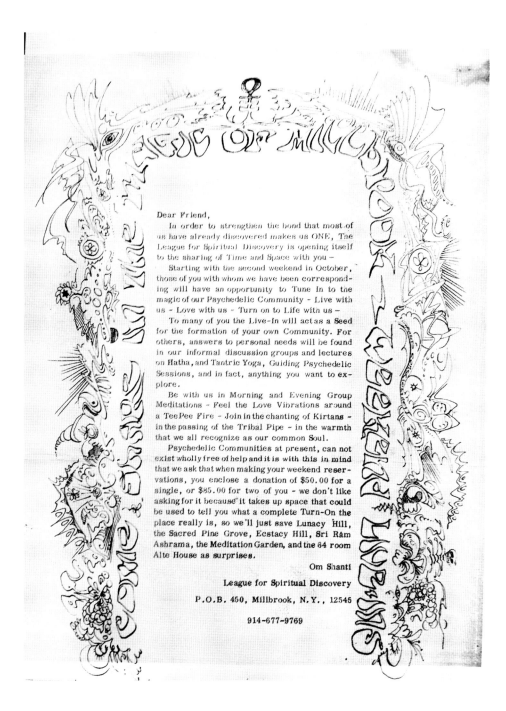

Dear Friend,

In order to strengthen the bond that most of us have already discovered makes us ONE, The League for Spiritual Discovery is opening itself to the sharing of Time and Space with you –

Starting with the second weekend in October, those of you with whom we have been corresponding will have an opportunity to Tune In to the magic of our Psychedelic Community - Live with us - Love with us - Turn on to Life with us –

To many of you the Live-In will act as a Seed for the formation of your own Community. For others, answers to personal needs will be found in our informal discussion groups and lectures on Hatha, and Tantric Yoga, Guiding Psychedelic Sessions, and in fact, anything you want to explore.

Be with us in Morning and Evening Group Meditations - Feel the Love Vibrations around a TeePee Fire - Join in the chanting of Kirtans - in the passing of the Tribal Pipe - in the warmth that we all recognize as our common Soul.

Psychedelic Communities at present, can not exist wholly free of help and it is with this in mind that we ask that when making your weekend reservations, you enclose a donation of $50.00 for a single, or $85.00 for two of you - we don't like asking for it because it takes up space that could be used to tell you what a complete Turn-On the place really is, so we'll just save Lunacy Hill, the Sacred Pine Grove, Ecstacy Hill, Sri Ram Ashrama, the Meditation Garden, and the 64 room Alte House as surprises.

Om Shanti

League for Spiritual Discovery

P.O.B. 450, Millbrook, N.Y., 12545

914-677-9769

Above: The League for Spiritual Discovery invites weekend visitors to "Live with us—Love with us—Turn on to Life with us" at Millbrook, as advertised in this "Come Share in the Magic of Millbrook, Weekend Love-Ins" poster, c. 1966–67.

the Civil Rights Act of 1964—convened the Subcommittee on the Executive Reorganization of the Senate Committee on Government Operations. Connecticut Senator Thomas Dodd convened a Special Subcommittee on Narcotics. Leary was asked to offer testimony. Although he stated the case for regulation, he was not able to convey his usual positive message regarding the drug. His testimony before the Senate judiciary prompted yet more headlines, before—"Leary Sees Crisis in the Use of LSD" in the *New York Times* (May 14, 1966)—and after—"Leary Proposes a Ban on LSD Except in 'Psychedelic Centers': Regret Expressed" in the *Washington Post* (May 27, 1966). The public backlash escalated and the criminalization of LSD and other psychedelic drugs loomed large. In response to this climate of criticism, Leary decided to dissolve Castalia and founded the League for Spiritual Discovery (L.S.D.) on September 19, 1966.

The League was established to continue the work of Castalia under the auspices of a quasi-religious organization with LSD, mushrooms, peyote, and other substances serving as its sacraments. Essentially, it was an attempt to legitimize the use of LSD and bypass legal prohibitions on psychoactive substances, such as the ban that came into effect in California on October 6, 1966. The League's symbol would be a mandala, its stated purpose being "the individual, communal, social worship of God, based on revelation and empirically validated methods for spiritual discovery,"[18] and its "clergy" consisted of guides to teach and prepare members for initiation. According to its founding documents, members were asked to devote at least one hour a day to withdrawal from social, symbolic activity "in order to attain sensory illumination." This could be achieved through mantras, with silence, meditation, music, or chakra exercises. In addition to this hour, members would be required one day a week to withdraw from "social-symbolic sensory activities to attain communication with evolutionary wisdoms preserved in cellular and molecular structures," or in other words, to take a "trip."

THE LEAGUE FOR SPIRITUAL DISCOVERY MISSION STATEMENT

The League for Spiritual Discovery is a legally incorporated religion dedicated to the ancient sacred sequence of turning-on, tuning-in, and dropping-out. Our aim is to help recreate every man as God and every woman as Goddess.

The LEAGUE magazine is a tune-in expression of the L.S.D. A record of our group trip. Each issue is a voyage log—a description of how we have turned-on, tuned-back-in, and how we go about the venerable and holy process of dropping out.

The seal of the LEAGUE is a mandala. The endless circle circumscribing a four-leaf lotus made by the double infinity sign. This interweaving of the infinite universe of male with the infinite universe of female forms the flower symbol of life—centered by the eye of God.

SUN.........DELIGHT.........LOVE.........SEED.........
DEATH.........LIFE

After founding the League, Leary published *Start Your Own Religion* (1967) as a manual for establishing similar churches, incorporating rituals and obtaining legal protection for distributing illegal sacraments, such as marijuana and LSD. The Native American Church that served as a gateway to the mind-altering experiences for nonnatives such as Huxley and the Beat poets during the 1940s and 1950s was held up as a model for legal exemption of the use of psychoactive substances on religious grounds. A version of Leary's "'Start Your Own Religion': A Manual for 'Turn-on' 'Tune-in' 'Drop-Out'" outlined the ancient and classical spiritual, emotional, and legal sequences involved in living that "LIFE OF SPIRITUAL DISCOVERY for which man has been designed by the Evolutionary Process, the Divine Plan, the DNA Code."[19] This manual was first published by the League at Millbrook under the imprint Kriya Press of the Sri Ram Ashrama in 1967.

START YOUR OWN RELIGION: A MANUAL FOR "TURN-ON, TUNE-IN, DROP-OUT"

Outlining the ancient and classic spiritual, emotional, and legal sequences involved in living that LIFE OF SPIRITUAL DISCOVERY for which man has been designed by the Evolutionary Process, the Divine Plan, the DNA Code.

Published by the League for Spiritual Discovery, Box 175, Millbrook, N.Y. 12545

The Purpose of Life is Religious Discovery: That intermediate manifestation of the Divine Process which we call the DNA Code has spent the last two-billion years making this planet a Garden of Eden. An intricate web has been woven—a delicate fabric—chemical-electrical-seed-tissue-organism-species. A dancing, joyous harmony of energy transactions is rooted in the 12 inches of top-soil which covers the rock-metal-fire core of this planet.

Each human being is born perfect. We were all born Divine mutants. The DNA Code's best answer to joyful survival on this planet. An exquisite package for adaption based on 2 billion years of consumer-research (RNA) and product design (DNA). . . .

Psychedelic churches began to spring up throughout the world, such as the Universal Life and the Psychedelic Venus Churches in California, the London Church of Aphrodite in Britain, the Church of All Worlds throughout the United States, and the Neo-American Church at Millbrook, founded by Art Kleps. Despite not being able to gain the same rights as the Native American Church, Kleps further developed his religion: the church's logo included the electric blue "Divine Toad" modeled after the *Bufo alvarius* native to Mexico and the Southwestern United States and known for secreting a psychedelic substance—hence, the saying "toad licking." This accompanied the logo, "Victory over Bullshit!" Kleps also established his own retreat "Morning Glory Lodge"; its newsletter was titled, "The Divine Toad Sweat." Kleps took his satirical approach to every element of religious doctrine, as exemplified by his *The Boo Hoo Bible: The Neo-American Church Catechism and Handbook* (1971).

Although inspired by Leary and, in part, as a way to legitimize continued experimentation, Kleps sought to distance himself from some of Leary's practices and even sent Leary a humorous "contract" for their sessions with the handwritten note "please amend, return or reject":

ART KLEPS'S "CONTRACT" WITH TIMOTHY LEARY

AK to arrive _____

AK to depart _____

AK will do the following:
1) Provide his own material for withdrawal of consciousness from externals.

CERTIFICATE of ORDINATION

In the NEO-AMERICAN CHURCH

This is to certify that *Timothy Leary*

is ordained a

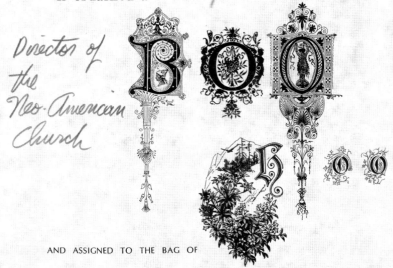

Director of the Neo-American Church

AND ASSIGNED TO THE BAG OF

ON THE *17* DAY OF *May* ,19 *67*

Arthur Kleps ,CHIEF BOO HOO

2) Accept without reservation whatever time and place assigned.
3) Accept recording procedures and standard ritual.
4) Will not make passes at girls who happen to be around.
5) Will sneak drinks privately, but will be sober at appointed hour.
6) Will not make cryptic remarks.
7) Will maintain an air of bland confidence and imperturbability, of approved Madison Ave. or Harvard variety.
8) Will not discuss epistemology until after session, even if asked.

TL will do the following:
1) Refrain from covert testing procedures prior to experience and take AKs [sic] word for it regarding his being ready or not ready.
2) Will encourage other members of community to suspend judgement until it is over.
3) Will assume that AK has as much right to be a kook as a nice guy type like Allan from Cornell, for example.
4) Will discuss, after session, the matter of living and working together in frank and practical manner.
5) If possible, will assign a date between the 23rd and the 4th, but if can't, will assign any date, and permit AK to decide for himself if he wants to risk job game.

Similarly, he created a questionnaire for potential devotees called "The Kleptonian Test of Spiritual Development":

THE KLEPTONIAN TEST OF SPIRITUAL DEVELOPMENT
Directions: rank choices from one to five in order of preference. If you disagree completely with two or more choices, rank according to which would be the most disagreeable in someone else. Or the most agreeable if you want to justify a prejudice or something. If you agree with two or more completely, switch to literary criticism, or something. Neatness counts. Anyone who tries to weasel out of this is an agent of Saturn, don't try to pull any of that egomaniacal "I am above such things" crap.
1) The "unity of all living things" is best explained in terms of:
   4 an "oversoul" of the Emersonian varity [sic].

1 solipsism, itisallinyourheaderism.

2 some other epistemological gag.

3 the genetic code.

5 a sentimental swooning over the cute little bunny rabbits, etc.

2) What good old Tim really means by "games" is

3 stuff like what your name is, what century you are living in, etc.

1 the whole bit, like even being a human on earth.

4 social role playing.

2 whatever seems to distinguish you as an entity from other life.

5 whatever someone else is doing that you don't want to bother about.

3) The best terminology for us wise guys to use right now is

2 scientific, neurological, chemical jazz.

1 occult, magical stuff.

4 oriental mysticism.

Kleps was all too aware of the precarious nature of his church and its sacraments and sought Leary's advice on how best to proceed in regard to the law:

FROM ART KLEPS TO TIMOTHY LEARY | UNDATED

Dear Tim, Just got a copy of the Pomeroy Act [drug legislation], and was not too surprised to find peyote included in list of prohibited substances.

I am holding off sending out my present orders until I here [sic] from you. What I would like from Castalia is assurance that I can get immediate bail by making a phone call, Is it possible to arrange this?

I am perfectly willing to test the law, but would like to avoid spending time in jail if at all possible. Also, it would be a big help if we could get the ACLU involved, or any lawyer with a personal, ethical or religious interest in maintaining internal freedom.

Please let me know if Castalia can help, if you have alternative plans, etc.

Naturally, this has to happen just when the church seems to be "catching on"—quite a mob coming this weekend.

Love, Art

Leary continued to support Art Kleps with his venture and corresponded regularly with him, urging him for more updates on his own explorations:

FROM TIMOTHY LEARY TO ART KLEPS | JANUARY 10, 1964

Dear Flower Christian, Each edition of your travelogue is awaited here with baited breath. They are really great. We are thinking of you and waiting for your return.

Captain Cook

TL/j

In this letter from Kleps to Leary, he comments on Leary's *Playboy* interview and the ongoing establishment of his church:

FROM ART KLEPS TO TIMOTHY LEARY | UNDATED

Dear Tim, All sessions going well—Harry (Chief Astrologer), Anna, Van, Carole . . . nothing spectacular, but O.K. The theme seems to be sex and sex determined relations and conflicts . . . *Playboy* arrived at the store 15 minutes after I talked to you . . . exactly the right angle . . . well done. All in sync.

The Neo-American flag will show an electric blue toad on a yellow circle with ragged edges and carry the motto, in Greek, VICTORY OVER BULLSHIT! Or shall we start getting stuffy? It seems very appropriate to me to put crap on a flag. . . .

Our problem with MGL [Morning Glory Lodge] is not quite solved, since it is in my name (the contract) and I have many old debts, thanks to my lawyer's inactivity—he was supposed to put me through personal bankruptcy, but didn't. Apparently, land contracts are fairly safe from attack by creditors, but there is some danger. It would be a good idea to transfer ownership to the church, but the [. . .] would probably refuse to allow it, as they may, under the terms of the contract if they can show that the transfer is (possibly) contrary to their interests. A solution might be to transfer the contract to some reliable person with means (who might then get a regular mortgage) and lease it back, or something like that. Difficulty #2 is that I will need capital to set up the bookstore—coffee shop—Head Quarters in Washington.

During this time, Leary was working on his autobiography, *High Priest*, which covered his experiences from 1959 to 1962. The period is broken down into sixteen trip reports, guided by his compatriots Aldous Huxley, Allen Ginsberg, Richard Alpert, Ralph Metzner, Huston Smith, and William S. Burroughs. Kleps received the book (which was eventually published in 1968) with glee:

FROM ART KLEPS, CHIEF BOO-HOO, NEO-AMERICAN CHURCH TO TIMOTHY LEARY | UNDATED

Timo, you old bastard!, That was very funny—only a deranged mind could have thought of it.

HP very good. I particularly enjoyed the Hollingshead chapter, naturally because you seemed to catch a few glimpses of what I see all the time . . . . But then, back to structural explorations. God damn it . . . . I suspect that if I went on one of your trips and you went on one of mine, we would freak out permanently. (what a godsend to humanity).

Despite the legal obstacles, psychedelic and parody religions and philosophies continued to surface[20] in the counterculture, later seen in Robert Anton Wilson's Discordian works (*The Illuminatus! Trilogy*, 1975) and Ivan Stang's *The Church of the SubGenius* (1979).

While based at Millbrook, Kleps penned a letter to Timothy Leary and Billy and Peggy Hitchcock on September 30, 1967 written on Neo-American Church Inc. letterhead regarding the status of Millbrook in their absence; the letter is a series of "in-jokes." Around this time, Leary and his then-girlfriend Rosemary took up residence at the large West Coast LSD-dealing operation The Brotherhood of Eternal Love in Laguna Beach, California.[21]

FROM ART KLEPS, CHIEF BOO-HOO, NEO-AMERICAN CHURCH TO TIMOTHY LEARY | SEPTEMBER 30, 1967

Greetings Tim, Billy, Peggy, Ron, Jackie, Indians. . . .

Not much is happening here. The place is like Forest Lawn. I suppose that is due to the fact that most of us are living at the Bungalow since the Hells Angels took over the Big House. You have probably heard all about the big group session Jack, Jimmy, Mary, and all the Clums and Hurdles took. I have never seen such a transformation in my life, but, alls [sic] well that ends well—they are now grazing peacefully in the pasture. It was necessary to geld Clum though—I don't care what the State Police say.

You will be delighted to learn we are off the money standard and have returned to the barter system, having worked out a deal with Marona's wherebye [sic] we get a week's worth of groceries for one strip of copper roofing. When it rains, the scene in the living room is truly surrealistic—we are taking movies.

The only fly in the ointment is the attitude of the Ashram (I suppose I should say former Ashram). I always felt they would end up as Baba lovers, and Karen . . . certainly makes a good leader, BUT, is it really necessary to spend all that time in town chanting "hare Krishna" and passing out Baba literature?

I really can't say that I blame the League, ably led by Susan . . . and Otto (the wedding was a gas) for resorting to violence in order to "clear the streets of vermin" as Susan put it.

I hope Billy understands the necessity of my taking over his invest-ment banking responsibilities during his absence. We are all amazed at the facility with which this could be accomplished by simply disguising one's voice over the telephone. Naturally, I can't be expected to "win 'em all" right off the bat, an initial period of floundering about and making mistakes is all part of the learning process. The S.E.C. should understand this too, but of course, they think Billy is doing it. I had no reason to be suspicious of what sounded like a perfectly respectable business proposition from that bastard in Rio. Well, live and learn.

I wish I could tell you more about the Big House, but we are sort of cut off from the place. . . .

Wendy is fine. She says her family is treating her very well now that she is home again leading a sane and safe existence. The *Daily News* is paying her a fabulous sum for her series of articles on the place—I never suspected she could write so well. . . .

Have fun and don't worry about a ting [sic]. You all deserve a nice long rest.

Om Shanti, Art

LEAGUE FOR SPIRITUAL DISCOVERY
SRI RAM ASHRAMA
NEO-AMERICAN CHURCH

STATE OF NEW YORK   )
) SS:
COUNTY OF DUTCHESS)

_____, being duly sworn and as a
condition of being a guest or upon the premises of the Hitchcock Cattle Farm and
The League for Spiritual Discovery headquarters thereon, hereby deposes and says:

1. Although I may or may not believe in the right of each individual to
possess psychedelic substances for spiritual aid and enlightenment, I am not in possession of any illegal chemicals such as cannabis or lysergic acid, nor shall I bring
any illegal substances upon the premises of the League for Spiritual Discovery, the
Sri Ram Ashrama, or the Neo-American Church.

2. I am not a law enforcement officer, agent, or informer, and I have never
been such, nor have I been requested to discover evidence against Dr. Timothy Leary
or anyone connected with Dr. Leary, The League for Spiritual Discovery, the Sri Ram
Ashrama, or the Neo-American Church.

3. This affidavit is made in penalty of perjury if any statements contained
herein are untrue. I understand that if either of the above statements are untrue, I
am a trespasser and without permission to be on the abovesaid premises.

                              Signed_____

Sworn to before me this
_____day of_____, 19_____.

_____
        Notary Public

Above: Blank affidavit to be signed by residents of
Millbrook as a legal disclaimer for the League for
Spiritual Discovery, Sri Ram Ashrama, and the
Neo-American Church regarding the possession

Timothy and Rosemary were married in California on November 11, 1967. A month later, Leary was arrested for marijuana possession in Laguna Beach, adding to his legal troubles. [22]

The Millbrook commune, which housed the newly formed League, was raided a number of times under orders by New York Dutchess County prosecutor G. Gordon Liddy beginning on April 17, 1966.[23] These raids continued over the next year. After a raid on December 9, 1967, eight individuals faced charges, including Timothy Leary, his son Jack, Art Kleps, and Billy Hitchcock.[24]

After one bust, Leary sent a telegram to the local Catholic church, St. Peter's in Poughkeepsie, New York, requesting assistance and support from the reverend and the church to "take every step to correct the unfortunate publicity and join with us in tolerance and understanding of the love of Christ. . . ." Leary described the events:

On Saturday Dec 9, twenty-five armed sheriffs of Dutchess County, NY raided the temples of three legally incorporated religions located in Millbrook NY: The League for Spiritual Discovery, the Neo-American Church and the Sri Ram Ashrama—a Hindu sect. Doors to the church buildings were smashed, shrines were desecrated and torn apart. The leader of the Neo-American Church, Arthur Kletp [sic], was arrested on the vague charge of conspiracy as was Williams Haines the spiritual leader of the Sri Ram Ashrama. A warrant for my arrest was issued and my son Jack was imprisoned. The authority for this raid was a search warrant based on an affidavit sworn to by a paid informer Finton O'Hare. Mr. Finton O'Hare stated on the sworn affidavit that he acted as informer at the request of his two brothers, William J. O'Hare, a former district [Justice] of Dutchess County, and Rev Daniel O'Hare of St Peters Roman Catholic Church Poughkeepsie NY. I request that you investigate the truth of this widely publicized statement which allegedly commits the Catholic Church to an act of religious persecution [sic]. I request that you ascertain whether father Daniel did indeed request, encourage or condone this violation of religious shrines. I remind you that the League for Spiritual Discovery, the Sri Ram Ashrama and the Neo-American Church, as legally incorporated religions, have the same rights under the United States constitution as the Roman Catholic Church. . . .

After the raids on Millbrook, Leary and the Millbrook-based League for Spiritual Discovery, Sri Ram Ashrama, and Neo-American Church shared an affidavit for members and participants to sign, serving as a legal disclaimer for the organizations.

It is not apparent how many of these were signed and notarized. These organizations were unsuccessful in gaining the right to use psychedelics based on religious freedom. No other churches gained this right, other than the already established Native American Church. It was a clear indication that it wasn't going to be that easy to "get around" the legislation.

FREE
TIM
LEARY
KIDNAPPED
BY
GOVERNMENT
OFFICIALS
RANSOM
$100,000.00

7
Leary versus the State, 1966–70

"What I feel or believe or experience is my business,
and what I do is all our businesses; and reward or
punish me according to whether I play the game
well—ethically and rightly—or unethically."

As quoted in "Leary calls LSD 'sacrament'" in *The Tech*
(November 8, 1966), p. 6

LEARY WAS arrested in Laredo, Texas in 1965 while crossing the Mexican border in possession of marijuana. He was charged under the Marijuana Tax Act of 1937 while traveling with his then girlfriend Rosemary Woodruff and his children. His daughter Susan hid the stash on her person and was also arrested. Leary was convicted and sentenced on March 11, 1966 to thirty years in federal prison—the maximum term allowed for the crime—and a $30,000 fine payable in Laredo. A few days later on March 15, he held a press conference, which was reported a month later in the *Berkeley Barb* with the headline "'License Pot' says Leary." His trial raised questions about marijuana as a gateway drug to heroin and other more serious substances.

"The question as to whether marijuana smoking is harmful was raised at my trial," Leary said at the conference. "The habitual use of any form of energy is probably harmful. If marijuana is used in large quantities, continuously, it could probably cause harm. But still, the use of marijuana is much less harmful than that of alcohol or nicotine." Although in 1966, the possession, use, and consumption of marijuana and LSD was not banned by federal law, officials did try to limit its spread in the United States through the enforcement of other laws against interstate commerce, mislabeling, and the illegal importation and administration of new drugs without a prescription.

Bernard Roseman and Bernard Copley were early LSD manufacturers and dealers (makers of the previously mentioned sixty percent pure green acid), and the first to be convicted in America for selling LSD.[1] They were arrested for drug smuggling, specifically concealing,

selling, and facilitating the transportation of LSD in violation of the
Federal Food, Drug, and Cosmetic Act (Bernard Roseman and Bernard
Copley v. the United States, 1966). Their case came about after pros-
ecutors claimed that their product was smuggled from Israel, and sold
unlabeled and without a prescription. Among the buyers were Myron
Stolaroff, President of the International Foundation for Advanced
Study, customers in Canada where one person was harmed but not
given medical attention, and an undercover agent. Roseman testified
that the LSD was actually manufactured in Los Angeles in 1960 in
collaboration with James Grossman of the California Corporation for
Biological Research; that he had buried the drugs in the Joshua Tree
National Monument, traveled to Europe and Israel, then returned two
years later and dug them up.[2]

A draft letter written by Timothy Leary in June 1964 to Judge George
Harris in support of Roseman and Copley touched on the gray area
of LSD legality at the time of their dealings (January–March 1963). He
commented on the competitiveness in psychedelic research and accused
a rival research group (possibly referring to the International Foundation
for Advanced Study) of aiding their entrapment. He admitted, "Everyone
involved in the psychedelic field agrees about the need for thoughtful
legislation. Like any other method for releasing energy—radio, airplanes,
fissionable material—LSD will eventually require licensing and government supervision. The form that this legislation takes must depend on
the scientific data. It will require decades to organize and interpret the
conflicting type of results produced by LSD. . . ."

FROM TIMOTHY LEARY TO HON. GEORGE B. HARRIS | JUNE 1964
(THIS WAS AN UNSENT DRAFT)

Dear Judge Harris, I am writing you in regard to the case of Bernard
Roseman and Bernard Coply [sic] who were recently convicted of
illegality in connection with LSD.

Since I have not seen the transcript, I cannot comment on the
legal aspects of this case. However, having talked with Mr. George
Walker, formerly an attorney on this case, I am familiar with some
of the extraordinary events which preceded and followed the arrest
of these men.

I am writing this letter to point out certain aspects of this important affair which are most relevant to disposition.

The interpretation and social application of the psychedelic drugs is still being studied and debated by scientists. The LSD controversy present [sic] the picture of large groups of competent and sincere scientists flatly and hotly disagreeing. The issue is still very much open; decades more research and observation will be required before we have the slightest idea how these drugs work and how they should be used. Far from being settled the scientific-social debate has hardly started. In the next six months at least seven books will be published—most of them demonstrating the promise of LSD. (The authors or editors of these books are Solomon, Blum, Leary, Alpert, Metzner, Osmond, Freedman.) A scientific scholarly journal on the subject has been successfully initiated. The United States Public Health Service is stepping up its support of studies which test the therapeutic-educational aspects of LSD. The popular press is presenting a second round of LSD stories—more thoroughly researched and less hysterical than the first round. (See enclosures.)

Scientific controversies in an open society must be settled by free research and scientists working in new areas must be free to pursue new leads. Any attempt to adjudicate or legislate what is basically an intellectual-empirical issue is alien and destructive to our political tradition. Government agencies and courts of law must bend over backwards to avoid involvement in scientific debates. The fact that government agencies are increasing their powers to support, approve and disapprove of certain lines of inquire [sic] is an ominous tendency which threatens the future of our science and way of life. That courts of law become involved in scientific controversies is unthinkable.

Bernard Roseman and Bernard Copley are dedicated scientist-scholars.

This letter, if it ever reached the Judge, didn't help their case. Roseman and Copley were sentenced to seventeen years in prison.[3] Their conviction on July 20, 1966 was closely followed by the criminalization of LSD in the State of California in October of the same year. After leaving the California Corporation for Biological Research, James Grossman became a research chemist at Philip Morris, Co.[4]

In response to Leary's own conviction, the Timothy Leary Defense Fund (TLDF): Committee for Reform of Marijuana Legislation was established in 1966, not only to help with his case, but to promote greater awareness of marijuana legislation. During this time, Leary held press conferences, talks, and interviews, including the aforementioned *Playboy* article. Based in New York City and out of Millbrook, the TLDF raised funds and campaigned on behalf of Leary, reaching out to other psychiatrists/psychologists, pharmacologists, other scientists, artists, and authors to help defend their beliefs in the positive power of psychoactive drugs. William "Billy" Mellon Hitchcock, Chairman of the Timothy Leary Defense Fund, owner of the Millbrook estate, and close friend of Leary and his associates, described Leary's dire legal situation in an appeal letter on April 27, 1966, written on TLDF stationery printed with a long list of supporters. Hitchcock noted that the outcome of Leary's case would have consequences for the forty thousand people then incarcerated for marijuana charges.

WILLIAM H. HITCHCOCK'S OPEN LETTER FOR TIMOTHY LEARY DEFENSE FUND | APRIL 27, 1966

Dear Friend, You may have heard of the harsh sentence Dr. Timothy Leary received for possession of one-half ounce of marihuana. Under the existing laws and rules, Judge Connally had no choice but to impose a maximum sentence of 30 years and $30,000 fine, pending psychiatric examination. In no case, however, is this reducible to less than five years—without parole or probation.

This is outrageous and unusual punishment of a prominent scientist, who has written 52 articles and books on psychology and consciousness. It has created a shock wave of disbelief. People from every walk of life understand that this is an attack on the constitutional freedoms of all us. Thought control is an imminent danger which must be opposed.

Dr. Leary's case is being appealed to higher courts, which will entail heavy expense. We are therefore asking you to contribute to the Timothy Leary Defense Fund. Because there are 40,000 people currently in prisons because of marihuana laws, most of them under age 25, the outcome of this case will be significant.

An envelope is enclosed for your convenience. Ask your friends to join in. Extra copies of these materials will be sent to you upon request and also to anyone you wish to suggest.

Sincerely, William M. Hitchcock, Chairman

One of the first benefits to raise funds and awareness for Leary was organized by Ron Davis and his politically activist Mime Troupe. It took place in the Colonial Room, St. Francis Hotel in San Francisco. Leary and Alpert offered this message to a crowd of 1,200 supporters, "The only way out is in. [The] way to get in is to find the center, and the way to find the center is to turn on, tune in, and drop out." Leary went on: "Everyone has a center. When you find the center of the life process, you'll find yourself floating in the center of the world of lattice-work. There are two things to keep in mind if you want to make this lifetime voyage. The key to get within is chemical. The judicious and planful [sic] use of drugs is involved. . . . You need a map to describe for yourself and others where you have been. Chemical without a language leads to confusion. The goal of the experience is a life of art, and that is why it's worth coming down."[5] He also warned that persons over thirty-five or forty years old should expect a bad "re-entry." Leary was forty-five years old at the time. Alternatively, Alpert described dropping-out as "starting slowly to reorganize our relations to our fellow men and the universe in such a way as to make each moment meaningful."

Leary was arrested a second time with Rosemary on December 26, 1968. They were pulled over while driving in Laguna Beach, California and found to be in possession of two marijuana roaches.[6]

Once LSD and other psychedelic use had spread from the artists, poets, psychologists, and others preoccupied with the study of the mind and spirituality to the wider youth population, a revolution was in the making, or so Leary and Alpert hoped. This was a threat to the establishment.

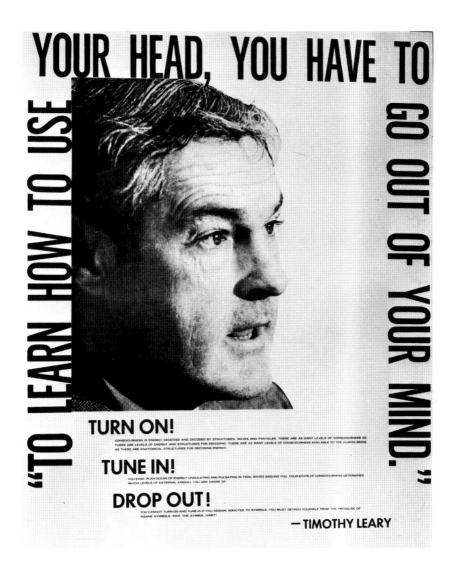

"TO LEARN HOW TO USE YOUR HEAD, YOU HAVE TO GO OUT OF YOUR MIND."

TURN ON!

CONSCIOUSNESS IS ENERGY RECEIVED AND DECODED BY STRUCTURES: WAVES AND PARTICLES. THERE ARE AS MANY LEVELS OF CONSCIOUSNESS AS THERE ARE LEVELS OF ENERGY AND STRUCTURES FOR DECODING. THERE ARE AS MANY LEVELS OF CONSCIOUSNESS AVAILABLE TO THE HUMAN BEING AS THERE ARE ANATOMICAL STRUCTURES FOR DECODING ENERGY.

TUNE IN!

YOU EXIST IN AN OCEAN OF ENERGY UNDULATING AND PULSATING IN TIDAL WAVES AROUND YOU. YOUR STATE OF CONSCIOUSNESS DETERMINES WHICH LEVELS OF EXTERNAL ENERGY YOU ARE AWARE OF.

DROP OUT!

YOU CANNOT TURN ON AND TUNE IN IF YOU REMAIN ADDICTED TO SYMBOLS. YOU MUST DETACH YOURSELF FROM THE PRESSURE OF INSANE SYMBOLS. KICK THE SYMBOL HABIT!

— TIMOTHY LEARY

Page 174: This placard at a protest outside the White House is testament to Leary's appeal to the younger generation, who saw his fight for liberty as their own.

Above: A poster proclaiming one of Leary's most well-known sayings, inspired by Marshall McLuhan.

Subpoena

This Subpoena requires your personal appearance at the time and place specified. Failure to appear may subject you to fine and imprisonment for contempt.

Above and opposite: Subpoena invitation to fundraising event "Coming Together" for the legal defense of Timothy Leary, also known as the Holding Together, Inc. fund. Supporters included John and Yoko Lennon, William "Billy" Hitchcock, Wavy Gravy, Allen

Mike Lang

John & Yoko Lennon

William M. Hitchcock

Wavy Gravy

Allen Ginsberg

Abbie & Anita Hoffman

Jerry Rubin

Alan Douglas

Wynn & Sally Chamberlain

John Giorno

Walter & Peggy Boart

Michael Kennedy

Michal Standard

Mr. & Mrs. James Coburn

Jeno

Mati

Ed Sanders

Caterine Milinaire

Mr. & Mrs. Jaakov Kohn

Invite You to a

COMING TOGETHER

COME TOGETHER

at the Village Gate

Monday   May 11, 1970   9:00 PM

— Heavy Musical Tribes —

— Earth Food from Woodstock —

for the Benefit of

HOLDING TOGETHER, INC.

a Fund for the Defense of

TIM LEARY

Imprisoned Without Bail

in the State of California

$25.00 per person.   We must raise $100,000.

This Party is a Beginning.

We Ask that You Search Your Soul

and Your Heart to Give More if You Can.

Above: Leary at a press conference in association with
the *East Village Other*, a periodical which he would
retain a strong association with until it folded in 1972.

FROM JOHN WILCOCK, *THE EAST VILLAGE OTHER* (*EVO*), TO
TIMOTHY LEARY | UNDATED

Dear Tim, *EVO*'s voting shares total 50, of which I own 13, and as Walter Bowart started the paper and has strong views on how to run it that differ from my own I have stepped out, at least for a few months. If it becomes fabulously successful it will make money for me and if it doesn't presumably my services will be requested.

Meanwhile I'm going to start a private-circulation newsletter, hopefully with a couple of thousand circulation, that will go first-class mail in a sealed envelope and will explore the newest trends in everything all over the world. (You wanna write a short piece for #1, appearing late Jan?) I'm hopeful that with the newsletter I'll be able to explore even further out than *EVO* can and keep one jump ahead of every other printed media.

On Dec 4 I'm off to California for a month to report on America's #1 battleground—the place where the kids are literally going to take control if they can. First target: the curfew, then the pot laws. While there, I shall be helping the *LA Free Press* in which I have a tiny investment. I'd like to buy some shares in it and also in the tough, growing *Berkeley Barb*. Then, in the spring, I'd like to get over to London and buy a chunk of the *International Times* which is exactly the same audience of hippies, heads and groupies that the *LA Free Press* has.

I mention these things to you because you once mentioned investing in *EVO* and as there is no voting stock available in *EVO* maybe you could acquire some stock in the others as an investment for the future? I don't have any specific proposals except to sound them out about us jointly buying stock if you're interested. But I thought you might like to know of the opportunities.

Hope to see you before I go.

Warm wishes, John Wilcock

The supposed threats to the establishment were portrayed in popular culture. The film *Wild in the Streets* released in 1968 depicted the country's anxiety about a youth culture run amok. President Nixon declared Leary to be "the most dangerous man in America." How did Leary respond? In 1969, he decided to throw his hat in the ring for Governor of California against Ronald Reagan. Paul Krassner was to serve as his press secretary. His campaign motto was "Come Together—Join the Party," which inspired John Lennon to write the lyrics for the song "Come Together," the opening track for the Beatles' album *Abbey Road* released in 1969. Lennon and his wife Yoko Ono also supported Leary by appearing at fundraising events for his cause:

FLYER ADVERTISING THE "COME TOGETHER" EVENT AT THE VILLAGE GATE

COME TOGETHER
at the Village Gate
Monday, May 11, 1970 9:00 PM
—Heavy Musical Tribes—Earth Food from Woodstock—
for the Benefit of HOLDING TOGETHER, INC.
a Fund for the Defense of TIM LEARY
Imprisoned Without Bail in the State of California
$25.00 per person. We must raise $100,000.
This Party is a Beginning.
We Ask that You Search Your Soul and Your Heart
to Give More if You Can.

After his initial charge for marijuana possession, Leary's trial challenged the law up to the Supreme Court in the 1969 case, Leary v. the United States. Leary's conviction for marijuana possession was overturned and the Marijuana Tax Law ruled unconstitutional. This paved the way for the United States Congress to pass further legislation, known as the Controlled Substances Act.

Before Congress passed the Controlled Substances Act in 1970, laws governing the importation, possession, use, and selling of drugs varied federally and by state. As mentioned, Leary was arrested in violation of the Marijuana Tax Law for not declaring marijuana to customs when entering Texas from Mexico. Yet, the possession of marijuana was illegal in the State of Texas. Leary argued that declaring marijuana when entering the U.S. was self-incrimination, violating the Fifth Amendment. For this reason, he successfully overturned his case and the law was ruled unconstitutional.

The 1970 Act laid out the current system of drug classification into Schedules according to addictive potential and lack of medicinal value. Psychedelic drugs, marijuana, and heroin fell into the first, most dangerous category, whereas opiate painkillers, methamphetamine, and cocaine were considered to have more medicinal value.[7] The Drug Enforcement Administration (DEA) was established in 1973 under President Nixon to help quell the tide of drugs available in the United States.

Ironically, Leary contributed to the very thing he had fought against—the criminalization of LSD. He had sought publicity to carry his message, but it worked against him after his Senate testimony. His court case created the opportunity for stricter legislation. His zeal towards "turning on" people to the joy of ecstatic experiences became the downfall of the movement. Possibly, if he had quietly conducted his drug studies at Harvard under controlled medical supervision, his story and that of the counterculture might have looked very different today.

8
From Sit-Ins to Be-Ins and Bed-Ins

"Think for yourself. Question authority."

Timothy Leary, *Sound Bites from the Counterculture* (1990)

WRITERS AND ARTISTS have often served as the voice of dissent, supporting the rights of free expression, whether considered subversive, obscene, or traitorous. Naturally, the counterculture reflected the political climate of the 1960s and sought to attack social injustice.

In the United States, the 1960s seemed to be marked by assassinations: President John F. Kennedy was killed on November 22, 1963 in Dallas, Texas; the black nationalist activist Malcolm X was assassinated in the Audubon Ballroom in Washington Heights, New York City on February 21, 1965; and JFK's brother, Senator Robert Kennedy was assassinated on June 5, 1968 at the California Democratic presidential primary in Los Angeles. However, perhaps the greatest assault on free speech came before then, with the assassination of Martin Luther King, Jr. in Memphis on April 4, 1968. The counterculture rose up in this climate of violent political turmoil, offering a voice to an entire generation of young activists and those intent on turning their backs on the establishment.

By 1965, the United States military had escalated its involvement in the Vietnam War. Branches of the left-wing organization Students for a Democratic Society (SDS) demonstrated against the war and perceived imperialistic and racist policies at academic institutions, staging "sit-ins"[1] and occupying campus buildings (1968–69).[2] At the same time, the fight against racial injustice had turned to more radical action, embodied by groups such as the Black Panther Party. Founded in 1966 by African-American political activists Huey Newton and Bobby Seale in Oakland, California, the Black Panthers adopted a militant style of self-defense in response to police brutality targeted towards black Americans.

Such armed resistance was immediately perceived as a threat to the rule of law and the Panthers, alongside other "subversive" movements like Leary's, were placed under surveillance by the United States government.

As the escalation of the Vietnam War continued, more radical groups splintered off SDS and new ones formed, such as the clandestine Weathermen, later known as the Weather Underground Organization, a militant left-wing group formed in 1969 that engaged in the targeted bombings of government buildings. The White Panther Party (WPP) was formed by white Americans to further the cause of the Black Panther Party. John Sinclair, a WPP founder and manager of the Detroit rock band MC5, fought against his own conviction for marijuana possession.

However, during the mid-1960s, Leary more naturally aligned himself with the burgeoning youth hippie movement, who saw him as a proponent of the liberal counterculture that they craved, and they were all too eager to expand their collective consciousness through the use of psychedelics with Leary as their ultimate guide. Indeed, some historians claim that the hippie movement was officially inaugurated at the "Gathering of the Tribes" Human Be-In held in Golden Gate Park, San Francisco on January 14, 1967. Leary was one of the key speakers, with his "Turn on, tune in, drop out" phrase becoming a mantra of the movement. Prior to the event, the gathering was advertised in underground newspaper the *San Francisco Oracle*, which planned to feature Leary and his "teachings":

FROM THE *ORACLE* PAPER TO TIMOTHY LEARY | MAY 11, 1967

Dear Tim, We had planned to interview you via phone last Thursday evening, but an extraordinary event intervened which should be of great interest to you.

We—the Oracle tribe—live in an old mansion that has a badminton court, a swimming pool, and a ballroom that will accommodate 300 people. We had a meeting with about fifty people representing various county and city agencies who are concerned about what they termed the "invasion of hippies" this summer. There were people from the Human Relations Commission, West Hollywood Coordinating Counsel, Teen Posts, Youth Workers, Health Department, as well as people from *LA Times*, *Herald-Examiner*, and *Newsweek*.

After a brief ceremony, in which we joined hands in a great circle and meditated silently on the forces that had brought us together, we got into a very heavy and productive exchange. It went on for four hours. Finally, an older gentleman from the Human Relations Commission (who had initially introduced himself by saying, "We are the establishment, and we…") stood up and volunteered to lease 160 acres of land he owns adjoining the Grand Canyon to *The Oracle* so that we could have a place for the Great Gathering of The Tribes Love-In next month.

Last weekend, Joe … (of *The Oracle*), Craig … (messenger between the Indian tribes), and Chealey Milliken (of the Indian Love and Light Committee) went to Arizona and checked out the site. It has a natural amphitheater surrounded by pine forests, and a giant semi-cleared area suitable for camping. It is in Kaibab National Forest, six miles from the rim of the canyon. There is a railroad stop adjoining the property, and a small town nearby.

We are making arrangements to provide trucked-in water, power, medical and sanitation facilities. An artist is drawing a map, a writer is writing directions and instructions, and someone else is designing a poster. We have commitments from six rcok [sic] groups so far, with more to come.

Today we received the lease from Tobias … the owner!

The forces of the universe are in harmony and the great evolutionary tide moves forward!

Your article on "How to Start Your Own Religion" will be published in the next issue of *The Oracle*, off the press May 23. It is precisely the piece we needed and should release a lot of energy.

Over twenty thousand people attended this Be-In as presented by Michael Bowen, artist and event organizer. The gathering came about in response to California's then recent legislation banning LSD on October 6, 1966 and Stanley Owsley—the largest distributor of LSD at the time—is said to have supplied the acid distributed at the event.

Alongside Timothy Leary, Richard Alpert, Allen Ginsberg, the essayist and fellow Beat Gary Snyder, Beat poet Michael McClure, and

Page 188: Allen Ginsberg and Timothy Leary at the Human Be-In held at Golden Gate Park, San Francisco on January 14, 1967. Photographed by Lisa Law.

Above: Gathering of the Tribes/Human Be-In poster, 1967. The artist and event organizer was Michael Bowen, and the designer of the poster was Stanley Mouse.

Above: Leary outdoors at the microphone with the
crowd and a flower in his hair. San Francisco, Sunday,
January 14, 1967. Leary made his first San Francisco
public appearance at the 1967 Human Be-in.
Photographed by Lisa Law.

civil rights activist and comedian Dick Gregory were also featured speakers. Popular rock music acts in the area performed, such as the Grateful Dead and Jefferson Airplane. As one oversized demonstration, the event inspired and influenced future Be-Ins and placed the San Francisco Haight-Ashbury area at the heart of the American (if not the worldwide) counterculture. It also cemented many of the tenets of the movement, including a rejection of conventional ideas and suburban morality, the power of the individual, the revolution against established political and cultural norms, communal living, the importance of nature, and, of course, the seeking of a higher consciousness (largely through the use of drugs).

Calcutta journalist and spiritualist Asoke Fakir accompanied a group of Baul singers from Bengal to perform at the Human Be-In. Fakir managed them under the direction of music executive Albert Grossman, who also managed popular musical acts at the time, including: Peter, Paul, and Mary; Bob Dylan; Janis Joplin; and The Band. Fakir named the group LDM after Lok Dharma Mahashram, the World's First Socio-Spiritual Research Institute for the Neo-Spiritual Movement, incorporated in 1968 and founded by Fakir. The LDM Spiritual Band included singer Purna Das Baul Samrat. The founder of a Vedanta center in Calcutta,[3] Fakir was a spiritual influence on Allen Ginsberg and Timothy Leary. Allen Ginsberg studied Baul spiritual practices during a trip to India he made in 1962–63 and recommended Fakir to Leary.[4] In a c. 1967 letter to Leary, Fakir refers to America as his true spiritual home, explaining why Leary, Ginsberg, and music executive Albert Grossman sought him out in India. He also announced that he was coming to live at Millbrook:

FROM ASOKE FAKIR TO TIMOTHY LEARY | UNDATED (c. 1967)

Blessed brother Tim, Your letter is angelic. Since last few days—a very strong and surprising feeling gradually rising in me . . . the feeling of a person who concealed himself in another country, among a different set of people and society for 41 years and now he is going home. I think, I am a SPY, who did a great lot of spiritual espionage work . . . forget that, he belongs to another country and suddenly one of his own countrymen meets him and says—"hellow [sic] boy, what are you doing here . . . come home!" and it's my home coming.

Right now, my pains are much. Because, maybe I am leaving all with whom I dwelt for 41 years. A great joy of homecoming—with a great pain of leaving somewhere I suffered, experience, learnt the pangs of life full of ignorance and miseries.

Your great and historical invitation at this point assures my statement doubly. After receiving life long b[?]—in India, now going to receive "joyous celebration of love and welcome" in my own country America by my true brothers and sisters.

My feeling is like this; an American died 41 years ago in USA with a great wish of coming to India and learn the Spiritualism which will be applied for a great cause of humanity; for a new world making—his spirit was born in my body . . . that was why . . . since childhood my thought structure always seemed so foreign to my own people . . . parents, friends, relatives, working associates at every field of my activities—did not fit with me from the age of 12/13 I became a lonely boy—who wanted to live alone . . . .

Brother Tim, I am coming home! Maybe, I was a Millbrook man . . . your very near man . . . once you have seen me . . . your spirit recognised me . . . as well as Allen's . . . and . . . Grossman's. . . .

I am coming home with a Panchamende (five skull s[et?]) to lay in Millbrook along with a Panchabati; (five in one) plant . . . to grow into a huge tree, sacred and holy with great spiritual power in Millbrook—and from here . . . the spiritual transplantation from India to America takes place. I have finished my espionage here . . . coming to report . . . am I not a subject or object for the "League for Spiritual Discovery?"

Sure, this spiritual travel from U.S.A. to India is a discovery . . . a self realization . . . knowing the unknown self . . . know thyself . . . atmanam Viddhi.

I will phone you . . . but would it be possible to come to San Francisco with sister Jean?

Love and smiles, Jai Guru Asoke

Despite the tenets of "love" and "peace" being preached throughout the counterculture, the last few years of the 1960s were turbulent ones as demonstrators across the United States clashed with authorities. One such key event was the 1968 Democratic National Convention

in Chicago, as members of the Democratic Party gathered to nominate their new presidential candidate. Members of groups aimed at stopping the war in Vietnam, including the Students for a Democratic Society, demonstrated alongside a number of other activist groups and individuals. Among those was the Youth International Party or yippies, founded in 1968 by social activist Jerry Rubin, journalist Paul Krassner, and activist/anarchists Abbie and Anita Hoffman. The yippie manifesto, written by Jerry Rubin and Abbie Hoffman, stated, "Nobody goes to work. Nobody goes to school. Nobody votes. Everyone becomes a life actor of the street doing [their] thing, making the revolution by freeing himself and fucking the system. . . ." The yippies held their own satiric party convention, nominating "Pigasus," a real pig, as their candidate in protest at the prevailing political culture. The disturbances and violence caused by the demonstrations in Chicago landed some participants in jail, charged with conspiracy to incite riots, and the leaders became known as the Chicago Seven. Abbie Hoffman and Jerry Rubin were included among the Chicago Seven defendants. The band MC5 performed outside the convention. Abbie Hoffman later offered his own "dropping-out" ideology, along with techniques on avoiding the capitalistic, corporate American system in his counterculture bestseller *Steal This Book* (1971).

However, not all revolutionary activity in the late 1960s was as radical as the yippies. The Sit-In began as an act of civil disobedience during the civil rights movement of the 1950s, such as the planned sitting of black and white Americans at segregated lunch counters. This tactic was later adopted by activists protesting the Vietnam War and other social issues during the 1960s. By 1969, Sit-Ins had morphed into Be-Ins (sparked by the gathering in San Francisco) and Teach-Ins. The Sit-Ins, Be-Ins, and Teach-Ins culminated in the famous Bed-In, organized by newlyweds John Lennon and Yoko Ono to raise media attention for the anti-war and pro-peace movement. Lennon and Ono lay in bed for a week in Amsterdam with the signs "hair peace" and "bed peace." Both staged additional Bed-Ins, one in Montréal during which Leary and his wife Rosemary, Allen Ginsberg, and others joined in singing the song "Give Peace a Chance" on June 1, 1969.

TRANSCRIPT OF INTERVIEW WITH TIMOTHY LEARY AND JOHN
LENNON AND YOKO ONO | MAY 24, 1969

YOKO: I've heard of Millbrook. I mean, it's famous.

TIMOTHY: Yes, and police informers and television people. But then we saw how geography was important. The land north of the house was uninhabited. As you got there, you got farther away from the people, and the games, and the television, and the police. What we've been trying to do is create heaven on earth, right? And we did have it going, for a while—in the forest groves where there were just holy people. Just people going around silently eating brown rice or caviar, and when you went there, you would never think of talking terrestrial. You never would say, "Well, the sheriff's at the gate."

JOHN: We were going to have no talking either, for a week.

TIMOTHY: Well, this was a place where you only would go if you just wanted to. It was set up somewhat like, you know, the Tolkien thing, with trees and shrines. There was another place where we lived, which we called Level Two, which was in a teepee, and people would come up there, and we would play, and laugh. And then you get down to the big house, and that was where you could feel the social pressures starting. And once you left the gate, then you were back in the primitive twentieth century. As soon as you walked out the gate, if you didn't have your identification, then they'd bust you. So it was all neuro-geography. The place you went to determined your level of consciousness. As you went from one zone to another, you knew you were just coming down or going up.

JOHN: That's great.

TIMOTHY: Now we've got that going again out in the desert.

ROSEMARY: We're living with a more intelligent group of people this time.

YOKO: What did you do with the place, Millbrook? Is it still going?

TIMOTHY: We were supposed to go there this week. Matter of fact, we may go there tomorrow night. It's still there. But it's the old story. In the past, societies fought over territory. They thought, "We'll hold this space, or we'll force you out." It's an old mammalian tradition. As you pointed out about Reagan, what we're doing in the United States is transcending this notion of the good-guy cowboy. That's

Governor Reagan: he's gonna shoot down hippies, shoot down blacks and college students. So we gave up Millbrook, because there's no point in fighting over the land, and making it a thing of territorial pride. If they want it so much that they're going to keep an armed guard there all the time, they can have it. We'll be back.

Just as John Lennon and Yoko Ono saw the media as a tool to make a statement, Leary and the myriad of counterculture movements embraced the combination of art and media to spread their messages. As a friend and admirer of media theorist Marshall McLuhan who coined the phrase, "The medium is the message"; Leary was highly influenced by his work. In fact, Leary's most famous catchphrase, "Turn on, tune in, drop out" originated from one of their conversations.[5] He understood the power of revolutionary slogans and through his collaboration with activists and artists, such as psychedelic artists USCO, performance art pioneer Yoko Ono, and the yippies, Leary was influential in the merging of countercultural activism and art. Such artistic activism was embraced by a youth culture regularly partaking in "grass" and "acid," who soon spurned the more straightforward picket line and parade in favor of artistic expressions and "happenings." A proto-performance art, happenings were first performed in 1952 by American artist John Cage at Black Mountain College in North Carolina.[6] They were interactive public presentations that became more prevalent during the 1960s as a form of performance art. Essentially, Ken Kesey's "Acid Tests" could be considered happenings.

Such groups of performers sprung up throughout America, including anarchist and radical theater group the Diggers, who were based in Haight-Ashbury, San Francisco.[7] Like the Merry Pranksters, the Diggers hosted parties with music provided by the Grateful Dead and Jefferson Airplane. Their performances and happenings were meant to provoke the establishment and attract attention from the media. They staged "Death of a Hippie" in 1967 with masked performers carrying a coffin with the text, "Hippie—son of media" through the streets of the Haight-Ashbury neighborhood—considered the unofficial North American headquarters for the peace, love, and hippie phenomenon. Like Leary, the Diggers were manipulating the media to spread their message.

The underground press also played a crucial role in disseminating information and ideas, by reporting on the activities of the counterculture and posting announcements for future events. Following the Be-In, the *San Francisco Oracle* was anxious to work more with Leary, as evidenced by this letter sent to Leary from the editor, Allen Cohen, in August 1967:

FROM ALLEN COHEN, EDITOR OF THE *SAN FRANCISCO ORACLE*, TO TIMOTHY LEARY | AUGUST 17, 1967

Dear Sir, Now is the time for philosophers, poets, artists and idealists to dare the sirens of temptation and guide America through the veil of its treachery and insanity.

The *San Francisco Oracle* has been communicating the vision of poets and artists and philosophers with the judo of mass-oriented tabloid style so that the time-lag between vision and reality is bridged and the envisioned can be realized.

Oracle #10 will try to blueprint the until now imaginary City of God on the seven-hilled beauty of San Francisco. The paradise of our dreams is realizable by our actions. We need your ideas about the ideal relationships of mankind toward his kind and toward his planet—economic, architectural, familial, sexual, ritualistic, cultural, governmental, ecological, technological and especially the state of mind or the state of grace that man must be in to pull the whole thing off.

We have about a three-week deadline but may either hold for perfection or do two consequent issues if it looks ripe. We eagerly await your response.

For the Peace and Love beyond understanding, Allen Cohen

That year, the *Oracle* also published a multiple-page transcript[8] of the "Houseboat Summit"—a gathering of the leading counterculture figures of the time: Timothy Leary, Allen Ginsberg, poet Gary Snyder, and Alan Watts, at Watts's houseboat, the *Vallejo*, in Sausalito in February 1967—discussing the current status and issues surrounding the use of LSD.

Underground newspapers and magazines proliferated throughout the 1960s and '70s, including the *Berkeley Barb*, *The Realist*, and the *San Francisco Oracle*, as well as the UK-based *International Times* (*IT*) and *Oz*. However, absurdist, satirical, obscene, and subversive material was not new to the baby boomer generation—*Playboy* and *Mad* magazines were founded in 1953 and 1952, respectively—but the counterculture allowed such works to reach a wider audience and served to develop an ever-growing youth culture that was ready to embrace and enact more radical ideas.

Yippie founding member Paul Krassner also edited the satirical publication *The Realist*. Pushing the boundaries of obscenity, *The Realist*, founded in 1958, featured provocative and graphic content. Contributors included cartoonists Robert Crumb and Wally Wood, and writers and comedians Terry Southern, Lenny Bruce, Ken Kesey, Woody Allen, Harry Shearer, and Norman Mailer. Timothy Leary was featured in an interview in Issue 69 in September 1966, headlined "An Impolite Interview with Timothy Leary" conducted by Robert Anton Wilson. During the interview, Leary discussed his claim for religious freedom to exercise the right of marijuana and psychedelic drug use in response to his charges for possession. Robert Anton Wilson, contributor to *Playboy* magazine, and later coauthor (with *Playboy* colleague Robert Shea) of the satirical science fiction work, *The Illuminatus! Trilogy*, was later recognized as a cult figure in the American counterculture. Books by Wilson and Shea were characterized as sardonic works that touched on the occult, secret societies, conspiracy theories, and Discordian philosophy, along with drug-induced encounters with extraterrestrials.

Leary was an advocate of journalism and used the underground and mainstream press to promote his ideas and theories to the widest possible audience. Throughout his life, Leary maintained his friendship with Paul Krassner who was involved in his legal defense efforts.

Krassner recently shared his memories of Timothy Leary in an interview for this book:[9]

In 1964, I featured a front-cover story in *The Realist* by Robert Anton Wilson titled "Timothy Leary and His Psychological H-Bomb." When that issue was published, Leary invited me to visit him at the Castalia Foundation, his borrowed estate in Millbrook, New York. There was instant rapport, and we became friends. I also became a friend of his colleague, Richard Alpert, later known as Ram Dass.

FUNERAL NOTICE

---•◆•---

H I P P I E

In the
Haight Ashbury District
of this city,
Hippie, devoted son
of
Mass Media

---•◆•---

Friends are invited

to attend services

beginning at sunrise,

October 6, 1967

at

Buena Vista Park.

Above: Diggers announcement for "The Death of the Hippie,"
Haight Ashbury, Buena Vista Park, October 6, 1967.

When questioned about Leary's convictions for drug charges and the influence of the counterculture movement, Krassner commented:

> Prohibition criminality was aided by fierce propaganda, and Leary went to prison—and escaped. He was a pioneer in trying to get rid of those cruel laws, and decades later medical and recreational pot have been legalized, step by step, state by state. Puritanical legislators believed in the lies of *Reefer Madness*, and greediness of the prison guard union and DEA informed their belief that inmates—victims of victimless crimes—deserve to live behind bars in cages. This injustice is the cornerstone of a police state.
>
> [Today] the evolution of freedom and technology has placed a light on subversion. There has always been counterculture in different forms: Bohemians, Beat Generation, baby boomers, hippies, yippies, punks, hip-hop, occupiers, millennials, on and on. The process continues. The seeds that were planted in the '60s, such as organic farming, have now been blossoming.

Robert Anton Wilson was also a lifelong friend who influenced Leary's writings later in life. After *The Illuminatus! Trilogy*, Wilson and Leary continued to correspond and collaborate, coauthoring with George Koopman and Daniel Gilbertson a collection of essays titled *Neuropolitics: The Sociobiology of Human Metamorphosis* (1977). Wilson expanded on Leary's eight circuits of consciousness theory in his book *Prometheus Rising* (1983). In this theory, Leary postulated eight stages of neurological evolution that operate in the human nervous system. Mirroring ideas of personal growth and progression, Leary often referred to humans as residing in the "larval" early stages, with enlightenment and extraterrestrial elements characterizing the more evolved stages.

Leary wrote an early iteration of this theory in a letter dated March 10, 1971, while living in exile at the Hotel Mediterranee, Algiers:

> The seven revolutions . . . 1. Survival 2. Political 3. Economic are the Do Re Mi. The first great Do is birth; most people live entirely at these three levels of consciousness—with cultural, sexual, religious, and neurological structures imprinted unconsciously and never made

conscious and thus accessible to liberation. A shock is needed to get beyond the first three. A turn-on of some sort which brings about a cultural liberation; you break out of unconscious tribal structure.

4. Cultural 5. Sexual 6. Spiritual 7. Neurological. Void . . . zero . . . and then descending, turning off 7, 6, 5, 4, 3, 2, 1 Void . . . then start up again. Survival-politics-economics are bring downs when you are high. From time into Space. Turn-off. But it is necessary to make some Space arrangements; to come down often enough. The decision about leaving SLO was whether to make the escape Political: i.e. return to heavy Space; or just drift off into Time. Kesey saw this. He said 'You should have disappeared to India.' We seem to be selected to play out publically certain high-energy dramas. We are all here to serve each other as energy particles in the vacuums of void. Ulysses voyaging. . . .[10]

Leary's influence in art, culture, and politics throughout the 1960s was wide-ranging. While President Nixon accused him of being out to corrupt the nation's youth into drug taking, many within the counterculture saw him as a visionary, who presented an alternative path to human fulfillment and harmony through consciousness expansion and the rejection of game-playing. However, for Leary himself the close of the decade was to see the limits of his vision decidedly challenged by the system.

The Realist

box
242
madison
square
station
new
york
n. y.
10010

gr 7-3490

thursday, 4/14

Dear Tim,

Glad to see that the Defense Fund is getting
off the ground so nicely. I noticed that,
although Billy Hitchcock read my name at the
press conference it was omitted from the
stationery. I assume this was because of the
lack-of-respectability factor, which I can
empathize with, and so I didn't try to in effect
embarrass the committee by asking that my name
be included in the Times ad.

Anyway, what are the chances of the Realist
printing the text of your "Politics and Ethics
of Ecstasy" talk at Town Hall? (This would
provide a healthy rationalization for the Realist
to contribute $100 to the Defense Fund.) Or,
you might prefer to write something new about
the recent LSD cases--the 5-year-old girl and
the murderer who is using psychedelics as an
-more-

Above: Missive to Leary from Paul Krassner, editor of
The Realist, suggesting new press to publicize the
Timothy Leary Defense Fund (TLDF). Known for its
controversial topics, *The Realist* published "An Impolite
Interview with Timothy Leary," conducted by Robert
Anton Wilson, September 1, 1966.

CALIFORNIA PRISON

B 26358

T F LEARY

3 18 70

9

From Prison to Space, 1970–74

"I am 100 percent in favor of the intelligent use of drugs, and 1,000 percent against the thoughtless use of them, whether caffeine or LSD."

Timothy Leary, *Chaos & Cyberculture*

AFTER BEING SENTENCED for drug possession on January 21, 1970, Leary was placed in a low-security prison in San Luis Obispo, California. At this point, his story becomes almost mythical. Incredibly, he was able to escape prison with the aid of his then wife, Rosemary, and radical leftist group the Weathermen, who organized (for a fee paid out by drug dealers the Brotherhood of Eternal Love) transport for him after he scaled the prison wall. Once free, he and Rosemary fled to Algeria where they stayed with Eldridge Cleaver and the Black Panthers. This feat was recounted in his book, cowritten by English author Brian Barritt, *Confessions of a Hope Fiend* (1973). Eldridge Cleaver, author of best-selling prison memoir, *Soul on Ice* (1968), was already living as a fugitive after skipping bail in 1968 on charges of attempted murder. He first fled to Cuba, but was living in exile in Algiers when the Learys arrived.[1]

After his prison escape, Timothy and Rosemary Leary were granted asylum by the Algerian government; since it had no extradition treaty with the United States. They initially lived in exile under the protection of the Black Panthers. During their time with the Panthers, the press reported that Leary had declared (in a taped interview) that youth should NOT "Turn on, tune in, drop out" and experiment with mind expansion, but follow the ways of the militant Weathermen and Black Panthers: "There is a time to expand, and a time to contract. This is a time to tighten up, organize."[2]

Unbelievably, Timothy and Rosemary had joined the revolution; their new slogan was "Shoot to Live/Aim for Life."[3]

EXCLUSIVE

NEW YEAR NEW LIFE

AN OPEN LETTER TO ALLEN GINSBERG
ON THE SEVENTH LIBERATION

Being Our Revelation About Armed Self Defense
At Crucial Survival Moment Against Mechanical
Violence To Maintain Life After Having Exhausted
   Every Other Means Of Preserving Life

Brother Allen
 It was about Time
For a Loving Call to Arms
Celebrated in mantra
SHOOT TO LIVE
     Which could have been
     AIM FOR LIFE
     But for energy needed to balance
     the SHOOT TO KILL of Police Robots
     And certain understandably angry
     Brave Young Revolutionaries

AIM FOR LIFE
As electrons
Obeying the Nuclear Code
At critical millisecond
Veer again from collision
     Yet anticipate
     That ultimate moment when Code
     Will fail to send Life Message
     Chanting instead
     Junk mantra SHOOT TO DIE

SHOOT TO LIVE/AIM FOR LIFE
As Seed Message moment of orgasm sends
Flash of sperm whirling thru fallopian barrel
Mantra of sunstars exploding outward
     Before moment of inverse implosion
     Disintegrates the Word
     La Chute to die
     Farewell to Arms
     Dying to be part
     Of the All again

SHOOT TO LIVE offered as
Our Seventh Liberation mantra
Existentially valid during passage
Through delimited space-time
Survival Zone: 8:25 p.m. PST Sept. 12, 1970
     San Luis Obispo, California
     Minute of climbing over fence
     In gunsights of two
     Guardtruck Sharpshooters
  Valid until: 5:31 p.m. CST Sept. 23, 1970
     O'Hare Airport, Chicago, Illinois
     Minute of Armed Federal Agents
     Passing within 12 inches of us
     On their way out TWA plane door
Slammed shut
On all of that for now
SHOOT TO LIVE no longer our mantra
Now being filed by archivists in Babylon
     Illham'dilla
Signalling NEW LIFE
In which Inshal'la
Hour Karma spins us
Away from Seventh Repression
     But we all ways pledge
     Deepest love and readiness to join
     All Brothers & Sisters passing thru
     Their space-time Survival Zone

Six Revolution-Liberation Cycles—
Rights of Passage 1960-1970:

1. Sacrament	Acid	Energy	OM TAO
2. God	Spirit	Center	OM MANI PADMA HUM
3. Mate	Tantra	Love	COME TOGETHER
4. Tribe	Brotherhood	Tolerance	LIVE & LET LIVE
5. Home	Possession	Sharing	GIVE & RECEIVE
6. Freedom	Politics	Strength	POWER TO THE PEOPLE

Our Loving Defense of them
Having made inevitable the Seventh Liberation—

7. Life	Body	Courage	SHOOT TO LIVE/
			AIM FOR LIFE

As those who have consciously
Made the Ancient Gamble
Spinning the Wheel of Life & Death
     Who choose to speak little
     Using the language of silence
     But grateful eye shares
As we shared with Sunny Weather
As we shared with Appolodoro Carbalho
     Brave Brazilian
     60-year-old Apollo
     Who kidnapped Amerikan Ambassador
     To free his comrades
     From torture prison
As we share with Angela Davis
     Raising her clenched fist
     In handcuffs in California

with Jonathan Jackson, age 17: This is it, gentlemen.
     I've got an automatic weapon.
     Everybody freeze.

with James McClain: Take these handcuffs off me.
     I've been in San Quentin 20 years
     And I want to be a free man
     So help me God.

with John Sinclair: If we don't survive
     We don't do anything else.

As we share with noble Cleaver
And his comrades Martian D.C.
     Fleet Mercurian Sakoo
     Quicksilver Larry
As we share with all
   Who aim for New Life
   In Babylons of the Planet

Beloved Brother Allen
We try as always to tell you
How it is with us
Out here in Free Space
Twin-stars Venutian
Spinning thru Free Time
Beaming Love to you
Orbiting round the same Sun

     "To us you will all ways be holy
     May we be holy to you"

Timothy + Rosemary Leary

ALGIERS, ALGERIA
DECEMBER 30, 1970

Page 208: Mugshot of Timothy Leary taken on March 18, 1970 while serving a ten-year sentence for marijuana possession in California. He escaped prison in September of that year.

Above: Penned by Timothy and Rosemary Leary, "An Open Letter to Allen Ginsberg on the Seventeenth Liberation," *Berkeley Barb*, January 1–7, 1971.

Above: Eldridge Cleaver and Timothy Leary in Algiers. Deeply enmeshed in the most prominent radical, militant organizations of the time, Timothy and Rosemary sought refuge with Cleaver and the Black Panthers after arriving in Algiers with the help of the Weather Underground, funded by the Brotherhood of Eternal Love. This photograph, taken by Larry Mack, was first published in *Newsweek*, November 1970.

Opposite: A handwritten message from Eldridge Cleaver to Timothy Leary. Timothy and Rosemary would soon leave Cleaver and the Black Panthers, but would continue to live underground.

Leary: 2-16-71

There are three
wise men here ~~this~~ who
~~see~~ want to see you.
One from India, one from
Ghana, and one from
Chilie. I told them
to check with us about
10:00 A.M. today (2/16/71).
Do you want to see
them? Give us a call.
                    Eldridge

The Learys responded to criticism over their militant image and alignment with the Panthers in the manifesto/poem "An Open Letter to Allen Ginsberg on the Seventh Liberation," written on December 30, 1971 and published in the *Berkeley Barb*.[4] They borrowed language from the Panthers, stating their case for armed self-defense, identifying themselves with other political prisoners such as Angela Davis and John Sinclair, and claiming—after completing six revolution liberation cycles during the 1960s—they had arrived at the seventh liberation: Life—Body—Courage. They ended the declaration with:

> Beloved Brother Allen
> We try as always to tell you
> How it is with us
> Out here in Free Space
> Twin-stars Venutian
> Spinning thru Free Time
> Beaming Love to you
> Orbiting round the same Sun
>
> 'To us you will all ways be holy
> May we be holy to you.'

The situation with the Black Panthers reportedly became difficult for the Learys, leading to their eventual "escape" from the group. By 1971, Timothy and Rosemary sought refuge in neutral Switzerland. During Leary's exile, he had received attention from like-minded scholars, authors, and artists, as well as others who were sympathetic to his cause. Despite his initial criticisms, his longtime friend Allen Ginsberg, a PEN (Poets, Essayists, and Novelists) club member, wrote the statement "Declaration of Independence for Dr. Timothy Leary July 4, 1971," which was signed by members of the San Francisco Bay Area Prose Poets' Phalanx including Ken Kesey, Robert Creeley, Lawrence Ferlinghetti, Anaïs Nin, and Diane di Prima.

Ken Kesey even penned a poem dedicated to the man he saw as a pioneer, entitled "Written Last Week on Psilocybin by Ken Kesey: 'St. Timothy Leary on the Freeway'" and published on July 18, 1971:

All the way down, of course, sanity going on with politic policy;

Craziness, on the other hand, a little shallow and sporadic.

Streets lined both sides with Karate teachers (DEFEND YOUR-
SELF!) fabricate enormous lies concerning the direness of our neighborhood. Manhole covers open up advertising Elysium with no down
payments. Rides needed outa town as soon as possible tomorrow
morning if possible help with gas and driving. Citizen band radios
charge each other with impossible atrocities (LET ME OUTTA HERE
DEFENDING MYSELF! All the way, still humming, humming, give
all you got, humming, humming, all you got) where fascists belch at
each other beneath the coffee tables, significantly.

You can't argue with the seven route interchange fulla segregated
schoolbusses, and you hitchhiking high the hell outta here. "Why!
Am ah treated so bad?" you cry with your thumbs out; but you can't
argue. "Where am ah goin' to? Will ah ever git thar?" But you know
you gonna get on whatever schoolbus stops for you.

"Look at the people this town ferchrissakes!" You say, hesitating.

"Nemmind that, kid; you get on board or aren't you."

"Don't ah got a right to known where you taken me?"

"Listen, kid, this your color bus or not? Or you wanta hang out the
rest of your life on the shoulder and watch the others get a education?"

"Alright. Anyplace better'n this town; but look at the people, I ask
you: why we makin' each other so ugly and shifty eyed?"

"I'm leavin', kid." Vrooom.

"Wait! No! wait . . . ."

In the streets behind you hear the Karate teachers charging the
open manholes, all narrated by conflicting radio reports (saving Grace,
humming there on the shoulder of the freeway all the day long all the
way down, humming, humming, feeling all right in spite).

I'd rather be real than right, tonight, with the freeway furor finally
dieing down . . . a quiet little rain is falling . . . the Karate classes are dark
. . . the manholes closed . . . oowumm . . . oooywouuummmmmmmm . . . .

You are a great man, Timothy: what else can we say? We will miss
you in this land but we'll lock you in none.

Leary received additional support from radio journalist Elliot Mintz, who interviewed him by phone in Algeria and Switzerland for his radio program and encouraged those who wished to help Leary's cause to write the Swiss Department of Justice, prompting letter writing and petition signing campaigns to the Swiss government to grant him asylum:

OPEN LETTER FROM HORACE MASTRONARDI, ATTORNEY AT LAW; BERN, SWITZERLAND

OM

Timothy Leary's research in the rehabilitation of biochemically violent criminals and other prisoners, and in the psychotherapeutic curing of mentally-retarded-autistic children, homosexuals, alcoholics, and the spiritually sterile, shows the promise of drastically cutting our crime rates, and tremendously cutting our tax costs in the maintenance of prisons and mental hospitals. His work and that of his contemporaries, Baba Ram Dass and Ralph Metzner, has been further verified by federally sponsored researchers, such as Dr. Stanislaw Groff [sic], at the Maryland Psychiatric Institute, all of whom agree that the psychedelic experience is primarily a religious one. Tim Leary and these men have brought our nation to a position we cannot afford to lose. We cannot and must not allow professional or political rivalry nor superstitious sensationalism [to] interfere with our legitimate and competent researchers.

The transient but integral manifestation of Spirit in the form of psychotherapeutic medicine has proven to be a specific biochemical alternative to a technologically polluted environment. At a time when noxious and toxic substances such as smog, radiation, and D.D.T. were damaging our nervous systems and thereby dulling our consciousness, psychedelics came on the scene to alleviate this state and expand our consciousness temporarily, showing us the direction to more permanent expansion through yoga discipline, right action, correct thinking, right eating, and meditation and prayer.

Psychotherapeutics temporarily alleviate the effect rather than the cause, that is they produce mental-spiritual relief, but do not directly eliminate the pollutants, those karmic-physical manifestations causing spiritual sterility, mental apathy and dullness. Similarly, anesthetics eliminate pain (effect), but do not eliminate the wound (cause). One can notice the tendency of psychedelic users as also yogis to be found in the forests, beaches, parks, and nature; an intuitive sponta- neous reaction to taking the drug. As an individual reharmonizes his personal environment and habits of thought and action, psychedelic medicines become obsolete to him, as they are no longer necessary. Biochemistry is being temporarily used to reharmonize our environ- ment and our selves, until both are in a self-sustaining natural balance. Yoga discipline is effective as the next step beyond drugs and as a substitute for drugs altogether. Tim Leary's work has caused much of the current interest in ecology and environment, as he has known all along that a proper environment is a substitute for necessity of medications, psychedelic or otherwise. The sociological blueprints of the economics of ecological-agricultural biomes for the support of present and future generations which have been developed through Dr. Leary's work is of vital interest to our space research, as the states of mind induced by psychedelics are similar to the states of mind produced by space travel, according to the theories of many experts. It is of utmost expedience that Timothy Leary remain free as he is a strategic member of those forces which provide for international peace and security . . . OM . . . TAO . . . .

A master of peaceable evolution, Tim Leary's strategic distribu- tion of psychotherapeutic medication in areas of potential turmoil has brought the elements of gentleness and nonviolence to the revolution. Violent, impulsive, irrational behavior is not normally consistent with the psychedelic experience. In the best interests of science, truth, and justice, Tim Leary must be freed. Those persons of spiritual integrity, faith and moral strength, who wish to help their brother Timothy are advised to send their donations by check or money order with Dr. Timothy Leary as payee to the following address: HORACE MASTRONARDI, ATT. AT LAW; BERNE SWITZERLAND

While in Switzerland, Timothy and Rosemary separated and soon after he met British socialite Joanna Harcourt-Smith. They instantly clicked and, according to Harcourt-Smith, consumed acid every day for forty days straight.[5] Joanna and Tim were traveling together when they were apprehended in Kabul, Afghanistan and forced back to the United States on January 13, 1973.[6] Leary's adventures as a fugitive from the law, living with the Panthers, his time in Switzerland, and associations with drug dealers and socialites while under constant fear of surveillance appeared to be ripped from the pages of a crime novel. It ended in similarly dramatic fashion, as reported on the front-page spread of the *L.A. Free Press* with the headline "The Capture of Tim Leary," with Harcourt-Smith offering details on their "illegal kidnapping" by the United States government, given that there was no extradition treaty between America and Afghanistan at the time.[7]

While Joanna publicly admonished the treatment of herself and Timothy, questions surfaced regarding her true role in successive events. Given the conspiracy theories of the day, some even suspected Joanna of being a spy with the mission of handing over Leary and other countercultural figures to the authorities.[8]

The fallout of the political and radical acts of the 1960s would help feed the paranoia of the 1970s. After President Nixon's Watergate scandal, and the public revelation of the CIA spying on dissident students from the Kennedy administration onward,[9] the veil had been lifted on covert government actions. Like Leary and Harcourt-Smith, individuals and groups involved in the counterculture would become riddled with suspicion and conspiracy theories. Leary's entanglement with the Panthers, Weathermen, Brotherhood of Eternal Love, and other drug manufacturers and dealers made several of his associates immediate suspects as narcs or informers. Although suspicion had begun since his dramatic return from Kabul, counterculture infighting and paranoia was justified considering the lives at stake.

After returning to America, Leary stood trial for his marijuana charges and prison escape and was reincarcerated at Folsom Prison in 1973. While in prison, he wrote *Starseed: Transmitted from Folsom Prison* (1973) regarding the Comet Kohoutek. The arrival of the comet triggered celebrations and anticipation of potentially apocalyptic change beginning in January 1974. Fundraisers were coupled with the Comet Kohoutek phenomenon. Yet, the comet's approach was anticlimactic, without much of a visual display.[10] Leary had for some time been fascinated by

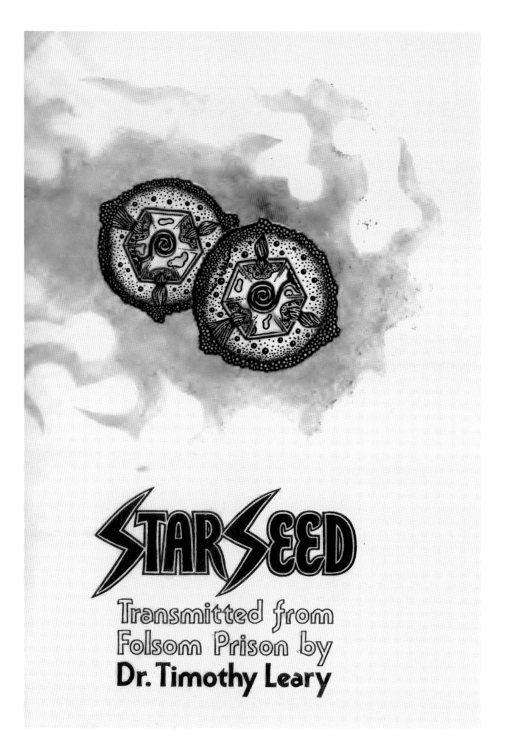

Above: The front cover of Leary's 1973 *Starseed* book,
designed by Timothy Leary and Dana M. Reemes.

space exploration and the idea of life beyond Earth, seeing the galaxy as a wider consciousness whose power, if it could be channeled, was potentially limitless.

After Leary was reincarcerated, Harcourt-Smith ran the Starseed Information Center and publishing business on his behalf. As with the Timothy Leary Defense Fund, Starseed served as the central operations for Leary's legal defense, issuing press releases, initiating letter-writing campaigns, and sponsoring fundraising events in the form of concerts and film screenings. A Starseed "Bulletin" issued in 1974 offered a status update on Leary's case:

> One year and three weeks ago Dr. Timothy Leary and Joanna Leary[11] were kidnapped and abducted by American narcotics agents from Kabul Airport in Afghanistan. This was in blatant violation of international law, since both Dr. Leary and Joanna held valid passports and traveling documents, and because there is no extradition treaty between the United States and Afghanistan.
>
> Dr. Leary is now serving a sentence of six months to ten years for possession of .001 grams of marijuana, and a six-month to five-year consecutive sentence for nonviolent escape. These sentences were pronounced consecutive by the Southern California judge presiding over the escape trial because of the twenty-nine-count indictment issued against Dr. Leary which demanded bail of five million dollars. Having served its purpose—to intimidate foreign governments into thinking of Dr. Leary as a dangerous criminal and to eliminate chances of asylum abroad—the prosecution in Orange County, California, a few months after his capture, dropped the entire twenty-nine counts.
>
> The charges outstanding against Dr. Leary in Millbrook, New York have also been dropped. Pending since 1966, these charges were the twisted machinations of the then assistant District Attorney of Poughkeepsie, G. Gordon Liddy, Watergate conspirator and burglar who, five days after Dr. Leary's return to the U.S., was himself thrown into jail. . . .

Starseed produced the documentary *At Folsom Prison with Dr. Timothy Leary* in 1973 to raise awareness about Leary's cause.

Starseed also sponsored several fundraising events on behalf of Leary which often included a combination of screening the documentary, speeches from members of the countercultural elite who were close to Leary, such as Allen Ginsberg and Ken Kesey, and musical rock concerts. Two tribute concerts were held at Zellerbach Auditorium at University of California, Berkeley. On March 10, 1974, musical group Man performed, opening for British psychedelic band Hawkwind. Leary had another surprising hand in the history of rock music. While still a fugitive in Switzerland in 1972, he had recorded an album, *Seven Up*, with psychedelic "Krautrock" band Ash Ra Tempel, which was released while he was in prison. Indeed, many musicians and music industry–types supported his cause, including Scott Piering, who went on to be a music publicist for popular British bands, such as The Smiths, Pulp, and Stereophonics.

At another event held on May 4, 1974, Sean McCarthy, a congressional candidate for Marin County, California spoke, along with music by Quazar. One event combined the Comet Kohoutek celebration, music by the J. R. Weitz band, and screenings of the Folsom documentary and the film *Rainbow Bridge*. The film, an encapsulation of the time, featured a New Age gathering at the "Rainbow Bridge Occult Center in Maui" with a performance by Jimi Hendrix.

While in prison, Leary also wrote *Terra II: The Starseed Transmissions* (1974), recording the transmissions received by his prison mate Lynn Wayne Benner regarding the evolution or migration of humankind from Terra I (Earth) to Terra II (space colony). This was a continuation of Leary's interest in space travel and human evolution, and a follow-up to the first *Starseed* book (1973). Dana M. Reemes shared his experience of designing the cover art for the *Starseed* booklet:

Michael Horowitz told me that Tim had written this short "Star Seed" thing and had an idea for the cover. I thought the project was a little silly, but was always happy to help. It seemed to me at the time that the whole message from space thing and Leary's subsequent ideas that we should all leave the planet were just the wishful daydreams of a man driven a little nuts by being incarcerated, and were really not very meaningful for anyone else. Leary had apparently read some then recent article about electron microscope studies of fragments of a meteorite believed to have originated from Mars. The fragments seemed to have traces of organic compounds formed when Mars still had an ocean and, more importantly, features that appeared to be fossilized remains of something like the epithelial cells found in simple organisms such as sponges. Leary made a simple sketch of two cells from this source, adding "Star Seed" lettering with a zigzag capital S like a lightning bolt—sort of "Buck Rogers" style. This original sketch was a very simple affair that I don't recall well, but was executed in pencil or (more probably) blue ballpoint on some simple scrap of paper like a napkin or the back of a small envelope. The image was significant to Leary because he thought that the Martian meteorite was evidence for the "panspermia" theory that life had been "seeded" on the planet from outer space. This was tied in with his prison escapist fantasies: since we were all originally from outer space, it was our destiny to return to outer space, Terra II, etc. I thought the idea was fun but ridiculous, and essentially irrelevant to the key insights of the psychedelic experience. Even if the Martian meteorite evidence was true (which is likely), it only meant that life had developed on Mars as well as Earth. There was, moreover, no way that such dead fossils could have have produced life here, and the whole "panspermia" hypothesis—even if true—just kicks the can down the road (though back in time rather than forward) about the origin of life in the universe and answers nothing. If life could originate somewhere else, then why not here?

Based on the original Leary sketch, I worked up final artwork for the Level Press booklet in india ink on a sheet of bristol board. I did the lettering "Star Seed: Transmitted from Folsom Prison by Timothy Leary" entirely by hand. Around the two cells I added the stylized "comet" flames in halftone. They wrap around to the back cover where they trail to a point. My inspiration for the flames was taken from the flaming nimbus seen around some tantric deities of Tibet and Japan. The flames were executed with a so-called "Ben Day"–type halftone sheet which was placed over the ink drawing, and then cut away with an X-acto knife. This was a standard graphic art technique of the time, but the "dot per inch" count of the halftone sheet I used was a little too fine for the somewhat amateurish printing technique of Level Press,

Up to 25 years in prison for 4 joints and 1 escape?

SEE

hear
feel
smell and
taste your freedom

Allen Ginsberg, Barry Melton, Michael McClure and the Sufi Choir

8 pm, Thurs. May 31, 555 Chestnut (Telegraph Hill Neighborhood Assoc.), $2. a benefit for Dr. Timothy Leary
A post Watergate appreciation of the persecuted visionary scientist—now held in Folsom Prison.

S.U.P.I.R.B. and STARSEED present

A TRIBUTE TO DR. TIMOTHY LEARY

featuring space rock live from England

HAWKWIND

plus special guests

in a five hour program including
TIMOTHY LEARY FILM and speaker JOANNA LEARY
SUNDAY, MARCH 10, 8:00 PM
ZELLERBACH AUDITORIUM,
U.C. BERKELEY
RESERVED SEATS: $3.00, $4.00 and $5.00

LOCATIONS: WALNUT CREEK: CIVIC ARTS BOX OFFICE; SAN RAFAEL: HOLIDAY BOX OFFICE; OAKLAND: MACARTHUR/BROADWAY BOX OFFICE AND NEIL THRAMS; STANFORD: TRESSIDER BOX OFFICE; SAN FRANCIS- CO: DOWNTOWN CENTER BOX OFFICE, SHERMAN CLAY BOX OFFICE, AND ALL MACY'S; BERKELEY: ASUC BOX OFFICE; SAN JOSE: SAN JOSE BOX OFFICE; OTHER UC CAMPUS BOX OFFICES: U.C. DAVIS; U.C. SAN FRANCISCO MEDICAL CENTER (MILBERRY UNION B.O.); U.C. SANTA CRUZ; AND AT ZELLERBACH HALL ON THE EVENING OF THE PERFORMANCE.

Top: Poster advertising a benefit for Timothy Leary, who is facing twenty-five years in prison. Performers include the poet Michael McClure.

Bottom: Advertisement for Starseed sponsored event. Psychedelic rock band Hawkwind was the headliner, along with a screening of Leary's Folsom Prison documentary and words from Joanna Leary (aka Harcourt-Smith).

Opposite: Starseed benefit poster featuring band Quazar, Berkeley, California, May 4, 1974.

STARSEED | THE ONE WORLD FAMILY

PRESENT

A Tribute To

DR. TIMOTHY LEARY

- **FILMS:** "At Folsom Prison with Dr. Timothy Leary"; "The Dancing Fools", showing Tim and friends in his Swiss exile
- **SPEAKERS:** Joanna Leary; Marin County congressional candidate Sean McCarthy
- **MUSIC:** The One World Family's "Quazar"

Time: Saturday, May 4, 8:00 p.m.
Place: O.W.F. Center, 2455 Telegraph at Haste, Berkeley
Admission: $2.50; for more info call 788-7180 or 848-9613
All proceeds go to the effort to free Tim Leary from prison

Above: An early Starseed fundraising music and comet event, November 18, 1973.

resulting in some drop out as you can see. It was disappointing to me, as the reproduction didn't quite do justice to the original art.

A few years prior, Leary had been visited in the California Medical Facility in Vacaville, California (before his escape) by astronomers Carl Sagan and Frank Drake after writing to them about his ideas on space colonization.[12] Known for the "Drake equation" used to determine the number of advanced civilizations in our galaxy, and the establishment of SETI (Search for Extraterrestrial Intelligence); he was a natural ally in Leary's mind. Although Drake proved pessimistic of such a venture, Leary was undeterred. When he found himself back in jail in 1973, his motivation to find "a way out" led to the publication of the Starseed books. He would seek further avenues for these ideas through the underground press, meeting with Ken Babbs and Ken Kesey in prison to discuss articles for the journal *Spit in the Ocean*. In an interview for this book, Babbs recalled their visit:

> We didn't see Leary again until the 1970s when we were doing our little magazine, *Spit in the Ocean*, which had a different editor for each issue, and we got Tim to do one, called "The Search for Higher Intelligence." Tim had been arrested by then and was in jail so we did all our communication with him through the mail until just before the issue was done. Kesey and I drove to San Diego and visited him in the Federal Prison. The prison was an ordinary high-rise building downtown, ordinary until you went in the front door and from there through thick steel doors with multitudinous locks. We met Leary on one of the upper floors in a sparse room with a table and chairs, an open door to the corridor, no guards around. We talked about the issue of the magazine and what still needed to be done and some editing things when suddenly Tim jumped up and went to the door and exchanged fist bumps and soul shakes with a big rusty five-o'clock-shadow-faced guy. Tim came back in and said, "That's so and so, he's in for murder, we play handball together."[13]

Meanwhile, Joanna Leary announced in a press release issued on February 20, 1974:

We are quickly building up a group of people who are contributing energy to Starseed in various forms, and we are happy that you are part of the molecular bond.

The purpose of this message is to announce an exciting venture that we are undertaking at this point in our evolution. At this halfway point in the life of our solar system it is time for humanity to accept its genetic mission. We suggest that life on the planet exists in an embryonic state. Life is programmed to be born; it is time for life to eject itself from the planet-worb and return home.[14]

Space travel was becoming a popular topic by 1974. Berkeley jazz group The Sun Ra Arkestra released the influential "afrofuturist" film, *Space Is the Place*; friend John C. Lilly claimed to have made contact with extraterrestrials through his use of ketamine;[15] and Carl Sagan was literally broadcasting messages to outer space using the Arecibo radio telescope. It seemed logical to assume space colonization would be imminent. As a prisoner, Leary naturally reflected on how to escape the confines of prison, if not physically, then mentally. This was to mark Leary's latest venture that would see him explore the idea of mind expansion from an entirely different perspective.

Sagan would visit Leary again and sent him a letter in February 1974 regarding his thoughts on space travel in which Sagan expresses how much he enjoyed Leary's idea in *TERRA II* of a "transgalactic gardening club" and discusses the viability of traveling to Mars.

For those who wanted to help Leary get out of prison but did not necessarily embrace the Starseed operation, efforts included the distribution of literature by Michael Horowitz and Robert Barker—Leary's archivists from 1970. Echoing the *Declaration of Independence for Dr. Timothy Leary July 4, 1971* petition to the Swiss government organized previously by Allen Ginsberg, Horowitz sought tributes from some of the same writers, once Leary found himself back in prison, to be presented in a "Festschrift for Timothy Leary."[16] Both projects posited Leary as a political prisoner persecuted for his ideas and writings. One of the writers asked to contribute was friend and mentor Marshall McLuhan:

FROM MARSHALL MCLUHAN TO MICHAEL HOROWITZ | JUNE 18, 1974

Dear Dr. Horowitz, How about Tim as the Ulysses of the inner trip? Or the Homer of the electric age? Electric technology, by virtue of its immediate relation to our nervous system, is itself a sort of inner trip, with drugs playing the role of subplot or alternate mode. It may well appear a few years hence that the panic about psychedelic drugs relates less to the chemistry than to the hidden terrors which people feel in the presence of electric technology. It was the same with the onset of the radio age in the twenties which inspired a booze panic.

Acoustic men are inclined to be alcohol addictive . . . that is, all preliterate societies, and also the post-literate, ourselves. It was in the TV Guide for September 15, 1973 that an article appeared, explaining the experimental discovery of the addictive character of TV as medium. Nothing to do with programs. Tim may be a martyr of this hidden addictive power of TV. Tony Schwartz in The Responsive Chord (Doubleday, Anchor book, 1973) points out that "TV uses the eye as an ear."

Best wishes, Marshall McLuhan

While the Festschrift did come to fruition, Horowitz published the booklet *Apologia for Timothy Leary: With a Selected Bibliography* in 1974, modeled after John Dee's *A Letter Containing a Most Brief Discourse Apologetical* (1599). Horowitz and his associates John James, Carol Tickner, Dana Reemes, Chip Roberts, Cindy Palmer, and Robert Barker, hoped such a work would help publicize Leary's legal struggle and improve his image.[17]

Although McLuhan died six years after writing this letter, his influence had a continued impact on Leary, the counterculture, and society in general. His insight into the effect and importance of media divorced of content, led to the concept of the "generation gap" still with us today. After his death, McLuhan's theories became even more influential with the rapid technological advances in personal computing and, eventually, the Internet.[18]

10
From the Counterculture to Cyberspace, 1976–95

"The PC is the LSD of the 1990s."

Timothy Leary, *Chaos & Cyber Culture*

TIMOTHY LEARY'S LEGAL TROUBLES came to an end once he was pardoned by Governor Jerry Brown[1] and released on parole from prison on April 21, 1976.[2] Yet controversies surrounding Leary and Joanna Harcourt-Smith didn't end with his release, but only sparked additional questions and accusations of duplicity and betrayal. John Bryan, founder of the San Franciscan *Open City Press* and former managing editor of the *Los Angeles Free Press*, published an account of Leary's life in a four-part series in the *Berkeley Barb*, from December 1976 to 1977, and in the 1980 book *Whatever Happened To Timothy Leary?*, exposing what many had believed: Leary was an FBI informant. This accusation was later corroborated with the release of FBI documents, but his testimony proved harmless to his friends and associates.[3]

In a letter to Michael Horowitz,[4] Leary lamented the situation in which he found himself:

> Michael, let me tell you a secret. I'm just beginning. I've just in the last year wised up. Learned how. Cut through the calculated stupidity and fear. Oh yes, Michael, the fear … FEAR. All the lonely frightened people. I had to carry the fear of so many millions etc. Sometimes I get caught up in the fears. Michael, I have no fear. That was never a problem, but now I have no fear of other people's fears. Truth. Truth. Truth. None of the people you mention on the back page have any interest in me or what we're doing. Most of them used me, used the times, used the hopes. None of them is going to let the game get a centimeter larger than their own larval little thing. None of them have any interest in

the future, have no idea about the future, and are dead-set, instinctively against anything that might free, even a few, from the past.

While Leary reacted to the backlash from his experience with federal authorities, he left prison nevertheless and was free to immerse himself not only in the underground, but the world at large. After parting ways with Harcourt-Smith, Leary took up residence in Los Angeles and continued his work writing, lecturing, and collaborating with artists and counterculture figures. He married Barbara Chase in 1978, adopting and raising her son, Zachary, as his own. Leary maintained his old friendships and formed new alliances.

Ironically, Leary reunited with G. Gordon Liddy—the prosecutor for Dutchess County in 1966 who had authorized the raids on the Millbrook estate occupied by Leary and the Castalia Foundation—for staged theatrical "debates." Liddy's career had taken a wrong turn after he had become embroiled in the Watergate scandal in 1972 during the Nixon administration. Liddy was one of the five who broke into the headquarters of the Democratic National Committee office. Coincidentally, Liddy and Leary met again while incarcerated at the same prison in California. After their release from prison, they reconnected in 1981 and agreed to engage in a public debate together. The irony of Leary and Liddy on stage proved popular, and they took their debate on tour, which was filmed as a documentary, *Return Engagement* (1983).[5]

Although Leary took on new roles and was a natural performer, his values in the pursuit of free expression remained unchanged. Leary and his cohort had a long history of shunning rules governing social mores and personal expression. After serving jail time for marijuana possession, it is not surprising that Leary and his acquaintances held Libertarian views. As previously mentioned, Robert Anton Wilson interviewed Leary regarding his views towards religious freedom and drug use in 1966.

In a letter to Leary, dated July 6, 1977, Robert Anton Wilson writes about heading to the Libertarian Convention—along with requesting permission to use his quotes in *Cosmic Trigger* (1977):

FROM ROBERT ANTON WILSON TO TIMOTHY LEARY | JULY 6, 1977

Dear Tim, Thanks for the GLORIOUS introduction!!!

Pocket Books wants me to get a letter from you saying that you give permission to use one of the quotes from your books, letters and conversations in *Cosmic Trigger.*

I'll be seeing you at the Libertarian Convention next week—and don't forget that you are scheduled for Dr. Steve Langer's radio show on Thursday, July 14 at one p.m.

Looking forward to seeing you, and thanks again for the introduction, Bob W.

Leary embraced the Libertarian political party. During the 1980s, First Lady Nancy Reagan promoted the "Just Say No" program to discourage recreational drug use. Leary responded with "Just Say Know" and went on to develop his KnoWare software, elevating knowledge over the stifling of personal freedoms, with partners and personal friends Vicki Marshall and Ron Lawrence.[6]

Leary continued to dabble in politics and was a supporter of 1988 Libertarian presidential nominee Ron Paul, hosting a fundraiser for his campaign. A floppy disk and sleeve doubled as an invitation with the text "If you're wise, digitize!" This floppy disk in many ways represented the coalescence of the counterculture, Leary's life experiences, and his advocacy of the personal computer and the power of the individual. Paul's bid was unsuccessful and the Republican nominee, George H. W. Bush was elected President.

The natural progressions of Leary's interests followed from consciousness exploration in the 1960s and space exploration in the 1970s, to the advent of personal computers and cyberspace exploration in the 1980s and '90s. This included the conceptualizing and development of computer games and programs, such as his first commercial software, "Mind Mirror" (1985), released by Electronic Arts. Adapted from his work on personality metrics developed at the beginning of his career, he came full circle and applied the same principles to this computer program. Marketed as a self-help tool, the software claimed to provide a sort of electronic psychoanalysis for the user.[7] He engaged in additional software development under the auspices of his new company Futique, meaning "the opposite of antique."[8] The advert for the software was typically Learyesque:

AMERICA 1984.

YOU'VE COME
A LONG WAY...
MAYBE.

ISLAND ALIVE presents a film by ALAN RUDOLPH

"A FASCINATING CONFRONTATION OF EXTREMES."

TIMOTHY LEARY   G. GORDON LIDDY
An ALIVE ENTERPRISES PRODUCTION "RETURN ENGAGEMENT"
Music by ADRIAN BELEW Photography by JAN KIESSER Edited by TOM WALLS
Produced by CAROLYN PFEIFFER Directed by ALAN RUDOLPH
ISLAND ALIVE in association with *new cinema*

Page 230: Leary quickly became one of the most enthusiastic proponents of the cyberdelic revolution.

Above: Reunited almost twenty years after G. Gordon Liddy raided Leary's Millbrook for drugs, the two found success and humor in taking their rivalry on tour in a series of debate performances.

If you're wise . . .

Above and opposite: The sleeve that held a floppy disk,
which formed part of the invitation to fundraiser
hosted by Leary, supporting Ron Paul as the Libertarian
Party candidate for the 1988 U.S. presidential election.

Digitize!

THINK FOR YOURSELF

"...take as your life goal the task of improving your thinking."
Dr. Timothy Leary

Upon reflection, most people would agree that the ultimate organ of pleasure, creativity, growth, and human contact is the MIND. The human brain comprises over 100 billion neurons, each with the information processing capacities of a microcomputer. This staggering array of idea-power is programmed by the MIND. Why not think of the MIND as the software which boots up and organizes that awesome main-frame that pulses behind your forehead?

But who programs our MINDS? Apparently we don't. Our minds are conditioned during our development by stimuli which are beyond our control. We choose neither the time, the environment nor the personnel of our birth and childhood. Consequently, many of our thoughts, conceptions and stereotypes, once formed, are rarely revised, even though they represent the very foundation of our perception of the universe.

MIND MIRROR is an interactive game of psychology designed to explore the thinking process and help understand or replace the vague ideas and concepts we carry around in our head. It is written by Dr. Timothy Leary and published by Electronic Arts. It is a "thought qualifying" device which allows you to "microscope" any thought in your mind into elements, plot these elements on MINDMAPS, reconstruct gamefilms of your life, compare your thoughts with those of others, and construct mind models of persons and places. It is interactive HEADWARE for the computer generation, and like Scruples or Trivial Pursuit, can be a fun and rewarding group experience.

The aim of the program is to use your MIND to make you laugh, cry, blush, giggle, create, remember, reflect ... but most of all to encourage and empower you to: THINK FOR YOURSELF

SKIPI, an acronym used for both Super Knowledge Information Processing Intelligence and Super Knowledge Information Processing Interface, was conceived to be the underlying engine for Leary's various software projects. In a draft of "SKIPI: The Personal Operating System"

Leary explained:

> The promise of the personal computer has yet to be fulfilled. Today's microcomputers are used as individual tools for business, education, recreation, but they are not truly personal.
>
> Computers should be tools for personal awareness, personal knowledge and personal improvement. Computers should be personal companions, advisers, friends. Computers should understand your personality as well as they understand BASIC [Beginner's All-purpose Symbolic Instruction Code]. They should do this now and they can. . . .
>
> The missing link in the chain of personal computer evolution/revolution has been the personal operating system. Today's machine operating systems have brought standardization to useful computer functions, but the most important computer functions—in truly personal software—have lacked the method for coding essential human characteristics. A personal computer can and should respond to your personality given the proper coding.
>
> SKIPI (Super Knowledge Information Processing Interface) is the first personal operating system. It creates an electronic database of essential personal characteristics. This information can then be accessed by personal applications programs in realms as varied as psychological therapy, self-help, education, and interactive fiction. . . .
>
> SKIPI can also stand alone as one of the most accurate personality profile tests available anywhere. It guides you through a series of questions and then translates the answers into visual representations of your personality traits on psychographs—easily read bull's-eye graph. The SKIPI program records 124 "memes," the essential codes of human behavior. During your initial session with SKIPI you will learn as much about yourself as SKIPI learns about you. You can always go back and retest yourself, updating SKIPI's personality data base at the same time.
>
> SKIPI is based on the research of Dr. Timothy Leary. In 1950, as the director of a Kaiser Foundation psychological research project, he developed one of the first computerized mathematical profiles for the interpersonal assessment of personality. Based on [a] series of binary

questions, the test provided data to be batch processed on a mainframe computer, yielding profiles and indices to be used by patients in the project. Delays caused by batch processing robbed this material of its immediacy. The real-time interactivity sought by Dr. Leary would have to await the advent of microcomputers.[9]

Leary's interest in psychological imprinting and behavior change expressed here paralleled that of neurophysiologist John C. Lilly, an advocate for reprogramming the brain. The term "human biocomputer" was coined by Lilly, referring to the systems in human anatomy, as described in his book, *Programming and Metaprogramming in the Human Biocomputer: Theory and Experiments* (1968). Yet, he is best known for the invention of the sensory-deprivation (isolation) tank (1954) and his work studying dolphin communication using LSD. He founded the Communication Research Institute around 1959[10] on St. Thomas in the United States Virgin Islands. Gerald Heard, a long-term friend of Leary and experimenter with psychedelics, makes reference to a visit to the Virgin Islands to "witness John Lilly [fraternizing] porpoise wise" in a letter to Leary on January 2, 1962:

FROM GERALD HEARD TO TIMOTHY LEARY | JANUARY 2, 1962

Dear Tim, Thank you indeed for card, endorsed with valuable news items. Delighted you have now a colleague in, or domus intentionalis. So there [is] still a life you might circuit as far as this extreme sector of the English speaking elapse? We want to get over to you sometime before the summer empties your lives, for your invitation is a top priority one. We take a swoop up to San Fran next week [route?] back after 4 days touch back here and then somersault into the Virgin Isles where we hope to witness John Lilly [fraternizing?] porpoise wise but any how, [J. M.?] B will be able to get down to [ref? condensely] on the third version of "Journey into Consciousness" which has now been injected the Bollingen Scholarship For Ages of Man will be there 4 or 5 weeks, when back here. Michael has love.

Bless you, Gerald

Above: One of many documents among Leary's
personal papers regarding his failed Neuromancer
project, c. 1986–87.

Lilly's writings and theories turned decidedly more fringe in the 1970s after experimenting with ketamine. Under the influence, he claimed to have communicated with extraterrestrial entities to stage coincidences, dubbed the "Earth Coincidence Control Office" or ECCO.[11] Lilly's work inspired the Academy Award–winning screenwriter Paddy Chayefsky to write the novel *Altered States* (1978) based on Lilly's psychedelic research with isolation tanks. Chayefsky's 1980 film adaptation starred William Hurt and Blair Brown; it received two Academy Award nominations for best score and sound. More recently, the science fiction television program, *Stranger Things* (2016)—starring Leary's goddaughter Winona Ryder—featured an isolation tank as a means for mind travel to another dimension.

Like Leary, Lilly's unconventional research methods would alienate him from the scientific community, but his quest in consciousness expansion would inspire artists and writers to introduce his work and life story to a larger audience.

In 1983, Leary published his autobiography, *Flashbacks*. The following year, William Gibson published his award-winning cyberpunk novel *Neuromancer* (1984), popularizing the term "cyberspace." Leary was enthralled and initiated a project to develop software based on the novel. It would be titled, "Neuromancer: An Electronic Mind Movie," created in collaboration with authors William Gibson, William S. Burroughs, and artist Keith Haring, and featuring music by new wave band Devo.[12] After making acquaintance with the band Devo, Leary's son, Zach, appeared on the cover of their 1984 album *Shout*. Musician David Byrne was also slated to play a character in this software program.[13]

Although this iteration of the project did not materialize, an adventure game based on the *Neuromancer* plot was successfully developed by Interplay Productions and released in 1988. Leary's archive contains correspondence and proposals between early gaming developers such as Interplay and EA, reflecting his interest and influence in virtual reality and cyberspace.

While living in Los Angeles, Leary surrounded himself with creatives and others from the counterculture scene, such as *Spin* magazine founder Bob Guccione, Jr., British film director Tony Scott, American actor Cheech Marin, Danny Sugarman (former manager of The Doors),

American filmmaker Spike Jonze, and American actress Winona Ryder. Long-term family friend and Ryder's father, Michael Horowitz was Leary's archivist and bibliographer. He first took custody of Leary's manuscripts and records in 1970 while Leary was living as a fugitive. This same year, Horowitz, along with his wife Cynthia Palmer, William Dailey, and Robert Baker, established a library consisting of psychedelic drug-related literature named, The Fitz Hugh Ludlow Memorial Library. With extensive knowledge of the writings of Leary, Horowitz cowrote *An Annotated Bibliography of Timothy Leary* (1988) with Karen Walls, Billy Smith, and Allen Ginsberg. Horowitz also edited *Chaos & Cyberculture* (1994), a collection of essays and interviews by Leary that featured counterculture figures, such as William S. Burroughs, David Byrne, William Gibson, Keith Haring, and Winona Ryder. The premise underlying each piece touched on the counterculture's embrace of technology, and Leary's theories within the cyberdelic continuum.

Into the 1990s, Leary and the counterculture continued to influence the upcoming Generation X, as seen by his contributions to magazine *Mondo 2000* (1989–98) and the book *Chaos & Cyberculture*. Leary understood the trajectory of electronic "transmissions" and interconnected virtual realities. He turned his own home and life into an Internet experiment with the creation of his website leary.com in 1993 with the help of web developers Joey Cavella and Chris Graves. Developed out of an earlier concept in simulated living, "Wonderland Park,"[14] his website would allow users to navigate through different virtual "rooms" in his home to access digitized items from his archive or publications.[15] This would be the culmination of his life's work and, for many, gave credence to the notion that the use of mind-expanding drugs and the counterculture helped to make the Internet possible.[16] Meanwhile, *Chaos & Cyberculture* was in many ways a tribute to the way in which his work threaded through the counterculture, addressing concepts such as artificial intelligence, cryonics, and the freedom that people would gain from personal computers and, ultimately, the Internet.

In the chapter on "How to Boot up your Bio-computer," Leary wrote about how the counterculture and psychedelics made personal computers and technological advances possible and could lead the way to new methods of programming the mind:

In 1976, the Apple computer was introduced. At the same time video games provided young people with a hands-on experience of moving flashy electronic, digital information around on screens. It was no accident that many of the early designers and marketers of these electronic appliances lived in the San Francisco area and tended to be intelligent adepts in the use of psychedelic drugs. . . . They could handle accelerated thought-processing, multilevel realities, instantaneous chains of digital logic. . . . Once again, external engineered tools helped us understand inner function. If the brain is viewed as bio-hardware, and psychedelic drugs become "neurotransmitters," and if you can reprogram your mind, for better or for worse, by "turning on," then new concepts and techniques of instantaneous psychological change become possible.[17]

Leary was a frequent contributor to *Mondo 2000*, a full-color glossy, extra-large cyberpunk magazine edited by Ken Goffman, aka R.U. Sirius. Sirius also coauthored Leary's last book, published posthumously, *Design for Dying* (1998). In the sixth issue of *Mondo* in 1991, Leary interviewed David Byrne, founding member of the art rock band Talking Heads, and wrote about his contributions to the art book *Reproduced Authentic*.[18] The premise for *Reproduced Authentic* involved Byrne, Barbara Kruger, and three other artists faxing images of their artwork via telephone lines from New York to Tokyo. A fax machine enthusiast himself, Leary reveled in the idea of transmitting content using technology. A friend and fan of Marshall "the medium is the message"[19] McLuhan, Leary was perfectly cast to report on this project and the ideas arising from it: the concept of "originality," the value of art, and the potential transformation and appropriation of it in electronic media. The transmissions resulted in the exhibition, curated by Joseph Kusuth, that was held at the opening of Barneys New York in Tokyo, Japan on November 3–16, 1990.

Leary's ideas regarding personal freedom and the progression from mind expansion to the Internet were encapsulated in his book *Surfing the Conscious Nets: A Graphic Novel by Huck Getty Mellon von Schlebrugge* (1995). Cyberdelic graphics were supplied by Howard Hallis and included illustrations by underground American cartoonist Robert Williams. The novel was set in a chatroom with Dr. Leary, covering sexual, drug, and cyberspace-related topics. The graphic nature of Williams's work combined with the content of the "chat," demonstrated Leary's vision of the Internet as a forum for free expression by the counterculture. In retrospect, the countercultural contributions to technology in personal computing, the Internet, and virtual reality reflect Leary and his colleagues' break from conventional thought to free the mind and imagine the world as an interconnected "web." Although Leary had always been associated with LSD and the 1960s, his insights would only really come into their own much later and would place him as one of the futurists born of the counterculture.

June 30, 1995

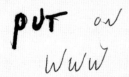

go down to electricity

HOW HAVE COMPUTERS EMPOWERED HUMANS?

By Timothy Leary

Homo Sapiens— "the species of bipedal primates...characterized by a brain capacity averaging 1400 cc (85 cubic inches) and by dependency on language and the creation and utilization of complex tools."

Random House Dictionary, 1987

NEW MEDIA CREATE NEW SPECIES

Species are defined in terms of varied characteristics usually including anatomy, means of locomotion & survival techniques.

It is interesting that **Random House** defines Human Species in terms of our enormous brains, our tool-making and language skills.

Indeed, the evolution of our species is often traced in terms of the language tools constructed and used at each stage.

THE MEDIUM IS THE MESSAGE

Medium: A surrounding substance in which a specific organism lives and thrives...also called "Culture"; A specific type of artistic technique or means of expression as determined by the materials used or the creative methods involved.
American Heritage Dictionary, 1975.

In McLuhanite terms, **Media** refers to the agencies used by **the Brain** to communicate and to fabricate the cultural realities which humans inhabit.

McLuhan's legendary, enigmatic epigram implies: that:

The materials, vocabularies, grammatical forms, methods, contexts ,

Above: Annotated by Leary late in life, with his instructions to "put on www" and aptly contains Marshall McLuhan quote.

REPRODUCED AUTHENTIC

by [signature]
12-28-91

"Reproduced Authentic" is a magnificently cloth-bound art-book containing five paintings by David Byrne and four other artists which were converted to 8 1/2" x 11" images transmitted from New York to Tokyo via telephone line by facsimile. They were exhibited at GALERIE VIA EIGHT.

possessive; feudal- reactionary

I consider this apparent oxymoron, "Reproduced Authentic" to be the most fascinating-controversial-liberating issue confronting us as we move from the solid materialism of the industrial stage to the relativity of electronic stage. Now that Newton's Laws *have* become local ordinances, the clunky, static art treasures of wood, marble, canvas, steel become crumbling relics, their value insanely enhanced by rarity. These archeological museum-pieces become commodities huckstered at Southeby auctions and guarded by armed guards in vault-like galleries.

curiosities

a shit

According to German philosopher, Walter Benjamin, "The authenticitiy of a thing is the essence of all that is transmissible from its beginning ranging from its substantive duration...to the history which it has eperienced." Rarity .."now is a ...mask of art's potential for meaning ...and no longer constitues the criterion of authenticity....Art's meaning then becomes socially (and politically) formed by the living."

Thus the wretched caste-class chauvinisms of Feudal and Industrial cultures which prized "rarity". Thus the $50 million market for canvases which the unauthentic painter van Gough could not exchange for a meal *to save his life and sanity.* To the Feudal aristocrat as well as the Manhattan Art Critic "authentic" means a "rare original" which is traded by gallery owners and monopolized by owners.

liberating, egalitarian, thrilling

This notion of "reproduced authentic" is the application of quantum dynamics and Einsteinian relativity to humanist communication. The implications are profound and timely.

[handwritten annotations at bottom, partly illegible]
authentic
this [...] of [...] artist is [...] any, -
the [...] of it this
→ the [...] are in [...].
then are the [...] owners and the [...]. This same [...] become active-

Epilogue

"You can always pick up your needle,
and move to another groove."

Timothy Leary (source unknown)

LEARY, LIKE MANY of his counterculture compatriots, had to find his own path to transition into the post-1960s world; some did so more successfully than others.

Aldous Huxley passed away on November 22, 1963, reportedly while under the influence of LSD.

Leary's research partner, Richard Alpert, certainly underwent dramatic changes. In 1971, he published a poetic meditation on spirituality, entitled *Be Here Now*, summarizing his transformation into Ram Dass under the guidance of his guru Neem Karoli Baba, and serving as a manual for "being" with guiding principles and resources. Ram Dass established the Hanuman Foundation in 1974 to further spiritual wellbeing in society through education, service, and spiritual training; publications and recordings; and to promote the study, practice, and teaching of spiritual knowledge.[1] Ram Dass continues to be a teacher and practitioner of "bhakti or devotional yoga focused on the Hindu deity Hanuman; Buddhist meditation in the Theravadin, Mahayana Tibetan, and Zen Buddhist schools, and Sufi and Jewish mystical studies."[2] Although their lives took very different paths, Leary and Ram Dass remained friends and reunited a few weeks before Leary passed away in 1996.[3]

Before Allen Ginsberg learned of his own terminal liver cancer, he was planning a trip to Italy, contemplating a newer Italian translation of "Howl," and visualizing a Milan apartment where he and Peter Orlovsky could cook.[4] A month later, on April 5, 1997, the year after Leary, he died from liver cancer in New York City. He was seventy years old. Peter Orlovsky died from lung cancer on May 30, 2010 at his home in Vermont. He was seventy-six.

Huston Smith edited the book *One Nation Under God: The Triumph of the Native American Church* (1995) detailing the United States Supreme Court case in 1990, which ruled peyote was not protected under the Constitution as a religious sacrament. In response, Smith engaged in a four-day peyote rite in Mexico at the age of seventy-five to better understand its usefulness. He helped to promote the American Indian Religious Freedom Act in 1994, legislation passed by Congress that overturned the 1990 Supreme Court's decision.[5] Smith passed away on December 30, 2016 at the age of ninety-seven.

Late in his life, William S. Burroughs returned to his Midwest roots; he was born and raised in St. Louis, Missouri. At the urging of his former lover and friend James Grauerholz, whom he met in New York City, Burroughs moved to Lawrence, Kansas in 1981, where he remained for the rest of his life. This was not a retirement, and he carried on creating works of art. Leary visited him at his home in 1987 and they continued to correspond throughout the rest of Leary's life. Burroughs also passed away the year after Leary, on August 2, 1997. He was eighty-three years old.

Ralph Metzner continues to study the medical and psycho-spiritual benefits of entheogens, authoring articles and books such as *Know Your Type* (1979) and in the 1980s was the Dean of the California Institute of Integral Studies, a private university founded in 1968 in San Francisco as a leading center for New Age approaches to personal growth. He has lectured extensively and was an active participant of MAPS, Multidisciplinary Association for Psychedelic Studies, founded in 1986 by Rick Doblin.

Timothy Leary was diagnosed with prostate cancer in 1995. Ralph Metzner wrote to him offering his help during Leary's last days:

FROM RALPH METZNER TO TIMOTHY LEARY | JANUARY 6, 1996

Dear Timothy, Years ago, I think in Zihuatanejo, or maybe Millbrook, when we were working on the *Tibetan Book of the Dead*, you and I promised each other that when the time came for one of us to die, the other would do the part of the Bardo guide, if possible.

I just wanted to let you know that I am willing to do that for you, if you would like me to. It would be an honor. So, if and when, you need me for that—just let me know, and I'll come immediately.

I can also facilitate a Huxley-type experience, if you like—but I imagine you might have all that prepared.

SEASON'S GREETINGS

all special bests
William

© 1989 William S. Burroughs

Page 248: Leary embraced life to the very end.

Top: Timothy Leary and William S. Burroughs on the porch of Burroughs's home in Lawrence, Kansas, 1987. Photographed by Philip Heying.

Bottom: A holiday postcard sent to Leary by Burroughs in 1989.

Opposite: Ram Dass. He and Leary remained close from their early days as Leary and Alpert to Leary's passing.

Ralph Metzner, Ph.D.
18210 Robin Ave.
Sonoma, CA 95476

WOW! LOVE

Timothy Leary
10106 Sunbrook Dr.
Beverly Hills, CA 90210

Fabulous!
my longest
term Pal!

"Mãe Natureza" Obra de Alexandre Segrégio, 1986.
Foto: Sérgio Polignano.

Top and bottom: Leary's notes during his last days,
expressing his love and gratitude for friend Ralph
Metzner, are scrawled on an envelope and the back of
a note from Metzner to Leary.

Anyway, please know I hold you in the highest regard and love,★ Ralph ★and I will always appreciate the role you played in my life.

Leary passed away on May 31 of that year.

What of Leary's afterlife? Organizations, such as Multidisciplinary Association for Psychedelic Studies (MAPS) and the Beckley Foundation, have been working to fund and promote research into psychedelic drugs. This research was suppressed in the United States for decades after the Controlled Substances Act of 1970. Many blame Leary. If he had not attracted so much media attention, would their research have been less alarming? If he had not become a spokesman or preached his message to "turn on" America, things may have turned out differently. Yet, would it be naïve to expect that Leary and all the others would not have undergone radical change after blowing their minds? Like Paul Lee's account of his first visit to San Francisco "he had witnessed the future." Is the CIA to blame for introducing LSD and unwittingly igniting the drug scene in the San Francisco Bay area? It could be that the youth movement would have been unstoppable and drug manufacturers like Owsley would have always been there to supply the demand. It could be that drugs (particularly psychedelics and marijuana) were only one element in the totality of the counterculture—albeit, a significant one.

With the aging of the baby boomer generation, attitudes towards drugs have become more liberal, leading to drug law reform. Unfortunately, Leary never saw medical marijuana legalized in California when enacted under Proposition 215 on November 5, 1996.

No one can argue that Timothy Leary didn't live a full life. He embodied the optimistic American archetype of pushing boundaries in consciousness expansion and personal freedom. Almost fifty years after being labeled "the most dangerous man in America," it is clear that he WAS dangerous . . . dangerous to the status quo establishment. Dangerous for trying to make the world a better place in his own way. He represented a change that many in society feared. Leary was both a participant and a guide. His life took on so many changes, involved a myriad of events—some on a global scale—and touched many people, both personally and publicly: as a professor, author, spokesman, activist, prisoner, fugitive, performer, celebrity, and futurist. His legacy will continue to be felt and examined for years to come.

After battling cancer, he died among his friends and family at his home in Los Angeles uttering his last word before leaving this world, "Beautiful."[6]

Endnotes

Introduction

1. Coined by Jack Weinberg. Writer, Charles Burress *Chronicle* Staff, "Free Speech Movement Turns 40/UC's Change of Heart—Celebrating Transformation of a Pariah into an Icon/ Weeklong Events Highlight Protesters' Campus-rights Fight," SFGate. n.p., n.d., accessed November 24, 2016.

2. Demonstrations reached a fever pitch beginning approximately in 1968 and into the '70s. For example, when students took over the Columbia and Harvard campuses in 1968, the Stonewall Riots in 1969, the Kent State shooting in 1970, and the Attica Prison riot of 1971.

3. As stated by President Richard Nixon, n.d.

4. Timothy Leary, Letter to Arthur Koestler, January 4, 1961, held in the Timothy Leary Papers, Manuscripts and Archives, New York Public Library. Astor, Lenox, and Tilden Foundations.

5. *Oxford English Dictionary*, s.v. "Psychedelic," accessed September 25, 2016, http://www.oed.com.

6. Albert Hofmann, *LSD, My Problem Child* (New York: McGraw-Hill, 1980), accessed September 25, 2016, http://www.psychedelic-library.org/child1.htm.

7. Omer Call Stewart, *Peyote Religion: A History*, 1st ed. (Norman: University of Oklahoma Press, 1987), 48–52.

8. Ibid., 53.

9. Wade Davis, *One River: Explorations and Discoveries in the Amazon Rain Forest* (New York: Touchstone, 1997), 61–63.

10. Schultes studied the peyote rites of the Kiowa in Oklahoma with Weston La Barre, author of the seminal book *The Peyote Cult* (1938).

11. @HeffterResearch. "About Dr. Heffter—Heffter." *Heffter.* n.p., n.d., accessed November 24, 2016, http://heffter.org.

12. George Plimpton, ed., *Beat Writers at Work: The Paris Review* (New York: The Modern Library, 1999), 217.

13. Interview with Jennifer Ulrich, September 25, 2016.

14. Janice Hopkins Tanne, "Humphry Osmond," *British Medical Journal* 328.7441 (2004): 713.

15. Ibid.

16. *Oxford English Dictionary*, s.v. "Psychedelic."

17. "(Henry) (Fitz) Gerald Heard," in Contemporary Authors Online (Detroit: Gale, 2003), accessed October 10, 2016, Gale Biography in Context.

18. Timothy Miller, "Notes on the Prehistory of the Human Potential Movement," in *On the Edge of the Future: Esalen and the Evolution of American Culture*, eds. Jeffrey J. Kripal and Glenn W. Shuck, (Bloomington & Indianapolis: Indiana University Press, 2005), 85.

19. Ibid.

20. Ibid., 80–81.

21. An existential form of psychology.

22. Una McGovern, ed., "MKUltra," in *Chambers Dictionary of the Unexplained*, (Chambers Harrap, 2007), accessed March 16, 2017, http://search.credoreference.com.

23. Subcommittee on Health and Scientific Research, Committee on Human Resources. Senate Select Committee on Intelligence. Senate Committee on Human Resources. Senate, *Project MKULTRA: The CIA's Program of Research in Behavioral Modification*, 95th Cong., 1st sess., August 3, 1977. Available from Proquest Congressional.

24. George Plimpton, ed., *Beat Writers at Work* (New York: Modern Library), 215.

25. Ram Dass, Andrew Weil, Allen Ginsberg, Winona Ryder, William Burroughs, Albert Hofmann, Aldous Huxley, Terence McKenna, Ken Kesey, Huston Smith, Hunter S. Thompson, *et al.*, *The Work: Timothy Leary: Outside Looking In: Appreciations, Castigations, and Reminiscences*. First published in memoriam (Inner Traditions/Bear, 1999).

26. Email interview with Robert Forte, January 2017.

27. Ann Charters, "Ken Kesey (17 September 1935–)," in *The Beats: Literary Bohemians in Postwar America*, ed. Ann Charters, vol. 16, (Gale, 1983), 306–16. Dictionary of Literary Biography Vol. 16. *Dictionary of Literary Biography Main Series*, accessed December 14, 2016, Gale.

Chapter One

1. According to Paul Lee. Interview with Jennifer Ulrich, October 8, 2016.

2. Stephen Strack and Leonard M. Horowitz, "Introduction," *Handbook of Interpersonal Psychology Theory, Research, Assessment and Therapeutic Interventions* (New Jersey: John Wiley & Sons, Inc., 2010), 4, accessed December 14, 2016, http://onlinelibrary.wiley.com.

3. Ibid., 6.

4. Michael B. Gurtman, "Circular Reasoning About Circular Assessment" in *Handbook of Interpersonal Psychology Theory, Research, Assessment and Therapeutic Interventions* (New Jersey: John Wiley & Sons, Inc., 2010), 304, accessed December 14, 2016, http://onlinelibrary.wiley.com.

5. Timothy Leary, "The Interpersonal System of Personality," Timothy Leary Papers, Manuscripts and Archives, New York Public Library. Astor, Lenox, and Tilden Foundations.

6. Series: 1960–1960, folders: Psychological Consultation Service—Orders, 1963–1972, Timothy Leary Papers, Manuscripts and Archives, New York Public Library. Astor, Lenox, and Tilden Foundations.

7. Don Lattin, *The Harvard Psychedelic Club* (New York: HarperOne, 2011), 38.

8. Timothy Leary, Allen Atwell, and Howard Hallis, *High Priest* (Berkeley, California: Ronin Publishing, 1995), 40.

9. As a representative of the Student Peace Union (SPU) at the University of Chicago, Philip Altbach obtained peace symbol pins from Campaign for Nuclear Disarmament (CND) rallies while visiting in London during 1960. The SPU adopted the symbol upon his return and its use spread. Alma Maldonado-Maldonado and Roberta Malee Bassett, eds., *The Forefront of International Higher Education: A Festschrift in Honor of Philip G. Altbach* (Dordrecht; New York: Springer, 2014), 4.

10. *High Priest*, 39.

11. Taken from a three-page report from Timothy Leary to David McClelland, Harvard University, November 15, 1960. Timothy Leary Papers, Manuscripts and Archives, New York Public Library. Astor, Lenox, and Tilden Foundations.

12. Ibid.

13. "C.I.A. Considered LSD Big Purchase," *New York Times*, August 5, 1976, accessed February 2016, http://www.nytimes.com.

14. Taken from a three-page report from Timothy Leary to David McClelland, Harvard University, November 15, 1960. Timothy Leary Papers, Manuscripts and Archives, New York Public Library. Astor, Lenox, and Tilden Foundations.

15. Later termed "set and setting."

16. Timothy Leary, Letter to Aldous Huxley, May 2, 1961. Timothy Leary Papers, Manuscripts and Archives, New York Public Library. Astor, Lenox, and Tilden Foundations.

17. Don Lattin, *The Harvard Psychedelic Club*, 53–54.

18. Ibid., 55–56.

19. Taken from a three-page report from Timothy Leary to David McClelland, Harvard University, November 15, 1960. Timothy Leary Papers, Manuscripts and Archives, New York Public Library. Astor, Lenox, and Tilden Foundations.

Chapter Two

1. Ibid., 103–04.

2. Carnegie Visiting Professor of Humanities.

3. Grover Smith, ed., *Letters of Aldous Huxley* (London: Chatto & Windus, 1969), 895. *On Art and Artists* was first published in 1960 by Chatto and Windus.

4. Ibid., 900.

5. Robert Greenfield, *Timothy Leary: A Biography* (Orlando: Harcourt, Inc., 2006), 126.

6. Allen Ginsberg and Bill Morgan, *The Letters of Allen Ginsberg* (Cambridge, Massachusetts: Da Capo Press, 2008), 223, accessed November 27, 2016, ProQuest ebrary.

7. Ibid., 230.

8. Ibid., 160.

9. Pantheon and Aperture editions published in 1958 without Kerouac introduction.

10. "Pull My Daisy" *IMDb.*, n.d., accessed November 27, 2016, http://www.imdb.com.

11. Morgan Falconer, "New York School" in *The Oxford Companion to Western Art* (Oxford University Press, 2001), accessed November 28, 2016, Oxfordreference.com.

12. David Anfam, "Kline, Franz," *The Grove Encyclopedia of American Art* (Oxford University Press, 2011), accessed November 28, 2016, Oxfordreference.com.

13. Christoph Grunenberg, *et al.* "De Kooning" in *Grove Art Online*; *Oxford Art Online* (Oxford University Press), accessed November 29, 2016, Oxfordonline.com.

14. Huston Smith, *The Huston Smith Reader* (Berkeley, California: University of California Press, 2012), 69, accessed November 28, 2016, ProQuest ebrary.

15. Grover Smith, ed., *Letters of Aldous Huxley* (London: Chatto & Windus, 1969), 895.

16. Participation of prisoners in medical and behavioral studies in the United States is now governed by Institutional Review Boards and the Office of Human Research. Incarceration could affect the ability of prisoners to make a truly voluntary and uncoerced decision to participate as subjects in research.

17. Rick Doblin, "Dr. Leary's Concord Prison Experiment: a 34-year Follow-up Study," and Ralph Metzner, "Reflections on the Concord Prison Project and the Follow-up Study," *Bulletin of the Multidisciplinary Association for Psychedelic Studies*, MAPS 9, No. 4 (Winter 1999/2000), accessed November 28, 2016, http://www.maps.org/news-letters/ v09n4/09410con.bk.html.

18. Bob Reece, "Anthony Brooke as Rajah Muda of Sarawak," *Borneo Research Bulletin* 42, (2011), 289–307, accessed February 2, 2017, EBSCOhost.

19. "Anthony Brooke," *The Telegraph*, March 6, 2011, accessed December 29, 2016, http:// www.telegraph.co.uk/news/obituaries/ politics-obituaries/8365045/Anthony-Brooke. html.

20. Gerald Heard, Letter to Timothy Leary, November 19, 1961, Timothy Leary Papers, Manuscripts and Archives, New York Public Library. Astor, Lenox, and Tilden Foundations.

21. Timothy Leary, Letter to R. Gordon Wasson, November 21, 1961, Timothy Leary Papers, Manuscripts and Archives, New York Public Library. Astor, Lenox, and Tilden Foundations.

Chapter Three

1. Robert E. Smith, "Psychologists Disagree on Psilocybin Research," *The Harvard Crimson*, March 15, 1962, accessed December 29, 2016, http://www.thecrimson.com/ article/1962/3/15/psychologists-disagree-on- psilocybin-research-pmembers.

2. Joel E. Cohen, "Drugs and Inter Freedom," *The Harvard Crimson*, October 25, 1962, accessed December 29, 2016, http://www. thecrimson.com/article/1962/10/25/ drugs-and-innter-freedom-pthe-professional.

3. R. Greenfield, *Timothy Leary: A Biography*, 179–80.

4. Memorandum from David McClelland to Richard Alpert, February 21, 1962, Timothy Leary Papers, Manuscripts and Archives, New York Public Library. Astor, Lenox, and Tilden Foundations.

5. Timothy Leary, Memorandum, April 10, 1962, Timothy Leary Papers, Manuscripts and Archives, New York Public Library. Astor, Lenox, and Tilden Foundations.

6. Fred M. Hechinger, "Harvard Debates Mind-Drug 'Peril'," *New York Times*, December 14, 1962 (1923–Current File), accessed December 19, 2016, http://ezproxy.cul. columbia.edu.

7. Interview with Jennifer Ulrich, September 22, 2016.

8. Timothy Leary, Letter to Albert Hofmann, March 6, 1963. Timothy Leary Papers, Manuscripts and Archives, New York Public Library. Astor, Lenox, and Tilden Foundations.

9. Displayed by Michael Horowitz on site Timothy Leary Archives, accessed December 29, 2016, http://www.timothylearyarchives. org/international-federation-for-internal- freedom-statement-of-purpose.

10. Ibid.

11. "Statement of Purpose," *Psychedelic Review* 1, No. 1 (June 1963), 6.

12. Joseph J. Downing, "Zihuatanejo: An Experiment in Transpersonative Living" in *Utopiates*, ed. Richard Blum (New York: Atherton Press, 1964), 156–57.

13. George Litwin, letter to Richard Alpert, September 4, 1963. Timothy Leary Papers, Manuscripts and Archives, New York Public Library. Astor, Lenox, and Tilden Foundations.

14. Timothy Leary, Letter to Albert Hofmann, February 13, 1963, 2. Timothy Leary Papers, Manuscripts and Archives, New York Public Library. Astor, Lenox, and Tilden Foundations.

15. Plimpton, *Beat Writers at Work*, 215.

16. International Foundation for Internal Freedom Memorandum, April 1963, Timothy Leary Papers, Manuscripts and Archives, New York Public Library. Astor, Lenox, and Tilden Foundations.

17. Arne Passman, "The LSD Conference," *The Realist*, 72 (December 1966), 21.

18. Louis J. Kern, "Reviews of Books," *The American Historical Review*, 107, No. 3 (2002), 911–12, accessed December 19, 2016, www. jstor.org.

19. c. February 4, 1974, Michael Horowitz Collection on Timothy Leary. Manuscripts and Archives, New York Public Library. Astor, Lenox, and Tilden Foundations.

20. Gerald Heard letter to Timothy Leary, July 17, 1962, Timothy Leary Papers, Manuscripts and Archives, New York Public Library. Astor, Lenox, and Tilden Foundations..

21. *Utopiates*, 146.

22. Coined by Alan Watts.

23. *Utopiates*, 142.

24. "Bernard Roseman and Bernard Copley, Appellants, v. United States of America, Appellee, 364 F.2d 18 (9th Cir. 1966)," n.p., n.d., accessed October 30, 2016, Justia Law.

25. *Utopiates*, 180.

26. Ibid., 150.

27. "Mexico Ousts 21 Researchers in 'Magic' Tests," *Los Angeles Times*, June 15, 1963 (1923-Current File), accessed December 19, 2016, ProQuest Newsstand.

28. *Utopiates*, 162–63.

29. Series: 1960–1976, folder: Clippings, Mexican Newspapers, June 12 and 19, 1963, Timothy Leary Papers, Manuscripts and Archives, New York Public Library. Astor, Lenox, and Tilden Foundations.

30. *Utopiates*, 151.

31. Ibid., 149.

32. "Castalia Foundation Experiential Workshops" [brochure], Timothy Leary Papers, Manuscripts and Archives, New York Public Library. Astor, Lenox, and Tilden Foundations.

Chapter Four

1. Michael Horowitz, *et al.*, *An Annotated Bibliography of Timothy Leary* (Hamdon, Connecticut: Archon, 1988), 102, accessed December 7, 2016, https://archive.org.

2. Michael Horowitz and Lisa Rein, "Never Before Published Photo of Timothy Leary with Aldous and Laura Huxley," Timothy Leary Archives, accessed December 7, 2016, http://www.timothylearyarchives.org/photo-of-timothy-leary-with-aldous-and-laura-huxley.

3. He wrote "Gerald Heard's Essay Toward a Natural Theology," *Journal of Religious Thought*, January 1, 1949 and "Remembering Aldous Huxley," *Journal of Humanistic Psychology,* 29, No. 3 (1989), 406–08.

4. Huston Smith, [Trip Report,] January 1, 1961, 4. Timothy Leary Papers, Manuscripts and Archives, New York Public Library. Astor, Lenox, and Tilden Foundations.

Chapter Five

1. Don Lattin, *The Harvard Psychedelic Club*, 102.

2. Published as *Magister Ludi* in the English language, 1949.

3. Timothy Leary and Ralph Metzner, "Herman Hesse: Poet of the Interior Journey," *Psychedelic Review*, 1, No. 2 (Fall 1963), 167–82.

4. Letter to Mr. Allen W. Dulles from Mr. R. Gordon Wasson [signed by Wasson's secretary], General CIA Records, Document No.: CIA-RDP80B01676R003700110086-8, https://www.cia.gov/library/readingroom/docs/CIA-RDP80B01676R003700110086-8.pdf.

5. "Georgei Ivanovitch Gurdjieff," *Encyclopedia of Occultism and Parapsychology* (Gale, 2001), accessed November 8, 2016, Gale Biography in Context.

6. R. Greenfield, *Timothy Leary: A Biography*, 218.

7. Ibid., 224–25.

8. "Mr. Nyland's Groups," W. A. Nyland Gurdjieff Groups, accessed December 19, 2016, http://www.nyland.org/34-2.

9. Sangsara refers to the Buddhist Wheel of Life—the eternal cycle of birth, suffering, death, and rebirth.

Chapter Six

1. Plimpton, *Beat Writers at Work*, 31.

2. "From Beat Scene Poet to Psychedelic Multimedia Artist in San Francisco and Beyond, 1948–1978," [Oral History], 19, accessed October 29, 2016, http://content.cdlib.org/view?docId=kt409nb28g&doc.view=entire_text.

3. Allen Ginsberg, "Howl," *Evergreen Review Reader* (New York Inc.: Blue Man Books, 1993), 25.

4. Interview with Jennifer Ulrich, September 25, 2016.

5. Stephen Durkee converted to Sufism and changed his name to Noorudeen. He lives in West Virginia.

6. Interview with Jennifer Ulrich, September 25, 2016.

7. Ibid.

8. Ibid.

9. Nancy Moran, "Sex, Poetry, Music: LSD Simulation Session Lures 16 to 'Ecstatic . . .'," *Washington Post, Times Herald* (1959–1973), November 1, 1965, ProQuest Historical Newspapers: *Washington Post*, B3.

10. Emma Brown, "'Bear' Stanley, Who Made the LSD on Which Haight-Ashbury Tripped, Dies at 76," *Washington Post*, March 15, 2011, accessed March 19, 2017, https://www.washingtonpost.com.

11. "*Playboy* Interview: Timothy Leary," *Playboy*, 1966, accessed March 19, 2017, https://archive.org.

12. R. Greenfield, *Timothy Leary: A Biography*, 279.

13. Arne Passman, "The LSD Conference," *The Realist*, December 1966, 19, accessed October 31, 2016, Independent Voices database.

14. Ibid.

15. Lawrence E. Davies, "LSD Conference Opens on Coast: Psychologist Divides Users Into Seven Categories," *The New York Times*, June 14, 1966, (1923–Current file), 44, accessed December 19, 2016, ProQuest Historical Newspapers: *The New York Times* with Index.

16. R. Greenfield, *Timothy Leary: A Biography*, 277–78.

17. Interview with Jennifer Ulrich, October 8, 2016.

18. "League" [for Spiritual Discovery], Timothy Leary Papers, Manuscripts and Archives, New York Public Library. Astor, Lenox, and Tilden Foundations.

19. R. Stuart, "Entheogenic Sects and Psychedelic Religions." *MAPS* [newsletter], 12, No. 1 (2002), accessed December 10, 2016, http://www.maps.org/news-letters/v12n1/12117stu.pdf.

20. R. Greenfield, *Timothy Leary: A Biography*, 331.

21. Ibid., 319.

22. William Borders, "LSD Psychologist Arrested Again: Dr. Leary, the Ex-Harvard Teacher," *The New York Times*, April 18, 1966 (1923–Current file), 31, accessed December 19, 2016, ProQuest Historical Newspapers: *The New York Times* with Index.

23. Letter from attorneys to Timothy Leary regarding raid at Millbrook; Art Kleps, December 13, 1967. Timothy Leary Papers, Manuscripts and Archives, New York Public Library. Astor, Lenox, and Tilden Foundations.

24. [Telegram]. Timothy Leary Papers, Manuscripts and Archives, New York Public Library. Astor, Lenox, and Tilden Foundations.

Chapter Seven

1. Caroline Jean Acker and Sarah W. Tracy, *Altering American Consciousness: The History of Alcohol and Drug Use in the United States: 1800–2000* (Amherst, Massachusetts: University of Massachusetts Press, 2004), 398.

2. "Bernard Roseman and Bernard Copley, Appellants, v. United States of America, Appellee, 364 F.2d 18 (9th Cir. 1966)," accessed October 30, 2016, Justia Law.

3. C. J. Acker and S. W. Tracy, *Altering American Consciousness*, 381.

4. Clipped from *The San Bernardino County Sun*, May 29, 1964, 7, accessed October 30, 2016, https://www.newspapers.com/clip/7168272/the_san_bernardino_county_sun.

5. *Berkeley Barb*, 24, June 1966, 2.

6. R. Greenfield, *Timothy Leary: A Biography*, 346.

7. At the time of this writing. "Drug Schedules," United States Drug Enforcement Administration, accessed October 30, 2016, https://www.dea.gov/druginfo/ds.shtml.

Chapter Eight

1. James M. Fallows, "SDS Members Protest Racism, Plan Sit-In," *Harvard Crimson*, November 12, 1969, accessed October 30, 2016, http://www.thecrimson.com.

2. "University Protest and Activism Collection, 1958–1999," Columbia University Archives, accessed October 30, 2016, http://www.columbia.edu/cu/lweb/archival/collections/ldpd_4080180.

3. Deborah Baker, *A Blue Hand: The Beats in India* (New York: Penguin Press, 2008), 167.

4. Deborah Baker, "For The Sake of the Song," *The Caravan*, November 9, 2016, accessed December 19, 2016, http://www.caravanmagazine.in/reportage/sake-song.

5. R. Greenfield, *Timothy Leary: A Biography*, 283.

6. Julia Robinson, "Happenings," in *The Grove Encyclopedia of American Art*, ed. Joan Marter (Oxford: Oxford University Press, 2011), accessed November 1, 2016.

7. David E. Lowes, "Diggers, the," *The Anti-capitalist Dictionary* (London: Zed Books, 2006), accessed November 8, 2016, Credo Reference.

8. "Changes," *San Francisco Oracle,* 1, No. 7 (1967).

9. Interview with Jennifer Ulrich, October 8, 2016.

10. Verso of letter to Bodhisattva (otherwise known as Michael Horowitz and Robert Barker). Michael Horowitz collection on Timothy Leary, Manuscripts and Archives, New York Public Library. Astor, Lenox, and Tilden Foundations.

Chapter Nine

1. Charles A. Gallagher and Cameron D. Lippard, eds., "Cleaver, Eldridge (1935–1998)," *Race and Racism in the United States: An Encyclopedia*, Vol. 1 (Santa Barbara: Greenwood, 2014), accessed October 30, 2016, Gale Virtual Reference Library.

2. "Leary Tells Young to Quit Drugs, Take Up Revolt," *The Washington Post*, February 25, 1971, in *Times Herald (1959–1973)*, accessed October 30, 2016, ProQuest Historical Newspapers.

3. Peter Conners, *White Hand Society* (San Francisco: City Lights, 2013).

4. "An Open Letter to Allen Ginsberg on the Seventh Liberation," *Berkeley Barb*, 26 (281) January 1–7, 1971.

5. R. Greenfield, *Timothy Leary: A Biography*, 442.

6. Arthur Kunkin, "The Capture of Timothy Leary," *Los Angeles Free Press*, January 26– February 4, 1973, (10) 445, 1, accessed November 1, 2016, http://voices.revealdigital.com.ezproxy.cul.columbia.edu.

7. Ibid.

8. John Bryan, "Whatever Happened to Timothy Leary," *Berkeley Barb*, December 24–20, 1976, 6–7.

9. M. Seymour, "Underground for the C.I.A. in New York: An Ex-Agent Tells of Spying on Students," *The New York Times*, December 29, 1974 (1923–Current file), accessed October 30, 2016, ProQuest Historical Newspapers: *The New York Times* with Index.

10. John Daintith and William Gould, eds., "Kohoutek" in *Collins Dictionary of Astronomy* (London: HarperCollins, 2006), accessed November 8, 2016, Credo Reference.

11. Although they were never legally married, Joanna Harcourt-Smith was referred to as Leary's fourth wife.

12. Keay Davidson and Carl Sagan, *Carl Sagan: A Life* (New York: John Wiley & Sons, Inc.,

1999), 236, accessed December 1, 2016, EBSCOhost.

13. Interview with Jennifer Ulrich, September 25, 2016.

14. Starseed press release, February 20, 1974; Timothy Leary Papers, Manuscripts and Archives, New York Public Library. Astor, Lenox, and Tilden Foundations.

15. John C. Lilly, *The Dyadic Cyclone* (New York: Simon and Schuster, 1976), 24.

16. Lisa Rein and Michael Horowitz, "Timothy Leary and Marshall McLuhan: Turned On, Tuned In," *Boing Boing*, June 3, 2004, accessed March 19, 2017, http://boingboing.net/2014/06/03/timothy-leary-and-marshall-mcl.html.

17. Michael Horowitz, *et al.*, *An Annotated Bibliography of Timothy Leary* (Hamdon, Connecticut: Archon, 1988), 264.

18. Tom Wolfe, "McLuhan's New World," *The Wilson Quarterly*, 1976–, 28, No. 2 (2004): 18–25, accessed March 12, 2017, http://www.jstor.org/stable/40261244.

Chapter Ten

1. Laura Mansnerus, "Timothy Leary, Pied Piper of Psychedelic '60s, Dies at 75," *The New York Times*, June 1, 1996, accessed October 30, 2016, http://www.nytimes.com/learning/general/onthisday/bday/1022.html.

2. Brown bestowed this act of kindness years after Joanna Harcourt-Smith tipped him off on a DEA plot to entrap him in order to thwart his election, according to Robert Greenfield, *Timothy Leary: A Biography*, 496.

3. Paul Krassner, "The Love Song of Timothy Leary," *Tikkun*, November 1999, 69, accessed March 12, 2017, Gale Biography in Context.

4. Folder: Letters between Horowitz and Leary, 1970–75. Michael Horowitz collection on Timothy Leary, Manuscripts and Archives, New York Public Library. Astor, Lenox, and Tilden Foundations.

5. Julia Lipkins, "Transmissions from the Timothy Leary Papers, Manuscripts and Archives, New York Public Library. Astor, Lenox, and Tilden Foundations: A Buddy Film Starring Timothy Leary and G. Gordon Liddy," New York Public Library, accessed October 30, 2016, https://www.nypl.org/blog/2012/08/15/transmissions-timothy-leary-papers-buddy-film-starring-leary-and-liddy.

6. Vicki Marshall, "How Tim's 'Just Say KNOW' Campaign and KnoWare Software Company Were Born," Timothy Leary Archives, accessed December 19, 2016, http://www.timothylearyarchives.org/how-tims-just-say-know-campaign-and-knoware-software-company-were-born.

7. "Mind Mirror—Tools for Self Understanding and Development—About Profiler," *Mind Mirror—Tools for Self Understanding and Development—About Profiler,* n.p., n.d., accessed November 27, 2016.

8. Timothy Leary, "SKIPI: The Personal Operating System," Timothy Leary Papers, Manuscripts and Archives, New York Public Library. Astor, Lenox, and Tilden Foundations.

9. "SKIPI: The Personal Operating System," Timothy Leary Papers, Manuscripts and Archives, New York Public Library. Astor, Lenox, and Tilden Foundations.

10. John C. Lilly, "Modern Whales, Dolphins, and Porpoises as Challengers to our Intelligence," *The Dolphin in History,* Ashley Montagu, ed., 52, accessed November 27, 2016, https://archive.org.

11. John Lilly and Antonietta Lilly, *The Dyadic Cyclone: The Autobiography of a Couple* (New York: Simon and Schuster, 1976), 26–27.

12. Alison Rhonemus, "Transmissions from the Timothy Leary Papers, Manuscripts and Archives, New York Public Library. Astor, Lenox, and Tilden Foundations: Keith Haring Makes a Mind Movie," New York Public Library, accessed December 19, 2016, https://www.nypl.org/blog/2013/01/25/transmissions-timothy-leary-papers-keith-haring-mind-movie.

13. Adi Robertson, "Timothy Leary's 'Neuromancer' Video Game Could Have Been Incredible," *The Verge,* October 1, 2013, accessed March 19, 2017, http://www.theverge.com/2013/10/1/4791566/timothy-learys-neuromancer-video-game-could-have-been-incredible.

14. "Wonderland Park: Home with the Leary Family," 1. Timothy Leary Papers, Manuscripts and Archives, New York Public Library. Astor, Lenox, and Tilden Foundations.

15. "Leary.com" Timothy Leary Archives, accessed December 19, 2016, http://www.timothylearyarchives.org/learycom.

16. Fred Turner, *From Counterculture to Cyberculture: Stewart Brand, the Whole Earth Network, and the Rise of Digital Utopianism,* 1st ed. (Chicago: University of Chicago Press, 2010), 4–5.

17. *Chaos & Cyberculture* (Berkeley, California: Ronin Publishing, 1994), 40–41.

18. "Two Heads Talking: David Byrne in Conversations with Timothy Leary," 68.

19. Marshall McLuhan, *Understanding Media: The Extensions of Man* (Cambridge, Massachusetts: MIT Press, 1964).

Epilogue

1. *Hanuman Foundation* [pamphlet], Timothy Leary Papers, Manuscripts and Archives, New York Public Library. Astor, Lenox, and Tilden Foundations.

2. "Biography," Ram Dass, accessed December 19, 2016, https://www.ramdass.org/bio.

3. Don Lattin, *The Harvard Psychedelic Club,* 197.

4. Allen Ginsberg and Bill Morgan, *The Letters of Allen Ginsberg* (Cambridge, Massachusetts: Da Capo Press, 2008), 445–46, accessed November 28, 2016, ProQuest ebrary.

5. Huston Smith, *The Huston Smith Reader* (Berkeley, California: University of California Press, 2012), 245, accessed November 28, 2016, ProQuest ebrary.

6. R. Greenfield, *Timothy Leary: A Biography,* 599.

Who's Who

Ken Babbs
(b. January 14, 1936)
Babbs attended Miami University and graduated in 1958, he later studied creative writing at Stanford University, where he befriended fellow student Ken Kesey. After serving as a Marine in Vietnam during 1962–63, he joined Kesey in a group known as the "Merry Pranksters," conducting pranks or "Happenings," and "acid-test" parties, as a nod to the government-sponsored psychedelic drug tests Kesey and others participated in. In 1964, Babbs rode in a bus called Further to Leary and Alpert's commune in Millbrook, New York. He helped edit Kesey's journal, *Spit in the Ocean* (1974–81).

Frank X. Barron
(June 17, 1922–October 6, 2002)
The psychologist studied at University of California, Berkeley and was a graduate student alongside Timothy Leary. He developed personality tests and studied creativity at the Institute for Personality Assessment and Research, as well as participating in psychedelic research at Harvard. He is credited with introducing Leary to psilocybin mushrooms in Mexico in 1960.

William S. Burroughs
(February 5, 1914–August 2, 1997)
Born in St. Louis, Missouri, the Beat writer became known for his copious drug use, international travels, and sardonic wit. Burroughs "accidentally" shot and killed his second wife in Mexico City in 1951. After his conviction for manslaughter, he went on to publish his most recognized novels: *Junkie* (1953) and *Naked Lunch* (1959); the latter was briefly banned in the U.S. due to obscenity laws.

Neal Cassady (February 8, 1926–February 4, 1968)
Born in Salt Lake City, Utah, Cassady grew up in Denver, Colorado. After his mother's death, his childhood was troubled and he became involved in petty crime at a young age. He was introduced to Jack Kerouac and Allen Ginsberg through a mutual friend, bonding quickly with them due to his gifted mind and taste for Benzedrine. As part of the Beat scene, he served as inspiration for Kerouac's *On the Road* and drove Ken Kesey and the Merry Pranksters in their *Further* bus across the U.S. during 1964.

Eldridge Cleaver
(August 31, 1935–May 1, 1998)
Born in Arkansas and raised in Los Angeles, Cleaver was in trouble with the law at a young age and was radicalized in prison. He became involved in the Black Panther Party while writing for *Ramparts* magazine. His essays were published in his critically acclaimed book *Soul on Ice* (1968). Timothy and Rosemary Leary stayed with Cleaver and the Panthers after Leary escaped prison and fled to Algeria.

Ram Dass
(b. 1931)
Born in Newton, Massachusetts as Richard Alpert, he was professor at Harvard and collaborated with Leary in the Department of Social Relations. Timothy Leary introduced him to psilocybin and both began a lifelong study of psychedelics and consciousness-expansion. He changed his name after traveling to India in 1967 and studying under the tutorship of his guru Neem Karoli Baba.

Rick Doblin
(b. November 30, 1953)
Doblin founded the Multidisciplinary Association for Psychedelic Studies (MAPS) in 1986, an organization created to promote research in the beneficial use of psychedelic drugs that is currently active and growing.

Allen Ginsberg
(June 3, 1926–April 5, 1997)
Born in Newark, New Jersey, he studied at Columbia University and became a renowned New York "Beat" poet with the publication of his explicit collection *Howl and Other Poems* (1956). In 1957, he faced obscenity charges for descriptions of homosexual sex acts in his work. His literary styles and embrace of drugs, sexual freedom, and Eastern spirituality was highly influential in his circle of writers and the greater counterculture.

Joanna Harcourt-Smith
(b. 1946)
Born in Switzerland, she met Timothy Leary during his exile from U.S. authorities when he was living in Switzerland and accompanied him when he was sent back from Afghanistan in 1973. She campaigned for his release from prison, helped to publish his writings, and promoted his cause under the Starseed organization.

Gerald Heard
(October 6, 1889–August 14, 1971)
Born in London, a writer and philosopher, like his friend Huxley, Heard immigrated to the U.S. and also became involved in the Vedanta. He founded Trabuco College, a short-lived center for the study of religion and spirituality, credited with being model to the Esalen Institute. Heard advocated for the therapeutic use of mescaline and LSD.

Albert Hofmann
(January 11, 1906–April 29, 2008)
Hofmann was born in Switzerland. He is
credited with being responsible for discovering
LSD-25 while employed as a chemist at Sandoz
Laboratories. He wrote about his experience
after ingesting the substance and riding his
bicycle home on April 19, 1943, later known as
"Bicycle Day."

Michael Horowitz
(b. 1938)
Born in Brooklyn, New York City. This rare
book dealer, and former archivist and
bibliographer for Timothy Leary, took custody of
his records at a critical time during his
imprisonment, prison escape, and exile.
Horowitz cofounded the Fitz Hugh Ludlow
Memorial Library of drug-related literature in
1970.

Aldous Huxley
(July 26, 1894–November 22, 1963)
The prolific English author and philosopher
moved to California in the 1930s, and due to
his interest in Eastern philosophy he became
involved in the Vedanta Society of Southern
California. Huxley experimented with
mescaline and subsequently wrote about his
experience in his book *The Doors of Perception*
(1954). He was already known for his dystopian
sci-fi novel *Brave New World* (1932).

Jack Kerouac
(March 12, 1922–October 21, 1969)
Born in Lowell, Massachusetts, Kerouac attended
Columbia University on a football scholarship.
He befriended other Beat writers in New York
City and engaged in drug-fueled road trips across
the U.S. and Mexico with Neal Cassady, as well
as participating in experiences with William S.
Burroughs and Allen Ginsberg, all of which
proved fodder for his stream-of-consciousness
novel *On the Road* (1957), considered emblematic
of the Beat Generation.

Ken Kesey
(September 17, 1935–November 10, 2001)
Born in Colorado, his family later moved to
Oregon, where he studied at the University of
Oregon and graduated in 1957. As a novelist, he
went on to become known for his experience
working at a mental health institution and
participation in the LSD drug studies that took
place in Palo Alto, California. These experiences
prompted him to write the well-received *One
Flew Over the Cuckoo's Nest* (1962). He also
headed the group the Merry Pranksters,
famously chronicled in Tom Wolfe's, *The
Electric Kool-Aid Acid Test* (1968). As leader of
the group, he directed the *Further* bus, driven by
Neal Cassady across the U.S. in 1964 to
advocate the use of LSD.

Art Kleps
(April 17, 1928–July 17, 1999)
Born in New York, Kleps attended Syracuse
University and graduated in 1959. He was a
practising psychologist who befriended Leary
and helped to found the Neo-American
Church, unsuccessfully seeking the legal right
for the ritual use of psychotropic drugs.

Paul Krassner
(b. 1932)
Born in Brooklyn, New York City. Satirist,
author, comedian, and editor of *The Realist*,
Krassner was part of the Merry Pranksters and
was a founding member of the Youth
International Parties (yippies) who staged a
protest at the 1968 National Democratic
Convention in Chicago.

Rosemary Leary
(c. 1936–February 2, 2002)
Born in St. Louis, Missouri, Rosemary became
Leary's fourth wife in 1967. In 1966, she was
arrested with him for marijuana possession in
Laredo, Texas. She helped him escape prison in
1970, after which they both fled to Algeria.
They separated soon after, but she lived
underground for approximately twenty-three years.

Paul Lee
(b. September 20, 1931)
Born in Colorado, Lee attended Harvard
Divinity School, where he gained his PhD in
1963. At the same time, Timothy Leary and
Richard Alpert held faculty positions in the
Department of Social Relations and Lee
participated in their psilocybin experiments,
such as the Marsh Chapel study held on Good
Friday 1962 to test the effectiveness of the drug
in inducing a religious experience.

G. Gordon Liddy
(b. November 30, 1930)
Born in Brooklyn, New York City, as Dutchess
County District Attorney, Liddy led the drug
raids on Millbrook throughout the commune's
residence. He was later convicted for burglary
connected to the Watergate scandal. After Leary's
release from prison, they reconnected and toured
in a debate performance.

John C. Lilly
(January 6, 1915–September 30, 2001)
Born in St. Paul, Minnesota, Lilly attended
Caltech and UPenn. He was known for
inventing the sensory deprivation tank, research
in dolphin communication, and his experiments
with LSD and ketamine.

Marshall McLuhan
(July 21, 1911–Dec 31, 1980)
Born in Alberta, Canada. McLuhan studied at
Cambridge and the University of Manitoba. A
communications scholar, he is best known for the

phrase "the medium is the message." He befriended Leary and provided inspiration for his media approach and slogans, such as his phrase, "Turn on, tune in, drop out."

Ralph Metzner
(b. 1936)
Born in Germany, he was a graduate student at Harvard University, where he gained his PhD and participated in the psilocybin research undertaken by professors Timothy Leary and Richard Alpert, and continued to collaborate with them at Millbrook, coauthoring the *Psychedelic Experience: A Manual Based on the Tibetan Book of the Dead* (1964). He is a psychotherapist and Professor Emeritus of psychology at the California Institute of Integral Studies in San Francisco.

Peter Orlovsky
(July 8, 1933–May 30, 2010)
Born on the Lower East Side of New York City, Orlovsky grew up on Long Island. A member of the Beat circle, he was also a poet and the long-term partner of Allen Ginsberg. By 1970, he and Ginsberg had moved out of the city to live on an organic farm.

Humphry Osmond
(July 1, 1917–February 6, 2004)
Born in Surrey, England, Osmond moved to Canada after his medical training. As a psychiatrist, he studied LSD and schizophrenia, and became known for introducing Aldous Huxley to mescaline and for coining the term "psychedelic."

María Sabina
(c. July 22, 1894–November 23, 1985)
María was one of the Mazatec curanderas (shaman) from the state of Oaxaca in Mexico credited with first introducing Westerners to the Mazatec ritual use of the psilocybin mushroom.

R. U. Sirius
(b. 1952)
Otherwise known as Ken Goffman, he was cofounder and editor of *Mondo 2000* (1989–93), an influential cyberculture magazine based in the San Francisco Bay area, during the burgeoning development of the Internet. He coauthored Leary's book, *Design for Dying* (1998).

Owsley Stanley
(January 19, 1935–March 12, 2011)
Stanley studied engineering at the University of Virginia and became an amateur chemist responsible for the manufacture of much of the LSD consumed in the San Francisco Bay area during the 1960s. He was also sometime supplier to Ken Kesey and the Merry Pranksters' acid-test parties.

Gerd Stern
(b. October 1928)
Born in Germany, Stern immigrated as a child to New York City. As an adult, the Beat poet relocated to the San Francisco Bay area during the 1950s, then returned to the East Coast and founded the artist collaborative USCO in 1963, along with engineer Michael Callahan and painter Stephen Durkee, he was a pioneer in multimedia art performances.

Robert Gordon Wasson
(September 22, 1898–December 26, 1986)
Vice President in Public Relations at JP Morgan & Co., Wasson was also an amateur mycologist. He is credited for first publicizing the Mazatec psilocybin mushroom ritual in an article for *Time* magazine in May 1957.

Alan Watts
(January 6, 1915–November 16, 1973)
Born in Kent, England, Watts moved to the U.S. and studied Zen Buddhism and theology, briefly becoming an Episcopal priest in 1945. He later taught at the American Academy of Asian Studies and became a radio personality at Berkeley's KPFA Radio station. He authored a number of books on Eastern religion, such as influential *The Way of Zen* (1957).

Andrew Weil
(b. June 8, 1942)
Weil attended Harvard as an undergraduate during the time Leary and Alpert were conducting their drug studies. As editor of the student paper, *The Harvard Crimson*, he helped to publicly criticize their studies, but later reconciled with them and has had a successful career promoting holistic and integrated medicine.

Robert Anton Wilson
(January 18, 1932–January 11, 2007)
Born in Brooklyn, New York. A novelist, journalist, and futurist, Wilson worked as an editor for *Playboy* magazine's "Forum" advice column and became acquainted with Leary and Alpert and other counterculture figures. His works commented on conspiracy theories, paranoia, and the occult.

Acknowledgments and Sources

I thought I was done thinking about Timothy Leary at the conclusion of my archival processing project. Like breaking up with a boyfriend, I cut off my hair and focused my energy on another subject. Yet, Leary is a hard act to follow. Luckily, editor Joanna de Vries contacted me with her vision and proposal. Skeptical at first, her enthusiasm and course of action convinced me to take the leap and hope for a soft landing at best, survival at least. I am truly indebted to her for putting her faith in me to complete such a work. This book would have never been written without the guidance, prodding, and—most importantly—editorial expertise of Jo, along with the exceptional team of Editorial Director Will Steeds and Publishing Director Laura Ward at Elephant Book Company, as well as the superb design skills of Paul Palmer-Edwards at Grade Design. They held my hand while simultaneously holding me accountable.

This book would not be adorning bookshop or library shelves without the enthusiasm and expertise of the team at Abrams Books, who had enough faith in our vision for the book that they selected it to sit on their eminent publishing program. Particular gratitude must go to John Gall, Devin Grosz, Eric Himmel, Gabriel Levinson, and Alicia Tan. As well as to Devin Grosz for his excellent jacket design.

I want to thank all of those who I interviewed, specifically Ken Babbs, Robert Forte, Michael Horowitz, Paul Krassner, Paul Lee, Gerd Stern, and Andrew Weil, who graciously allowed me to mine their first-person accounts of Timothy Leary. I found myself amazed and entertained by their candid recollections and self-effacing wit. Additionally, I am grateful for their recommendations of other resources and individuals to pursue. Thanks to Dana Reemes for his permission and information on the Starseed cover art, and to Joanna Harcourt-Smith for her insight.

I wish to thank my dear colleagues in the New York Public Library, particularly Thomas Lannon, the Curator of Manuscripts, and the reference staff in the Brooke Russell Astor Reading Room, Tal Nadal, Nasima Hasnat, and John Cordovez, for their assistance in my research. With additional thanks to Tom Lisanti and his staff in the Permissions and Reproductions Department for their unfailing patience and support to ensure that we could showcase the original material from Leary's collection in these pages. All of this was inspired by my work as Project Archivist years prior, which was not possible without the collaboration and support of my former colleagues, Digital Archivist Don Mennerich, Interns Julia Lipkins, Alison Rhonemus, Rebecca Weintraub, Boni Joi Koelliker, and David Olson, and of course, the leadership of Lea Osborne, Head of Archival Processing and William Stingone, former Curator of Manuscripts.

This book would not have been possible without the support of Leary's estate, the Futique Trust, and that of Zach Leary. I am very thankful for his foreword, and for sharing his personal relationship with his father who had such a public legacy.

Last, but not least, I thank my own family for their support, especially my husband John.

As you will have gathered from reading these pages, Timothy Leary corresponded with a huge range of figures and his life and work touched many people. This book would not have been possible without the kind permission of the estate holders of all the works reproduced herein. It has been a Herculean effort to track down the copyright holders and we are grateful to them for their cooperation. However, while we have made every possible effort to trace and obtain permission for the material included, if we have been unable to do so or unwittingly misattributed or overlooked an item, we sincerely apologise and please do contact Elephant Book Company at: info@elephantbookcompany.com to notify us so we can ensure that material is fully referenced in future editions.

The vast majority of the material reproduced in this book is held within the Timothy Leary Papers, Manuscripts and Archives, New York Public Library, Astor, Lenox, and Tilden Foundations. Permissions for material original to Timothy Leary held in the archive remain under the Futique Trust, who are the executors of Timothy Leary's estate. Unless otherwise stated below transcriptions of and quotations from material original to Timothy Leary within this book are reproduced courtesy of the Futique Trust:

Text permissions and transcriptions are from the following collections:

Anthony Brooke: courtesy of The Brooke Trust: pp. 63–64,

Asoke Fakir: The Estate of Asoke Fakir, by kind permission of Dr. Kaniska Sarkar: p. 196–97

Allen Ginsberg: Letters to Timothy Leary by Allen Ginsberg. Copyright © Allen Ginsberg, 2008, used by permission of The Wylie Agency (UK) Limited: pp. 47–48, 49–52, 53, 54–55, 55, 57–58, 72–73, 92–95

Gerald Heard: Copyright © 2018 by The Barrie Family Trust. By permission of John Roger Barrie in care of Harold Ober Associates Inc.: pp. 62–63, 82, 240

Dr. Albert Hofmann: Copyright © The Estate of Dr. Albert Hofmann: pp. 59–60,

Aldous Huxley: Reprinted by permission of Georges Borchardt, Inc., on behalf of the Estate of Aldous Huxley. All rights reserved: pp. 65, 84

Ken Kesey: Reprinted by permission of SLL/ Sterling Lord Literistic, Inc. Copyright © Ken Kesey: p. 215

Art Kleps: Copyright © Joan Kleps, The Original Kleptonian Neo-American Church: pp. 164–66, 166–67, 167, 168, 169, 169–70

Marshall McLuhan: Copyright the Estate of Marshall McLuhan: p. 229

Humphry Osmond: Copyright © The Estate of Humphry Osmond: p. 66

Robert Anton Wilson: The Estate of Robert Anton Wilson: p. 234

Their letters are reproduced in transcription by kind permission of the following individuals: Ram Dass/Richard Alpert: pp. 81, 141–43; Paul Lee: pp. 101–06; Ann Litwin: p. 112; George Litwin: pp. 108–11; Ralph Metzner: pp. 89–91, 251–55; Eleanor Kendra Smith: pp. 113–17; Joan Watts and Anne Watts (on behalf of the Alan Watts Estate): pp. 126, 131; Gunther Weil: p. 117; John Wilcock: p. 185

Material reproduced from Leary's published work: Copyright 1994: Timothy Leary; 2014: Futique Trust. From Chaos and Cyberculture, pp. 40–41, by permission of Ronin Publishing. All rights reserved: p. 244.

Picture Credits

Images are from the following collections:

Alamy: pp. 24 (Richard Mittleman/Gon2Foto/ Alamy Stock Photo); 30 (Science History Images/Alamy Stock Photo); 44 (Everett Collection Inc/Alamy Stock Photo); 97 (Moviestore collection Ltd/Alamy Stock Photo); 174 (Tim Brown/Alamy Stock Photo); 198 (Pictorial Press Ltd/Alamy Stock Photo); 235 (Everett Collection, Inc./Alamy Stock Photo);

Berkeley Barb, with kind permission of the estate of Max Scherr: p. 211

The Estate of Frank X. Barron (reproduced from copy held in The Timothy Leary Archives): p. 43. This artifact is also reproduced by permission of Peters Fraser & Dunlop (www.petersfraserdunlop. com) on behalf of the Estate of Arthur Koestler

Copyright © William Burroughs, used by permission of The Wylie Agency (UK) Limited: p. 252 (bottom)

Getty Images: pp. 19 (PL Gould/IMAGES/ Getty Images); 27 (Michael Ochs Archives/ Alvan Meyerowitz/Contributor); 56, 68, (Bettmann/Contributor); 86 (Denver Post/ Steve Larson/Contributor); 104, 105 (The LIFE Picture Collection/John Loengard/ Contributor); 118 (Archive Photos/Santi Visalli Inc./Contributor); 127 (Archive Photos/Images Press/Contributor); 137 (Hulton Archive/Alvis Upitis/Contributor); 153 (Premium Archive/ Fred W. McDarrah/Contributor); 181 (Hulton Archive/A. Jones/Stringer); 184 (Bettmann/ Contributor); 195 (Corbis Premium Historical/ Ted Streshinsky Photographic Archive/ Contributor); 208 (Michael Ochs Archive/ Donaldson Collection/Contributor); 219 (Bettman/Contributor); 230 (Redferns/Frans Schellekens/Contributor); 248 (Hulton Archive/Alvis Upitis/Contributor); 253 (Michael Ochs Archive/Robert Altman/ Contributor)

Letters to Timothy Leary by Allen Ginsberg. Copyright © Allen Ginsberg, 2008, used by permission of The Wylie Agency (UK) Limited: p. 51

With kind permission of photographer Philip Heying: p. 252 (top)

The Timothy Leary Archives, the New York Public Library; the collection of The Futique Trust: pp. 33, 35, 36, 37, 39, 67, 79, 123, 124, 125, 128, 129, 134 (by kind permission of Ram Dass), 135 (top: by kind permission of Ralph Metzner), 136, 139, 144, 147, 152, 155, 156, 161, 165 (by kind permission of Joan Kleps, The Original Kleptonian Neo-American Church), 171, 182, 183, 188 (by kind permission of Lisa Law), 193 (by kind permission of Stanley Mouse), 194 (by kind permission of Lisa Law), 207 (by kind permission of Paul Krassner), 213 (by kind permission of Eldridge and Kathleen Neal Cleaver Family Archive), 220 (by kind permission of Dr. Dana Reemes), 224–26 (by kind permission of Joanna Harcourt-Smith), 236, 237, 241, 246, 247 (by kind permission of R U Sirius/Ken Goffman), 254 (both by kind permission of Ralph Metzner)

Pixie Records: p. 159

Rex/Shutterstock/Larry Mack: p. 212

The Harvard Review: p. 76

The New York Times: p. 121

Index